NUMBER 71

Yale French Studies

Men / Women of Letters

Yale French Studies

Charles A. Porter, *Special editor for this issue*
Liliane Greene, *Managing editor*
Editorial board: Peter Brooks (Chairman), Ellen Burt, David
    Civali, Lauren Doyle-McCombs, Mary Lou Ennis,
    Shoshana Felman, Richard Goodkin, Christopher Miller,
    Charles Porter, Allan Stoekl
Staff: Peggy McCracken
Editorial office: 315 William L. Harkness Hall
Mailing address: 2504A Yale Station, New Haven,
    Connecticut 06520
Sales and subscription office:
    Yale University Press, 92A Yale Station
    New Haven, Connecticut 06520
Published twice annually by Yale University Press

Copyright © 1986 by Yale University
All rights reserved.
This book may not be reproduced, in whole or in part, in any
form (beyond that copying permitted by Sections 107 and 108
of the U.S. Copyright Law and except by reviewers for the
public press), without written permission from the publisher.

Designed by James J. Johnson and set in Trump Medieval
Roman by The Composing Room of Michigan, Inc. Printed in
the United States of America by The Vail-Ballou Press,
Binghamton, N.Y.
ISSN 0044-0078
ISBN for this issue 0-300-03697-3

Pénélope écrivant à Ulysse. Photo du Musée de la Poste, 34, boulevard de Vaugirard, Paris.

CHARLES A. PORTER

Foreword

In the beginning was the . . . letter.

The letter "a," a love letter, men of letters, arts and letters, *belles-lettres.*

Just what is the text we call "a letter"? What does it have to do, if anything, with "literature"?

After perusing the following studies our reader may well come to the conclusion that one of the few undisputed characteristics of "a letter" is that it is *written.* It may be appropriate after all to call the missive or epistle after its basic unit, the *letter* (or character)! Now the "missive letter" need not have been written by its "author": no one disputes that that person may have dictated it orally to another person, who wrote it down. Nor will all agree that in order to be a letter it need to have been sent, or even addressed, to some identifiable other person or persons. But I think all will concur that the letter must be set down in written (or typed, or printed) characters. A telephone message is *not* a letter: indeed, for many, the ease of that kind of communication in modern life has contributed greatly to the decline of the letter. (Will, then, computer-generated "electronic mail" contribute to a renaissance?)

English Showalter, Jr., in the pages following, states what a letter is, at least in terms of its "specific functions": "a message-bearing object delivered from one person to another." One surmises that, like the lady in our cover engraving, he takes a dim view of the *unsent* letter; it is not certain that the scowling woman dressed in black in the background would agree with them! The Robert dictionary of French defines a letter as an "Ecrit que l'on adresse à quelqu'un pour lui communiquer ce qu'on ne peut ou ne veut lui dire oralement" [Writing addressed to

1

someone in order to communicate to that person what one cannot or does not want to say to him orally]: the "cannot" situation is that of good Penelope in our frontispiece. It seems appropriate to go along with Showalter and the Robert at least so far as to allow three further certain characteristics: the letter then becomes, at the very least, a *written,——message-bearing——object——from——*someone.

The remaining illustrations in this volume (letters written by Chateaubriand, Lamennais, Victor Hugo, and Proust; envelopes addressed by Mallarmé) are examples of handwriting and the "shape" of the "object." They illustrate yet another aspect of the letter: how its message is enhanced, illustrated, or perhaps obscured by its writer's hand and the kind of ink and paper used.

On the basis of preliminary observations like these, we may now begin to trace a working definition of "the letter." It must include further characteristics of the letter that are almost invariable, since up till this point we have described almost anything that is written.

(1) The letter has an *author* known to or readily *identifiable* (even if vaguely) by the intended reader. Likewise it is *addressed* by that author (even if at times only implicitly) to an identifiable person or collectivity, sometimes well-known to the author, and usually addressed *only* to that person or collectivity. The fact that the author is identifiable links the letter to such familiar literary genres as the diary and the autobiography, while the address differentiates it both from the diary, "addressed" normally to its author alone, and from the autobiography, which usually does not have an identifiable—at least a single—addressee and is not ordinarily a "private" communication. One can imagine a "zero degree" case on the addresser-addressee scale: that of a letter *really* addressed *only* to its author; its opposite could be an "eyes only" message from an anonymous spy to be destroyed by its addressee immediately after reading. Such "no addressee" or "no addresser" letters are doubtless rather rare; the typical letter remains essentially a *private communication between* two persons.

(2) The letter ordinarily is written, more or less directly, out of its author's experience or wishes or aspirations. Its *"I" refers to its author* directly, again like the diary and the autobiography. As in the diary and to a lesser extent the autobiography, the "I" expresses itself in the immediacy of the moment and surrounds itself with what Showalter calls the "particularity" of the I's own experience. Like the diary and the autobiography, of course, the "I" of the letter is to some extent a fabrication or "fiction," *not necessarily identical* to its author.

(3) Like the diary, less frequently the autobiography, the letter or its

parts are ordinarily *dated, or presumably datable.* The date is not only a part of the information presented in the letter (allowing its reader, for example, to measure the writer's statements against what relevant knowledge he or she could have had at the time of writing) but also a *terminus ad quem* the significance of which changes radically depending on whether one considers the letter individually or as part of a "correspondence" (as, to take a particularly radical example, in the case of a suicide letter which by date takes its place near the beginning or in the middle of a series of letters emanating from the same person).

(4) Series of letters, like a diary but quite unlike the major part of most autobiographies, are *written "forward,"* with no certainty about the future and thus little possibility of *surely* tracing a "destiny." Except in the relatively rare case of a series of letters intended by its author (or later by an editor of the author's correspondence) to include only the accomplishment of a specific foregone conclusion (as, for example, a series of letters from author to publisher regarding the specifics of an agreed-on publication), letters, even between the same two correspondents and in sequence of dates, are *discontinuous, multidirectional, fragmented.* Now the diary will take much of its eventual meaning from the play among the various dated segments: for we understand the diary to reflect, according to its dates, the continuous development of a more or less unified personality, and we expect every piece to be relatable to all those preceding and following. The dates help to measure and evaluate the rate and direction of evolution. In letters, on the other hand, the sequence of dates may be much less interesting. It is hard to know to what extent, necessarily, a letter depends for its proper reading (except in certain specific cases) on other letters, not necessarily yet written, for, unlike entries in a diary, letters at their date are *independent* entities. For instance, a text which claims something its writer knows to be false can be read one way as an example of rhetoric, another according to its intended function, and still another if we use it to examine the psychology of the writer. All three of these readings are clearly part of such a text's message in a diary, but that is much less certain in the case of a letter.

Since the diary does not necessarily presuppose a reader other than the author, and since it presumes to be a continuous reflection of its author, one assumes at the least that every possible "meaning" it may have is in some degree generally intended at that date to contribute to overall self-understanding, or ongoing self-delusion, or something of that sort. But the letter, always addressed at a given time to a given other person, will commonly have *a precise intention* (to seduce, to deceive, to request, to respond, or to continue a subject already begun, for example); its peripheral "meanings" will be so very secondary to that intention that any interpretations based largely on them will often seem—or be—"forced." The dates of a diary often do no more than mark a sequence, while the date of a letter is bound up with its message. The order according to the dates, even of letters to the same addressee, does not necessarily describe an evolution; series of letters are much "more discontinuous" than diaries. Indeed they are discontinuous almost from the point of origin: as Showalter points out, once a letter has been sent, even its author cannot modify it in the light of future letters.

(5) Moreover, the individual letter, like the diary, in Béatrice Didier's words, is characterized by "le morcellement, le discontinu, l'absence d'élaboration et de composition" [fragmentation, discontinuity, the absence of development and formal arrangement].[1] Often, and particularly between intimates or family members, the letter appears to aim at being *"written speech,"* "long-distance conversation," following in its rhythms and discontinuities as well as in its vocabulary and style the relative informality as well as the directness of spoken (as opposed to written) language. "J'aime à vous écrire; je parle à vous, je cause avec vous" [I like to write you; I speak to you, I talk with you], writes Madame de Sévigné to her daughter on 9 October 1675.[2] As Mireille Bossis reminds us below, "For writer and recipient the letter is above all an extension of daily life." But we will note also that, as Martine Reid points out in her discussion of Stendhal's struggles with the letter, there is always an "internal contradiction" between the letter's implied "spontaneity, naturalness, and originality" and the inevitable artifice of its form.

(6) For the letter is instantly and almost without exception recognizable *as a letter* by (in a placement and order that vary from time to time and place to place) its address, folding, date line, salutation, signature—which in turn lead to presumptions of identifiability, directness, and so on.

(7) Lest all of the preceding make it appear that the letter, despite differences, is generically most like a diary, one must hasten to note two major divergences. A reader ordinarily presupposes the sincerity of a diary (at least a "real"—as opposed to fictional—diary), whereas the reader is always *obliged to seek to measure the sincerity* of the letter.

1. Béatrice Didier, "Autoportrait et journal intime," *Corps écrit* 5 (février 1983), 173.
2. Quoted by Roger Duchêne, *Madame de Sévigné ou la chance d'être femme* (Paris: Fayard, 1982), 264.

Furthermore the letter is a different sort of object: it is a relatively small thing, susceptible (particularly when it is a "love letter") of becoming a "fetish."

That it is *written*, bears a *message*, is an *object*, and emanates *from* someone: these traits characterize a minimal letter. The address and signature, relatively unproblematic first person, datation, fragmentation, primacy of intention, informality, fixed form, and indeterminable sincerity within its own boundaries, are further characteristics that will not usually be questioned. Length, style, language, presence or absence of rhetorical figures, on the other hand, will only in extraordinary circumstances be useful defining characteristics. At the outset, then, we appear to be close to a *formal definition* of the letter. The eventual *literary status* of the letter, on the other hand, will almost certainly require a definition centered more on function, that is, if the notion of "literary" is to keep its traditional content involving elements of intention, a selection of stylistic level, and a discernable form or structure. It will be harder to arrive at a functional definition that would be agreed upon by all "letterary" critics.

Many would agree, however, that a letter usually *is a reply* to another letter and/or *invites a reply*. Earlier we mentioned the interest of knowing whether or not a letter was part of a series of letters by the same author. Now we must ask whether a letter must be treated as part of a chain of letters and responses—and what then of third parties who may become involved? Ought letters to be considered "in dialogue," like the constituent parts of epistolary novels, rather than like fragments of autobiographical writings? In any case it seems certain that a letter's function can be determined only with some consideration of its relationship to other letters of other writers—even if the latter are replies that failed to be written. A single, perfectly independent letter would be hard to distinguish from, say, an essay.

Furthermore, few writers of letters write to only one correspondent or for a single purpose. It would seem that a functional definition of the letter should include therefore the description of admissible correspondents (a friend, surely—but a newspaper editor, if the letter is intended for publication?) and of admissible subjects (one's feelings, no doubt, but what of an ordered declaration of one's beliefs or the demonstration of a scientific principle?). Is a letter by Pascal to Fermat the same kind of "literature" as a letter written by Madame de Sévigné to Madame de Grignan? Should Chateaubriand's collected correspondence include the descriptive and lengthy "Lettre à Fontanes [at the period one of the owners of the *Mercure de France*] sur la campagne romaine"? Can we distinguish between a "real" letter and some other kind of writing that borrows the external form of the letter? Is an "epistolary novel" composed of letters, or of imitations of letters?

At this point it is helpful to take into consideration writers like Rousseau, who provide ample examples of both fictional and "genuine" letters, or like Flaubert and Chateaubriand, who are known to write under differing kinds of self-imposed constraints depending on whether they are writing to individual correspondents or "for publication." It should be possible, at the very least in the case of a single author, to arrive at formal and functional definitions that separate "real" from "fictional" letters, and it should also be possible to measure, at least in individual cases, the quantity of stylistic and rhetorical information that can appropriately be sought from a writer's letters about his or her way of writing.

But when we choose examples like Rousseau and Flaubert, authors of voluminous and much appreciated "correspondences," we are also reminded that a letter by itself, written at a given date, for a purpose, to a given addressee, is not the same kind of literary object as a "correspondence" made up of many of those letters: for once letters have become a "correspondence" they have lost, as far as their reader is concerned, their independence. Even if its author has abandoned control over a sent letter, the reader has not. And if it is hard to define "a letter," it is almost impossible, as the polarized debate among editors shows, to define "a correspondence."

Let us return for a moment to our cover and frontispiece. They are amusing reflections of further traits not infrequently associated with letters: surreptitiousness and guilt, in the case of "Honni soit qui mal y pense," longing and hope, in the case of medieval Penelope. And how does it happen that both writers are women, while all the other letters in our illustrations have been authored by men?

The lady mailing off to her lover an assignation (not an improbable interpretation of the cover picture) is using the letter to convey a message to one person while concealing it from another; the situation portrayed is dramatic and suspenseful, since not only can we not know whether the watchful duenna is to be trusted but the letter itself as object has potentially a life of its own, being capable of reappearing in unintended contexts, such as before her husband's eyes, or in court. The interpretation of this letter, surely, will have to take into account its intention: its reader must look for tearstains and passionate irregularities in the handwriting; the date, position in a sequence of replies, use of emotional language are all of great relevance. Penelope, on the other hand, betrays little nervousness here; her different surreptitiousness, weaving and unweaving, has perhaps strengthened her hand, as she now writes, to judge from Ovid's *Heroides*, in full command of the arts and artifices of persuasion. We will not be surprised to find confirmation of strength of character in the decidedly "composed" message of Penelope's letter, as Ovid has worded it; its classically ordered development must be quite unlike the broken phrases and hasty emotional outbursts that will characterize the letter being posted in the romantic cover picture. The urgency with which each of the two women will press for a reply will certainly also differ: indeed Penelope will tell Ulysses not to answer but rather come back in person. The ultimate fate of Penelope's letter will depend on the fortune of the sea and the winds, as she entrusts it to the captain of one of those ships depicted in the harbor beneath her window, to give to Ulysses if by chance he should meet him. Our cover girl, on the other hand, benefits from the efficiency and relative anonymity of the modern postal service: indeed the presence of the mailbox makes us wonder whether the postage stamp has already been invented, in which case her lover will almost surely not even have to pay to receive her message.

Not all letters are addressed by loving women, and only some letters are "confidential." But when *we*, that is, students of "letters," read letters from the past, not originally addressed to us, we are in a sense breaking into a confidence, uncovering something private, seeing something we were probably never meant to see. We must recognize that our understanding of these letters is mediated by the ways in which they have come before our eyes. The letter before us, if for no other reason than the passage of time, is *not* identical to the letter that was read by its original addressee, and even that letter was not quite the same as the letter the author thought he or she was sending.

Whereas at first glance it may have seemed important to identify only an

$$\text{addresser} \longrightarrow \text{message} \longrightarrow \text{addressee}$$

we must now consider at the very least, in order to account for a letter's writing and its reading, the following sequence, in which the "letter" (the message) is even further from "the beginning":

received form, formula, or "code" of "the letter" $\longrightarrow$ addresser $\longrightarrow$
    worded message + appearance of the "object" $\longrightarrow$ mode and

length of time of delivery ⟶ addressee ⟶ means of
transmission to us ⟶ ourselves

None of these factors is simple, and they are not independent of each other. The "addresser" will use, or submit to, or play with the "code," in accordance with his or her intentions, will select a paper and writing implement, and will frame his or her message while taking into account the time needed for delivery before it will be read. The "addressee's" reading will be affected by his or her expectations as well as by the physical appearance of the "object," the words of the message, and changes that may have occurred since the letter was solicited or its message set down. After making the crucial decision of committing handwritten or variously lettered originals to the authority—and relative clarity and permanence—of print, the later editor of the "correspondence" will have had to make decisions concerning the presentation of the letter (with or without notes and commentary, for instance; as part of some or all the letters of the addresser or as part of a correspondence including letters and responses) that will affect its interpretation by "us," just as we will be helped or hindered by the state of our understanding of the "code," of the language and linguistic habits of the period, of peripheral matters referred to by the addresser, and of the conditions of mail delivery at the time and place of departure and arrival.

Here we come directly to the subject of this issue of *Yale French Studies.* "Men/Women of Letters" seeks to address three kinds of issues. The first, the definition and description of "a letter," we have already begun to examine. Almost all the studies here (in particular that by Mireille Bossis), and many more to which our authors will make reference, will return to that question; Janet Altman will examine, among other matters, the constitution and rôle of "letter books," while the article by Marie-Claire Grassi surveys, in a series of letters written in a single social group over a century and a half, evolving aspects of the "code" as, reflecting the shifting norms of a changing society, it affects the expression of emotion in personal letters. The second, the question of "literary status," will be of particular concern to Altman, as she traces the evolution of both correspondences and "literature" from the Renaissance into the nineteenth century, and to the authors of articles on different writers' correspondences. Some of the latter will use the letter primarily as a source of information about the writer and his or her times (Louis Le Guillou and Deidre Dawson, in different ways, for example); others (in particular Martine Reid) will see a writer's letters as a constituent part of that writer's literary work; English Showalter, Jr., will examine various ways in which the letter can become "literary." Finally, in a period which has seen the appearance and in some cases already the completion of an extraordinarily rich variety of publications of great writers' letters, several of their editors will describe the particular difficulties they have faced and the material and moral dilemmas they have tried to resolve in the course of their labors (Showalter on Madame de Graffigny, Pierre Riberette on Chateaubriand, Le Guillou on Lamennais, Sheila Gaudon on Victor Hugo, Philip Kolb on Proust). If these editors by no means agree on all aspects of the editorial task, they do in any case all show strikingly how literary an effect plunging into a particular correspondence has had upon them. With reference to them one might quote, slightly altering her expression, Reid's conclusion concerning Stendhal: "as soon as language has become involved in letters, life is a novel."

First, the letter. Next, the postal service.

Even before the arrival of the Romans, messages could be sent in what is now France via runners established from place to place: and so in Caesar's day important happenings in Orleans could be known the same day in Auvergne. Mounted couriers were well enough established that they managed to get two letters from Caesar in Brittany to Cicero in Rome, one in twenty-six and the other in twenty-eight days.

Anything resembling modern mail delivery had to await at least the fifteenth century, however. Till the time of Louis XI (reign 1461–1483) organized postal service (the word, "post," referring to the place where the runner or horse was stationed, as in "Hôtel de la Poste" or "post-chaise") was in the service of the king or the military, or monasteries, corporations, large towns, big merchants: that is, those who could both write or employ a writer and also afford a messager. One must add the University, for already in the thirteenth century the University of Paris had a veritable postal service aimed at facilitating relations between students and their families. Louis XI is credited with the creation of relays for post horses, and from 1479 postal routes were being constituted.

Observing that the postal service could be a source of needed revenue, Henri III created an office of "messenger royal" in 1576, with the monopoly of official business but also with permission to accept private correspondences. In the period of Henri IV and Louis XIII post offices were opened in the cities of Paris, Lyons, Bordeaux, and Toulouse, with fixed dates for the departure and arrival of mail between those cities.

There were almost a thousand provincial offices in 1735. In 1672 Louvois made postal service a state monopoly, headed by a *fermier général*, although the "messageries de l'Université" continued their separate existence until 1719. There was, in addition, in Paris, briefly from 1653 and then after 1759, an establishment known as the "petite poste," united with the "grande poste" in 1780. The increasingly elaborate structure helps to explain the rise of extensive personal correspondences in the seventeenth and eighteenth centuries: Mme de Sévigné could expect to know when her letters would leave and when they should arrive, and Mme de Graffigny could write from Paris to the Lorraine and get an answer within a week.

The Revolution and the governments of the nineteenth century built on these achievements, maintaining the state's direction of the postal service, gradually improving and extending services and simplifying and reducing charges. There were several daily pickups from mail boxes in various quarters of Paris after 1821. From 1830 on every French *commune* was to have at least one delivery every two days, and upon the payment of a surtax (later revoked) home delivery became possible. The year 1844 saw the first mail train service, on the Paris-Rouen line. It was possible by Mallarmé's day to mail a letter in London in the morning and have it delivered the same afternoon in Paris. A notable event in nineteenth-century postal history in France was the adoption of the postage stamp in 1848; its rapid success can be seen in the following comparison: before 1849 only about ten percent of letters were mailed prepaid; eighty-five percent were in 1855.[3]

Eugène Vaillé, concluding his shorter *Histoire des Postes françaises jusqu'à la Révolution*, remarked on the gradual change in the nature of correspondence over its long early history. Up through the Middle Ages the vast majority of letters concerned political or governmental affairs. Then came the development of letters concerned with private or commercial interests, but even when they were between husband and wife, their correspondents would refrain from expressions

3. This unoriginal and very general survey has been gleaned from Eugène Vaillé, *Histoire générale des Postes françaises*, vol. 1. "Des origines à la fin du Moyen Age" (Paris: Presses universitaires de France, 1947); Eugène Vaillé, *Histoire des Postes françaises jusqu'à la Révolution*, "Que sais-je?" (Paris: Presses universitaires de France, 1946); Eugène Vaillé, *Histoire des Postes françaises depuis la Révolution*, "Que sais-je?" (Paris: Presses universitaires de France, 1947); *Larousse du XXᵉ siècle* (Paris: Librairie Larousse, 1932); *Grand Larousse encyclopédique* (Paris: Librairie Larousse, 1963); Société d'histoire littéraire de la France, *Les Editions de correspondences*, Colloque 20 avril 1968 (Paris: Librairie Armand Colin, 1969); Duchêne, *Madame de Sévigné*; and the articles following in this issue.

of familiarity or affection. The Renaissance saw the rise of intellectual correspondence among humanists, but not before the seventeenth century can be dated the advent of sentimental correspondence—a development that is charmingly confirmed in genre paintings of the period. Indeed, as late as 1750 a *Directeur des postes* estimated that letters inspired mainly by affection made up only one-tenth of the whole

It would be interesting to attempt a parallel between the evolution in dependability and speed of postal correspondence, on the one hand, and the rise of "autobiographical" writing, on the other. Regular "scientific" correspondences have become possible in the Renaissance. The seventeenth century sees both the rise of confessional (mostly religious) writing and Mme de Sévigné's correspondence with her daughter.[4] The increase both in postal services and in sentimentally inspired correspondence in the eighteenth century is contemporary with the publication of Mme de Sévigné's letters, the rise of the epistolary novel, and Rousseauist autobiography. Finally, in the age of the development of rapid postal exchanges, in a matter of hours or days, there is the flood of personal literature that accompanies the outburst of emotional expression characteristic of Romanticism. These could be some of the privileged moments in such a parallel.

After the letter, with its diversity of messages all filling the same space and the same words, has been delivered to its addressee, after its addressee has interpreted the letter and its words according to what his or her personal preconceptions will permit or encourage, the letter-object remains. All kinds of things can then happen to that object, from fairly rapid destruction, to faithful or unfaithful reproduction, to eventual readdressing—perhaps to us. The modes of this eventual redistribution are more complex yet than the history of any national postal system, and Pierre Riberette's article concerning the ongoing publication of Chateaubriand's correspondence, or Philip Kolb's on Proust's, will give some hints of the complexities.

The number of ongoing or recently completed French writers' correspondences is truly extraordinary, and the following table is certainly incomplete. It is, however, an indication of the devotion and energy being expended by the scholarly community in the midtwentieth century.

4. "Only a few years earlier [Madame de Sévigné] wouldn't have been able to receive and send her letters with the same regularity." Duchêne, *Madame de Sévigné*, 256.

Voltaire (Besterman) 51 vols., 1968–1977
Mme de Graffigny (Dainard, Showalter, et al.) 1 vol. to date, 1985–
Jean-Jacques Rousseau (Leigh) 43 vols., 1965–1984
Diderot (Roth and Varloot) 16 vols., 1955–1970
Mme Riccoboni (Nicholls) 1 vol., 1962
Helvétius (Smith et al.) 2 vols. to date, 1981–
Isabelle de Charrière (Candaux et al.) 5 vols., 1979–1983
Mme de Staël (Jasinski) 5 vols. to date, 1960–
Benjamin Constant (Roulin) 1 vol. (Pléiade), 1955
Chateaubriand (Riberette) 4 vols. to date, 1977–
Lamennais (Le Guillou) 9 vols., 1971–1981
Stendhal (Del Litto and Martineau) 3 vols. (Pléiade), 1962–1968
Balzac (Pierrot) 5 vols., 1960–1969
Hugo (J. Gaudon, S. Gaudon, Leuilliot) 1 vol. to date, 1979–
George Sand (Lubin) 20 vols. to date, 1964–
Sainte-Beuve (J. Bonnerot and A. Bonnerot) 19 vols. to date, 1935–
Barbey d'Aurevilly (Centre de recherches Jacques-Petit, University of Besançon) 4 vols. to date, 1980–
Flaubert (Bruneau) 2 vols. (Pléiade) to date, 1973–
Zola (Bakker, Mitterand, et al.) 4 vols. to date, 1978–
Proust (Kolb) 12 vols. to date, 1970–

In preparation are editions of many other writers' correspondences: Lamartine (Croisille, Morin), Vigny (Ambrière, Pierrot), Michelet (Viallaneix), Nerval (Pichois), Musset (Pierrot et al.), Gautier (Laubriet, Lacoste), Renan (Balcou), Romain Rolland (Duchatelet), Gide (Martin), Colette (Pichois), Apollinaire (Decaudin), Giono (Citron) are some that have come to my attention.[5] These editions are supported by foundations and universities (particularly in North America), government funding (particularly, in France, via the Centre national de la recherche scientifique and the Centre national des lettres), and—occasionally— the editor's personal funds; it is only in the rarest cases that their publishers have sponsored them as sound commercial ventures.

Further witness to the extraordinary interest in such editions and the kinds of critical inquiry that become possible once they are available can be seen in the recent flurry of colloquia and publications devoted to

5. Louis Le Guillou et François Lesure, "Les Correspondances littéraires et musicales," *Le Courrier du CNRS*, 49 (janvier 1983), 21–25; *Dix-Neuvième Siècle*, Bulletin de la Société des Etudes romantiques, 1 (avril 1985), 6–17.

correspondences: the Nantes colloquium of 1982 that Mireille Bossis reviews below; a second Nantes colloquium two years later, whose Acts are to appear in 1986; a colloquium in Aix-en-Provence in 1983, another in Fribourg (Switzerland) in May, 1984, and still another in Urbino in July, 1984; the recent issue of the *Revue des Sciences humaines* concerning the "Lettre d'écrivain"; the day to be devoted in 1986 by the Association Internationale des Etudes Françaises to "l'art épistolaire." A "décade" is planned in July, 1987, at the International Cultural Center of Cerisy-la-Salle on "L'épistolarité à travers les siècles: geste de communication et/ou geste d'écriture."[6] As regards editions of correspondences perhaps the most hopeful recent sign is the establishment by the Centre national de la recherche scientifique of a "Gréco"—a working group for coordinated research—directed by Louis Le Guillou, to encourage and facilitate the publication of nineteenth- and twentieth-century French correspondences.

The letters we are mostly concerned with in this special issue of *Yale French Studies*, the "real" letters of well-known French writers of the past, contain all kinds of allusions which we cannot be expected to understand. Our reading of such letters is literally "unauthorized," and we need help if we are to understand them fully. This is one of the major responsibilities of the editor of a writer's correspondence. Not only must that editor find the letters, decipher them, decide which to include, obtain permission from their owners first to see and then to publish them, decide on a suitable arrangement of the letters selected, figure out what to do about idiosyncratic or inconsistent spelling and punctuation, the editor must also attempt to insure the eventual reader's comprehension. Why are so many scholars now devoting themselves, often for the better part of a lifetime, to such arduous investigations? On behalf of whom? To accomplish what?

To the reasons suggested below by Louis Le Guillou, Pierre Riberette, and others—in an age where biographies and memoirs are popular among readers, correspondences add to their interest; the popularity of the epistolary novel among students of modern European literature leads naturally to scholarly interest in a novelist's correspondence; despite all the cautions that have repeatedly been raised, the quality and quantity of information provided in correspondences re-

6. For further information interested readers are encouraged to write to either of the codirectors: Mireille Bossis, University of Nantes, or Charles A. Porter, Yale University, in care of *Yale French Studies*, Box 2504A Yale Station, New Haven, Connecticut 06520–7445, USA.

mains superior to what historians and biographers may often otherwise find; sociologists and psychologists may find in correspondences from the past confirmations, illustrations, or troubling exceptions to their theories which are not available elsewhere—to these and other possible reasons, we add, particularly in a number of *Yale French Studies*, a further reason in this present day in which some critics of narrative fiction have discerned a "return of the plot." Surely a very basic human curiosity to know "what" and "why" motivates this search. Behind all the efforts recounted in this volume aimed at the definition of "letters" and behind the strategic conundrums their editors have encountered, there seems to lie a fundamental question: Just exactly *what is the "plot"* of a writer's correspondence?

Even if the editors think they are only trying to assure the reader's maximal comprehension, it is clear that they do more. Since with the editors' help we know at least parts of the future unknown to both the author and the addressee of the letters that have come down to us, letters in a series, all the more when they involve persons otherwise known, necessarily become parts of what in narrative and drama would be called plot. Forming as well as reflecting changing relationships between people, letters contain mysteries and a suspense that are in constant evolution; as they are successively opened they are illuminated from different angles. Perhaps letters have no "literary status" until, having been collected and edited, they have become the "strange genre" Showalter writes about, that genre in which the author has lost his customary "prerogative . . . of conceiving and implementing a coherent organization." To what extent is it the editor's responsibility to *make* "literature" with "letters"? To what extent can he or she avoid doing so?

And thus the questions that have led to the articles that follow. What are the characteristics of letters, of correspondences? What do certain existing correspondences signify to us belated readers? and how do they do it? Finally, how does the editor of a writer's correspondence responsibly perform his or her task?[7]

7. The special editor wishes here to thank all who have collaborated in this venture, and particularly the authors of the following articles, Liliane Greene and Peggy McCracken of *Yale French Studies*, and Mesdemoiselles Bodin and Fabre of the documentation and library staff of the Musée de la Poste in Paris.

$$\frac{Men}{Women}$$ *of Letters*

JANET GURKIN ALTMAN

The Letter Book as a Literary Institution 1539–1789: Toward a Cultural History of Published Correspondences in France

"Trouver une phrase qui irait moins à toi qu'à la postérité, j'en suis bien incapable."
—Alcmène to Amphitryon, I:3

"Je vois que vous parlez très suffisamment. D'ailleurs les poètes de la postérité se chargeront de votre conversation de cette nuit."
—Mercure to Alcmène, II:5
Giraudoux, *Amphitryon 38*[1]

"Real" letters have an ambiguous status among literary critics. For the historian or the biographer they have long had a recognized value as source documents. For literary critics schooled in modes of close reading that privilege "closed" or at least "definitive" texts and genres that are clearly fictive, real correspondences have not been a tempting terrain; indeed, although the last two decades have considerably swelled the numbers of critical editions of literary correspondences available for potential literary readings, relatively few have appeared. A scan of the *MLA Bibliography* suggests that more articles in language and literature journals are devoted to publishing newly discovered letters by literary writers than to interpretive readings of already available correspondences.

1. Alcmène to Amphityron (I:3): Uttering words that would be less for you than for posterity is beyond my ability. Mercury to Alcmène (II:5): I can see that you speak more than adequately. Besides, the conversation that you have tonight will be handled by the poets of posterity. (All translations from the French in this article are my own. For editions of letter books, whenever the original French is cited, I have respected the spelling and punctuation of the edition used.)

It is not my purpose here to offer a "literary" reading of a real correspondence. Exemplary literary readings exist, and are likely to spawn others.[2] Rather, I would like to look broadly at the various forms that published correspondences by literary figures have assumed in a specific cultural milieu (France), and press their authors (publishers, editors, writers) to give us a sense of what literary values were at stake for the author and the reading public in the publication of a real correspondence. By "literary" value, I here mean the value attached to writing embraced by the institutions of literature at a given point in a culture's history, insofar as we can still read this value today.

I shall be looking at a rather heterogeneous group of published correspondences and shall deliberately focus my attention on some letter books and some aspects of letter books that have been least commented upon by literary historians. What I shall be tracing is the way in which *published* correspondences, whenever they address their paradoxical function of *preserving* the *ephemeral*, institutionalize themselves as literature or as literary documents and in so doing project or reinforce certain images of the "Republic of Letters" at given moments in history.

A single letter, when it is dispatched as a truly missive letter, pro-

2. In these days of increasing lack of consensus about what "literature" itself is (see, for example, Paul Hernadi's recent anthology of diverse views, *What Is Literature?*), I find it more productive to speak of "literary" readings. By a "literary" reading, I simply refer to any commentary on a work which emphasizes the ways in which the work's production of meaning is affected by figurative language, rhetorical strategies, narrative or dramatic structures, thematic development, stylistic choices, and other qualities that have traditionally been considered "literary." The following readers of real correspondences have been particularly attentive to their literary workings: Lionel Duisit, *Mme Du Deffand épistolière* (Genève: Droz, 1963); Bernard Bray, "Quelques Aspects du système épistolaire de Mme de Sévigné," *Revue d'Histoire littéraire de la France* 69 (1969), 494–500; Louise K. Horowitz, "The Correspondence of Madame de Sévigné: Letters or Belles-Lettres?" *French Forum* 6 (1981), 13–27; Dalton Krauss, "The Voices of the Hydra: Diderot versus Falconet," *The Eighteenth Century* 24 (1983), 211–26. Others could be cited. In addition, a new kind of historical reading of correspondences has emerged, which seeks less to extrapolate from a correspondence the "facts" of a real existence than to explore the relationship between lived experience and the artistic qualities of letters that refer to that experience. Roger Duchêne's work on Mme de Sévigné has pioneered in this area. Finally, I discern in the work of Lionel Duisit and in Bernard Bray's work on both Chapelain and Mme de Sévigné an interest in what I would call the "literary consciousness of the letter writer," which I find to be a productive interest. By focussing on the writer's own statements about her or his writing, Bray has extrapolated from Sévigné's and Chapelain's correspondences a complex epistolary poetics that illuminates specific literary strategies within their respective correspondences. In my own work, I shall simply extend this notion of literary consciousness to include the broader context of the way in which addressed writing positions a writer within society during a particular period of literary history.

jects an image of its author at a given point in time and negotiates a relationship with a particular reader. It is to some extent both auto-biographically *undressed* (potentially offering insight into the author's "private" life and thought at that moment) and rhetorically *addressed* (constituted as a speech act to have an effect on a specific addressee on a particular day). Its acknowledged life is that of the *ephemera*, "for one day." When it is reinscribed in a book for publication, however, the letter is *readdressed* to a new readership and often *redressed* (corrected, revised, truncated, contextualized) by the publisher (be it original author, reader, or a new publisher), who negotiates a new, more perdurable relationship between the letters and the reading public for whom the correspondence is now intended. What I shall be focussing on in the next few pages are the latter two activities—redressing and readdressing—in an attempt to read some of the literary values that have been implicit in the reinscription of letters as books within the world of print culture. It will become clear that these literary values are not separable from other social and cultural values.[3]

The earliest published collections of letters in the French vernacular are largely the work of the humanists.[4] They are inspired by Latin and Italian models and inherit the burden of medieval rhetoric, in which letter-writing is a privileged activity for cultivating the *ars dictaminis*. Etienne Du Tronchet (1569—*Lettres missives et familieres*) and Etienne Pasquier (1586—*Lettres*) are the first to "defend and illustrate" the French language by cultivating the classical epistolary genre.

3. For a thoroughgoing critique of the assertion that noncontingent distinctions *can* be drawn between aesthetic and nonaesthetic value, see Barbara Herrnstein Smith's "Contingencies of Value," *Critical Inquiry* 10 (1983): 1–35.
4. Thanks to recent research, it is no longer possible to assert—as Daniel Mornet did in 1940, still echoing Gustave Lanson—that the epistolary genre in France was born with the polite society of the Précieuses. (See his chapter on "La Littérature épistolaire: Mme de Sévigné" in *Histoire de la littérature française classique*, 318.) After the careful work of Bernard Bray, Marc Fumaroli, Alain Viala, Lajos Hopp, Roger Duchêne, and others, we can now begin to perceive a vast and complex network of relationships between Latin epistolography and a nascent poetics of letter-writing in French during the Renaissance and early seventeenth century. Thus far, unfortunately, very few bridges have been built between those working on Latin rhetoric and epistolography in the Renaissance (Marc Fumaroli having made the most important contributions in this area recently) and those who have been pushing inquiry into epistolary discursive practices under French Classicism beyond study of Balzac, Voiture, and Sévigné. Antoine Viala has written one of the few attempts to bridge this gap in an article on "La Genèse des formes épistolaires en français et leurs sources latines et européennes," which appeared in the *Revue de littérature comparée* 218 (1981), 168–83.

In practice they benefit from the loosening of the ossified Ciceronian model, through the theory and example of Erasmus in his *De conscribendis epistolis* (1522), in which Erasmus argued for diversity in content, form, and style. Both Du Tronchet and Pasquier claim to be publishing their own real letters, directly composed in French, and exhort others to write letters in their "mother tongue,"

> en laquelle ils descouvrent leurs sens. Et, de ma part, escrivant en mon vulgaire, pour le moins escry-je en langage auquel j'ai esté allaicté dès la mammelle de ma mere.

> in which they discover their meaning. And, for my part, by writing in my vernacular, at least I am writing in the language which has nourished me since my mother's breast. [Pasquier, Book 1, Letter 1 (1586)]

Particularly emphatic in Pasquier's poetics is the notion that writing and reading personal letters in the language learned "at the mother's breast" is the way in which writers can most readily "descouvrir" (produce and "uncover," and subsequently "discover") "leurs sens," the perdurable but plural meanings of a life and culture.[5]

Readers also seem to have found perdurable meaning in Pasquier's letters. Five editions were published during Pasquier's lifetime alone; his letters continued to be printed in subsequent centuries, and his epistolary work is still highly readable today in recent editions (Droz, 1956 and 1974). The original publication of this letter book doubtless contributed a great deal toward legitimating the missive letter composed in French as a literary form. Pasquier's work is that of a cultivated man of letters and personal stylist, an epistolarian who reflects on a variety of serious issues, dedicates himself to a lifetime of learning and questioning, and is a subtle observer of the civil wars that he lived through. His preface makes clear his ideology and his program. Through publication of these letters he hopes to promote eloquence in the newly formed nation-state; all other nations that have cultivated eloquence have approved "this way of exposing to the public the letters that noteworthy people (*les gens de marque*) wrote each other privately" (1:1).

---

5. Pasquier's poetics is already quite close to Diderot's concept of letters as conversations, ostensibly disjointed, but in fact held together—like writing in the unconscious—by "imperceptible links," as Diderot writes to Sophie Volland: "Look at the circuitous paths we have taken. The dreams of a delirious sick person are not any more heteroclite. And yet, just as nothing is disconnected in the head of a dreamer or a madman, everything holds together likewise in conversations; but sometimes it would be quite difficult to reconstruct the imperceptible links that held so many disparate ideas together" (*Correspondance*, ed. G. Roth, 3, 172–73).

Pasquier quite comfortably includes himself among the "gens de marque" and publishes his private correspondence as the civic duty of a famous lawyer and already established writer: he is simply following the principle that *noblesse oblige*—the nobility particular to the Republic of Letters, that is, as distinct from the writer's original social class, for Pasquier's origins are bourgeois. As lawyer, however, he belonged to a class whose numbers had grown dramatically within the university and in the new nation-state during the fifteenth century,[6] and whose rhetorical practice, scholarship, and writing entitled them to a privileged position within the humanistic Republic of Letters. Publication, for Pasquier, is on a logical continuum with the original activity of letter writing, which Pasquier conceives as *already* literary, because it is produced by writers with literary consciousness, lawyers and other humanistically educated "gens de marque" who leave their literary mark in all of their writing. Pasquier is careful, however, not to identify model writers with any particular social class or profession. In Book 2, Letter 12 he makes it clear that model writers are not to be sought at the royal court or even in the "Palace of Lawyers," for both of these milieux have far too many practitioners who shun the work (*estude*) of writing. Pasquier's republic of letters essentially remains open to all who infuse their writing with a broad, ongoing commitment to learning from books and from experience.

Slightly less comfortable with this business of publication is Pasquier's contemporary Du Tronchet, who has asked others to assist him in improving upon his letters prior to publication and who takes great pains to tell us that these letters were written and dispatched without thought of publication. (Contrast Pasquier who in his epistolary poetics encourages writers to publish imaginary letters, thereby openly disagreeing with his master Erasmus, who "wants an epistle to have been authentically sent"—Book 2, Letter 2). Whereas Pasquier fully assumes the activity of authorship as his chosen civic identity and responsibility, Du Tronchet appears the literary parvenu, arriving at authorship by patronage (the title page dedicates his work to the Comte de Retz and the book includes many letters soliciting patronage), translation (he freely admits "pillaging" the Italians and includes several letters from Aretino among his own), and the assistance of "editors" (one of his letters requests a correspondent's assistance in the revision of his book

6. See Michel Rouche, *Histoire générale de l'enseignement et de l'éducation en France*, 1 (Paris: Nouvelle Librairie de France, 1981), 521–30, for a discussion of the growth of law schools within academic and humanist institutions in the latter half of the fifteenth century.

manuscript). Whereas Pasquier in his letters boldly rivals the Italians, opposing his voice to theirs, Du Tronchet is largely content to plagiarize them.

In these initial moments, these inaugural gestures of two sixteenth-century writers who are publishing their correspondence in what they perceive to be an unprecedented way, we catch a glimpse of the way in which authorial consciousness and identity get constructed within society at an early moment in print culture. Pasquier's explicit and elaborate program promotes the development of a national literature through real and even imaginative letter writing: Pasquier urges a young poet to turn to the letter genre to develop his literary persona, since verse seems to him to have exhausted its creative potential (2:2).

In Pasquier's epistolary practice, moreover, the exercise of the literary imagination is largely a function of an engaged historical consciousness. Pasquier the historian is attentive to the particular in both his own life and the life of his nation: childbirth, the marriage of a son, and various incidents in the wars of religion are equally worthy of original tropes. In putting together the first ten books of his letters, published in a single handsome quarto volume when he was fifty-seven years old, Pasquier rejoices in the diversity of the book, likening his letters to the mixed merchandise of a hardware store (calling them the "denree meslee" of a "quincaillerie"), and attributing the book's pluralism to the fact that these letters are a "general tableau of all of my ages in life,"

> in which you will see at one point my springtime, at another my summer, and then my autumn vividly portrayed—by this I mean my letters, molded by the ages that have diversely determined my opinions. [1:1]

Pasquier refuses to weed out the "folastre" from the "sage": in fact, he refuses to engage in any "pruning," arguing that the "beautiful leaves" of his letter tree will stand out all the more against the background of the bad ones (10:12). In preparing his letters for publication, he has amputated only their "heads" and "feet," that is, the lengthy, formulaic greetings and closings whose conventionality he rejects, calling them "a waste of time and nothing but filler" (1:1). These ossified heads and feet clearly are not part of Pasquier's anatomy. For publication, Pasquier substitutes instead a straightforward "Adieu." As a result, the remaining opening and closing gestures of his letters are each anchored in highly particularized temporal, geographical, and interpersonal relationships.

Pasquier's organic metaphors identify the letters as metonymies of a self engaged in historical process. The familiar letters do not belie this vision: each locates a voice that is highly positioned (temporally, geographically, and ideologically) as friend, barrister, and historical observer, and whose persona is complexly interlocked in contextualized dialogue. Moreover, Pasquier creates no preface for the book, to frame it for a general public. Instead, two letters to his close friend Antoine Loisel (1:1 and 10:12, first and final letters of the 1586 volume) readdress the letters as a missive book sent under the aegis of affectionate friendship. Anticipating the various objections that other readers will make to this "denree meslee," Pasquier indulges in some playful impersonation of his critics in his final letter, not in order to defend himself but rather ultimately in order to pronounce rather gleefully, "objections sustained." For after all, "the opinions of men are too diverse to conform in everything and everywhere with mine. . . . my friends, I have not undertaken to satisfy all of you generally, but rather some of you in particular, and especially myself" (10:12). Pasquier's book of letters, like Montaigne's *Essais*, celebrates the infinite diversity of the human personality as it affirms its pluralistic existence in time through a non-hierarchical display of language; and it grants to readers (inscribed as friends entitled to differing opinions) the same privilege.

Du Tronchet's motivations for publication are vague and mixed in comparison to Pasquier's coherent literary project. Pasquier publishes as an accomplished, independent, mature writer, seeking chiefly to encourage other writers to do the same in their own language and way. Accordingly Pasquier infuses his letters with a strong personal style, making his book into a collection of highly autobiographical essays that could be read alongside those of his friend Montaigne (essays which, incidentally, Montaigne suggested he would have written in letter form, had he had a close friend as correspondent).[7] Du Tronchet, however, conceives his missive letter collection rather as a model for epistolary writers functioning in a fixedly hierarchized society. His preface dis-

7. In his essay "Considérations sur Cicéron" (1:40), Montaigne confides, "Concerning letters, I want to say this word: that this is an area in which my friends claim that I have some talent. And I would have preferred that form for publishing my sallies, if I had had someone to whom I could speak. I would have needed, as I formerly did have, a certain relationship which attracted me, sustained and elevated me." Montaigne thereby alludes to the death of his friend La Boétie as determinant, but goes on to describe in detail how he goes about letter-writing in his daily life. Like Pasquier he shows considerable impatience with the current modes of courtly letter-writing, with their endless codified formulaic openings and closings, "harangues, offers, and pleadings." For a subtle reading of the way in which epistolary discourse nonetheless functions—from a Lacanian and Derridean perspective—in Montaigne's essays, see François Rigolot, "Montaigne's Purloined Letters," *Yale French Studies* 64 (1983), 145–66.

tinguishes between good ("legitimate") and bad ("bastard" or "barbarous") secretaries, and his letters divide stylistically into three basic categories, according to a hierarchy of social relations: "familieres" (letters to members of the family or persons of lower rank), "graves" (letters to persons of highest rank, conducting affairs of state), or "communes" (essentially letters of compliment for persons of middle, i.e., less than princely, rank).[8] Since Du Tronchet's collection predates Pasquier's by seventeen years and is unacknowleged by Pasquier in his list of predecessors, even though Pasquier had received a copy of Du Tronchet's book, we might ask ourselves whether it is just another courtesy book.

When Du Tronchet published his *Lettres missives et familieres* in 1569, letter manuals for courtiers already were beginning to flourish in the vernacular print world, the earliest being the anonymous *Le stille et masniere de composer, dicter et escrire toutes sortes d'epistres ou lettres missives*, published in Lyon in 1555. In 1568, only a year before Du Tronchet published his *Lettres missives*, the first manual to use the name "Secrétaire" appeared: *Le Secretaire, comprenant le stile et méthode d'escrire en tous genres de lettres missives, extraits de plusieurs scavans hommes* by G. Chappuys, who had translated Castiglione's *Cortegiano*. What distinguishes Du Tronchet's work, however, from these letter manuals influenced by courtesy books is the fact that his letter collection develops a persona that can readily be correlated with all of the biographical details that we know through other sources about the historical Etienne du Tronchet, secretary to several prominent nobles, and ultimately to Catherine de' Medici. And the persona that emerges from this rudimentarily autobiographical letter book (Du Tronchet's *Lettres missives*) is both an aspiring poet and court secretary; it is therefore quite possible to imagine that most of the letters in his published correspondence, even the ones borrowed from Italian authors, were actually sent—authored or reauthored—by Du Tronchet, during the course of his quite active career. Unlike other letter manuals, which are typically anthologies, Du Tronchet's book can be read as traces of a secretary-poet's life. There is enough personal detail and enough personal style, particularly in the familiar letters, to warrant the careful reconstruction of an author's life and work that Sister Mary Sullivan published in 1931.[9]

8. In his *Finances et Thresor de la plume françoise* Du Tronchet elaborates this tripartite typology of letters, using the terms cited. In his *Lettres missives* the letters are randomly presented, but the differences in style respect these three ranks of addresses.
9. Sister Mary Saint Francis Sullivan, *Etienne du Tronchet: Auteur Forézien du*

Indeed, if we agree with Sister Mary Sullivan that the "serious" letters (those conducting affairs of state or addressed to persons of highest rank) are the most garbled, bombastic, and unreadable ones today, we can choose to read them as evidence of the strain that Du Tronchet was under when he tried to create a noble style. His letters testify to the dilemma of the secretary as author in an age when royalty itself was seeking a literary voice and when nobles frequently had to borrow the voices of secretaries, who, in turn—when pressed to find a noble style— often translated badly from the Italian. Read as autobiography, Du Tronchet's letters trace the life and record the stylistic efforts of one of the earliest hack writers who had to live by their pens—both literally and figuratively—in the age of transition to print. Du Tronchet was by all reports an excellent calligrapher, and there are indications that this quality was rare in the sixteenth century. When he published his *Lettres missives*, however, he clearly had invested more than a calligrapher's ego in the act of publication. He includes in the *Lettres missives* the letters of encouragement that he received from friends who assure him that these letters, which are the very "portrait" of his "virtue" and talent, will guarantee his immortality. This inclusion of fan mail in a published correspondence was not, however, enough to convince the poet Ronsard of Du Tronchet's status as "author." Du Verdier, in *La Bibliothèque Française* reports that Ronsard, on hearing Dorat call Du Tronchet an excellent "auteur," answered "dites *écrivain*," implying that Du Tronchet's chief talents still lay in calligraphy.[10]

Du Tronchet's letters were to be his first and primary claim to authorship, but they enjoyed a success even greater than Pasquier's. That they were frequently reprinted between 1569 and 1623 but not at all thereafter, however, suggests a readership that regarded these *Lettres missives* primarily as a letter manual, to be superseded by the book that was to corner the market in the field: Puget de la Serre's *Le Secrétaire de la cour ou méthode facile d'écrire selon le temps*, whose first edition privilege dates from 1623. Thus, although Du Tronchet's polemics and title (*Lettres missives*) identify his book with the humanist tradition— as a collection of *sent* (rather than *sendable*) letters, as art rather than

---

XVIe siècle. *Etude biographique et littéraire* (Washington: L'Université Catholique d'Amérique, 1931).

10. I owe the Ronsard quotation from Du Verdier to Sister Mary Sullivan's *E. du Tronchet*, 3. She points out, moreover, that "écrivain" would have been a synonym for "scribe" or "calligrapher" at the time, and adduces the reported quotation as further evidence of Du Tronchet's reputation as a calligrapher. Each age thus develops its own hierarchies of "writers," reinvesting the lexicon with its own system of values.

commodity—Du Tronchet's letter book seems to have been received as a *Secrétaire.* Such is the potential fate of the work of art in the age of mechanical reproduction: by recasting his letters as art to be copied, and in so doing eliminating much personal and historical detail in order to make these letters into acceptable models,[11] Du Tronchet-the-editor began the commodification process that was to undermine Du Tronchet-the-writer's pretensions to authorial status and immortality through print.

Publication of letters in the vernacular was not common in the sixteenth century. Three other instances are worth discussing, if only because they reveal the value that more private citizens than Pasquier and Du Tronchet attached to the publication of missive letters during the early history of print. In the same year that Du Tronchet published his *Lettres missives,* 1569, a certain Gaspar de Saillans, who for thirty years had dealt in saltpeter for his majesty's artillery, published the letters he and his wife had exchanged before and after their marriage. His handsomely adorned letter book, intended as a gift for his wife's cousin and for his own newly born son, offers a fairly detailed image of daily domestic life and conjugal communication in a specific milieu, one menaced by plague and religious wars. Gaspar de Saillans published the book for no other reason than "afin de laisser en quelque endroit mon nom viure apres ma vie corporelle" [to create a place where my name might survive my body], calling it *Premiere liure de Gaspar de Saillans* ["Gaspar de Saillans's First Book"].

In 1586, the same year in which Pasquier published his letters, Mesdames des Roches, a mother and daughter who presided over a literary salon in Poitiers, privately published their own missive letters. These are essentially embellished greeting cards: letters of compliment, letters sent on occasions of illness, and the like. Although they were never to be reprinted, they were viewed as literary works by Pasquier, who mentions this volume as an immediate predecessor in the genre that he considers himself as initiating. Indeed, he appends a postscript to Loiseul, just prior to publication of his own letters, noting that these ladies have jumped the gun on him:

> All the same, I must not forget to tell you that five or six weeks after
> my letters were in press, Mesdames des Roches had a collection
> printed which also bears the title *Epistles,* in which you see some

11. Sister Mary Sullivan, who has studied the Du Tronchet manuscripts, points out that in editing his letters for publication, Du Tronchet omitted many names and details as being of purely local and historical interest (Sullivan, 51).

beautiful writing and clever niceties. And verily I shall not be upset to figure symbolically together with her whom I infinitely respect and honor among the beautiful, honest, and virtuous Ladies of France. [10:12]

The very first missive letters published in French, however, insofar as I can determine, were the *Epistres familieres et invectives* of Hélisenne de Crenne, in real life Marguerite Briet, a young woman from a village near Abbeville, who had been married at age twelve but subsequently left her husband to lead an independent life as a writer, publishing a successful novel *Les Angoysses douloureuses* (1538), an essay *Le Songe* (1540), and a translation of Virgil (1541). In 1539 her collection of "familiar and invective letters" was printed by the publisher Denys Janot. The familiar letters are highly personal, addressed largely to persons in distress, primarily women friends. In the invective letters, Hélisenne argues against several adversaries: (1) her husband, (2) a correspondent who contends that women are capable only of spinning, and (3) fellow citizens who have criticized her literary activity. The progression of the eighteen letters of the volume, from private exchanges to increasingly public defense of a woman's right to speak with a literary voice, suggests that part of Hélisenne's purpose in publishing these letters was to defend and illustrate her sex. Her book will inscribe a woman's name in a long history of forgotten women's names:

> Cornelia, mother of the Gracchi, gave them an excellent education in eloquence. Valery, a Roman virgin, was so expert in Greek and Latin letters that she interpreted Virgil's verse and versification. Aspasia was so filled with great knowledge that the respected philosopher Socrates was not ashamed to learn from her. [Invective Letter 4]

For Hélisenne, Marguerite de Navarre incarnates all the preceding qualities, combining Cicero's eloquence with Socrates's reason, and is admired as the most recent exemplar of women's writing. Hélisenne de Crenne's letters, which went through two reeditions, found a larger readership than those of Gaspar de Saillans, but were eclipsed by Du Tronchet's in 1569 and not included among Pasquier's acknowledged predecessors, even though he alludes to Hélisenne's writing (2:12).

What then can we conclude from this brief survey of published correspondences in the sixteenth century? The letter books of Hélisenne de Crenne (1539), Gaspar de Saillans (1569), Du Tronchet (1569), Mesdames des Roches (1586) and Etienne Pasquier (1586) are all published by the authors themselves, during their own lifetimes; in this practice alone they differ significantly from the published correspondences of the seventeenth, eighteenth, and nineteenth centuries, which will be largely posthumous. Indeed, the most personal of the writers—Hélisenne de Crenne, Gaspar de Saillans, and Pasquier—publicly assume full editorial responsibility for their correspondence, insisting on the fact that no one other than they has redressed or readdressed their letters. Although each of these five epistolarians has different motivations for transforming a private correspondence into a printed book, ranging from Gaspar de Saillans's simple desire to save his name from oblivion to the more complex literary and historical consciousness of Pasquier, each presents her or his book in some sense as a commemorative self-portrait. Seen in this light, as rudimentary autobiography, sixteenth-century letter books are yet another sign of the individual self-consciousness that had already emerged in Renaissance art and portraiture.

We can note, moreover, that of the five letter books discussed, the only three that were to survive more than one printing were those whose authors self-consciously situated their work within the larger literary enterprise. By including either letters or prefaces that in some way designate the book's place in an ongoing literary history (as women's writing or as a continuation of Greek, Latin, and Italian epistolography) Hélisenne de Crenne, Du Tronchet, and Pasquier readdress their work to a readership which is called to respond to their work in a literary way: to imitate their example and write in turn. Each uses the letter to illustrate vernacular eloquence within a particular "republic of letters," thereby in part constituting and designating the status of that group as a legitimate Republic of Letters, be it Hélisenne's lineage of eloquent women, Pasquier's humanist circle, or Du Tronchet's world of courtiers. Each writes with a sense of literary mission, rendered explicit in the organization and framing of the letters in the act of publication.

The literary status of correspondences in the seventeenth century has long been recognized, and the art of individual epistolarians has been amply discussed in recent years. The epistolary poetics and practice of Malherbe, Balzac, Voiture, Madame de Sévigné, Costar, Godeau, Chapelain, Tristan l'Hermite, Maynard, and even Hercule Audittret have been closely scrutinized by a group of literary critics in France who have been most attentive to the complex ways in which the real missive letter was constituted as a literary genre during that period.[12]

12. The 1978 issue of the *Revue d'Histoire littéraire de la France* (vol. 78, no. 6),

Particularly lively has been the debate between Roger Duchêne and Bernard Bray over the literary consciousness of Madame de Sévigné, over what the forging of her unique style owed to the unique historical reality of a lived experience—separation from her daughter (what Duchêne calls Mme de Sévigné's "réalité vécue")—and what it owed to an inherited code of literary language and culture (what Bray discerns as her "système épistolaire").[13] Duchêne argues that Mme de Sévigné's letters owe their special qualities and spontaneity to the author's lack of literary consciousness, to her refusal to write for any public beyond her daughter. In his view, Sévigné breaks with the practices of all previously published epistolarians, producing an "immediate transcription of reality" that owes nothing to books or to "literary" choices (*Madame de Sévigné et la lettre d'amour*, 297). Bray, however, who has worked extensively with the relationship between love letters in letter manuals and the development of the novel in the seventeenth century,[14] and who has closely studied the poetics and practices of other epistolarians of the period,[15] points out the extent to which Mme de Sévigné's writing is mediated by larger systems of discourse which were part of her milieu and which functioned as conscious literary models for her: the language of passion developed in fictional letters; the conventions that govern

---

devoted to "La Lettre au XVIIe siècle," gives an excellent view of work currently being done and offers references to previous work. See also the prefaces to recent critical editions of seventeenth-century epistolarians (e.g. B. Bray's 1966 edition of Chapelain, C. Grisé's 1972 edition of Tristan L'Hermite, G. Couton and Y. Giraud's 1975 edition of Hercule Audittret). Roger Duchêne's *Ecrire au temps de Mme de Sévigné: lettres et texte littéraire* (Paris: Vrin, 1982) gathers articles that Duchêne has written between 1962 and 1981 on Sévigné and the epistolary genre.

13. The chief publications in this debate are Bernard Bray, "Quelques Aspects du système épistolaire de Mme de Sévigné," *RHLF* 69 (1969), 494–500; Duchêne's *Madame de Sévigné et la lettre d'amour* (Paris: Bordas, 1970) and his "Réalité vécue et réussite littéraire: Le statut particulier de la lettre," *RHLF* 71 (1971): 177–94; Fritz Nies, *Gattungspoetik und Publikumsstruktur* (München: W. Fink, 1972); Bernard Beugnot, "Débats autour du genre épistolaire: réalité et écriture," *RHLF* 74 (1974), 195–203; Duchêne's response to Nies, "L'Esthétique de la négligence," *Oeuvres et Critiques*, 1,2 (1976): 113–27; Bray's review of Nies's book in *RHLF* 78 (1978), 120–21; and Louise K. Horowitz's article cited in note 2 (1981).

14. See B. Bray, *L'Art de la lettre amoureuse: des manuels aux romans* (The Hague and Paris: Mouton, 1967).

15. Two particularly noteworthy articles are "L'Epistolier et son public en France au XVIIe siècle," *Travaux de linguistique et de littérature* 11 (1973), 7–17, and Bray's lengthy introduction to his critical edition of Jean Chapelain, *Soixante-dix-sept lettres inédites à Nicolas Heinsius* (La Haye: Nijhoft, 1966). In both of these articles, Bray argues (against Lanson and others) for more serious and nuanced consideration of real correspondences as literary works constrained by generic codes.

transfer of news from one circle (Paris and the court) to another (the province); and the aesthetics of negligent style.[16]

Although the debate between Bray and Duchêne may have polarized the conceptual opposition between historical consciousness and literary consciousness, masking what the one owes the other, it has been productive even within its very polarization of Sévigné scholarship: Duchêne, Bray, and the others who have written on Mme de Sévigné since the 1960s have significantly deepened and nuanced our understanding of the complex relationships between letter writing, postal systems, publication (informal and formal), literary models, and lived experience in the seventeenth century.

Unfortunately the very existence of Mme de Sévigné's monumental correspondence, which has been compelling (not to mention compulsory) and formative reading for so many generations of writers and students of literature, has tended to obscure somewhat the nuances of the epistolary practices that preceded publication of her letters. Even Duchêne's careful work induces the perception that "Enfin Sévigné vint," that prior to Mme de Sévigné published epistolarians were all writing their letters for literary glory, banning "the direct expression of life's realities" and the particularities of interpersonal relationships from their letters (*Mme de Sévigné et la lettre d'amour*, 77). Duchêne, like Daniel Mornet before him, tends to deal summarily with other epistolarians, putting Pasquier, Du Tronchet, Guez de Balzac, and even the authors of letter manuals in pretty much the same category—as writers of impersonal letters.

To be sure the "divine Marquise" rightfully enjoys her position—comparable to the status enjoyed by Richardson, Rousseau, Laclos, and Goethe for the letter novel—at the summit of the epistolary genre; the publication of her letters unleashed and laid barer than ever before the creative energies that blur the distinction between personal writing and living. But Mme de Sévigné's striking originality in her letters to her daughter, we should note, is not so different, strategically, from Pasquier's. Indeed both Pasquier and Sévigné find their strongest, most unique voices by deliberately cultivating the "mother tongue" as an idiolect; both explicitly eschew more universal language formulas, forging instead strong interpersonal ties through imaginative exploration of the "breast-feeding language" (what Pasquier calls the "langage auquel j'ai esté allaicté dès la mammelle de ma mere"). Both use the mother tongue, moreover, in a way that interweaves personal and national his-

16. To reinforce this argument, Bray adduces the work of Fritz Nies on Mme de Sévigné, *Gattungspoetik und Publikumsstruktur.*

tory, positioning themselves autobiographically as observers and com-
mentators on contemporary phenomena.

In Duchêne's history of letter writing, the publication of Mme de
Sévigné's letters figures as the developmental summit of a mutation
beginning with Voiture. Duchêne's evolutionary view recognizes af-
finities only between Sévigné and two immediate predecessors: Voiture
and Bussy, both of whom innovate with respect to previous practice by
addressing their letters exclusively to one specific reader or circle of
readers, thereby paving the way for the publication of Mme de Sévigné's
more intimate letters to her daughter.[17] Duchêne's history is now a
widely accepted one. Elizabeth Goldsmith, for example, uses it to position Bussy's correspondence within Duchêne's history of correspondences.[18] Citing Duchêne, she sees Bussy's correspondence as offering
"a new stress on the letter as the expression of a person," which she
believes to be previously absent from published correspondences in
France (240). I shall argue that it is important to see this stress not as
"new" but as "renewed" under particular historical conditions. Duchêne's history is an illuminating one, but it omits some stories that yield a
slightly different map of seventeenth-century epistolary space. In particular, once we bring Renaissance epistolography into the picture, and
in equally close focus, this evolutionary progressive view breaks down,
and it becomes possible to read the dominant epistolary practices of the
seventeenth century instead as a long rupture with the Erasmian practices of the sixteenth century, which Mme de Sévigné's letters profoundly renew.

Between 1586, when Pasquier's first book of letters was published,
and 1725–54, when four successive editions (1725, 1726, 1734, 1754)

17. See Duchêne, *Mme de Sévigné et la lettre d'amour*, 67–114, and "Le Lecteur de
lettres," *RHLF* 78 (1978), 977–90 for an outline of this history. For Duchêne, the crucial
distinction is between what he calls the deadly "lettre érudite" (cultivated—as he sees
it—by the early epistolarians Du Tronchet, Pasquier, and Balzac) and the lively "lettre
mondaine" (illustrated by the later epistolarians Voiture, Bussy, and Sévigné), the latter
being more linked to relationships with people in society. According to Duchêne, on
978–81 of the article cited, Pasquier was writing only for "those who like generalities
and 'beautiful subjects'" and eliminated all references to his personal life from his
published letters. (Needless to say, I find Duchêne's reading of Pasquier a bit hasty.)
Duchêne, like most other literary historians, does not discuss Hélisenne de Crenne,
Gaspar de Saillans, and Mesdames des Roches.

18. In "The Politics of Sociability and Sincerity in the Letters of Bussy-Rabutin,"
French Forum 8 (1983), 232–42.

brought out an increasingly voluminous proportion of the letters of Mme de Sévigné to Mme de Grignan, the literary institutions of France had undergone profound changes. The aesthetic, political, and social forces that conditioned epistolary poetics and practices in the seventeenth century, I shall argue, work against the publication (though not necessarily the writing) of letters like Pasquier's and Mme de Sévigné's, which are conceived as metonymies of a historically localized and singular self, as it affirms its evolving relationships with close friends and relations.

The ease with which Pasquier and even Hélisenne de Crenne and Gaspar de Saillans assumed authorship, publishing personal letters during their own lifetimes, suggests a different attitude toward the letter book from the attitudes that we encounter among seventeenth-century epistolarians. For the Renaissance writers, print is a logical extension of the territory staked out for the self in the handwritten letter. Just as the letter, by Erasmian principles,[19] is a space for personal growth and linguistic development of the self as it interacts with others, the book is essentially the record or trace of that growth. Pasquier articulates this vision of the letter book most fully with his organic metaphors: the tree's leaves, left unpruned, as they grew. But even Gaspar de Saillans before him had used the same metaphor to insist on the value of the idiolect, as long as it bears substantive fruit. In preparing his letters for publication, Gaspar notes that he has not concerned himself with orthography, since it reflects the particularity of individual pronunciation; moreover, anyone who would show more concern for spelling than for the "writing's savory intelligence" ("le goust de l'intelligence de l'escriture") would resemble those who are more interested in the tree's bark than in the substance of its fruit (31). There is a markedly individualistic, pioneering spirit in these Johnny Appleseeds of the early French republic of letters, who abandon their trees to the four winds and posterity without ostensibly pruning or prescribing a social use for them.

By the seventeenth century, however, the social uses of the letter will have been thoroughly codified by letter anthologies that define a limited number of "epistolary situations," and offer model letters and responses for each situation. Thus the standard collection will always contain letters of compliment, gratitude, consolation, and so forth. These epistolary situations are repeatable, social, aristocratic, and

19. For a fuller discussion of Erasmian epistolography, see Marc Fumaroli, "Genèse de l'épistolographie classique: rhétorique humaniste de la lettre, de Pétrarque à Juste Lipse," *RHLF* 78 (1978), 886–905, esp. 888–93.

above all public; epistolary communication in the letter manuals and anthologies—from Rosset (1608), Puget de la Serre (1623), and Faret (1627) at the beginning of the century to Furetière, (1689) Richelet (1690), and Vaumorière (1690) at the end of the century—reflects the social rituals of courtly and salon life.[20]

Epistolary style, when it is discussed in these manuals and anthologies, is not the *apte dicere* promoted by Erasmus. Erasmus's *apte dicere* admits infinite variety, because it is forged by personal *ingenium* and therefore reflects the infinite diversity of the human personality as it changes over time.[21] Epistolary style in the anthologies is instead the *decorum* prescribed by social rank and current public taste: noble and sublime in the early part of the century, when Balzac's eloquence is the primary model, more lively and playful when Voiture's letters replace Balzac's as the epistolary ideal. The editors of these anthologies, when they include a section of "Remarks on the style" of individual authors, will limit themselves to spelling, grammar, and decorum, criticizing whatever deviates from an increasingly standardized code. In short, the anthologies stake out a space for the letter which is essentially uniform, public, and limited to persons of a particular social status.[22]

20. François de Rosset, *Lettres amoureuses et morales des beaux esprits de ce temps* [privilège for first edition: 1608]; Jean Puget de la Serre, *Le Secrétaire de la cour ou méthode facile d'écrire selon le temps* [privilège for first edition: 1623]; Nicolas Faret, *Recueil de lettres nouvelles. Dédié à Monseigneur le Cardinal de Richelieu* (Paris: chez Toussaint de Bray, 1627); Pierre Richelet, *Les Plus belles lettres des meilleurs auteurs françois, avec des notes* (Lyon: Bailly, 1689); [Antoine Furetière], *Essais de lettres familières. Sur toutes sortes de sujets. Avec un Discours sur l'Art Epistolaire. Et Quelques Remarques nouvelles sur la Langue Françoise. Oeuvre postume de Monsieur l'Abé*** de l'Académie Françoise* (Paris: chez Jacques Le Febvre, 1690); Pierre d'Ortigue de Vaumorière, *Lettres sur toutes sortes de sujets, avec des avis sur la manière de les écrire et des réponses à chaque espèce de lettre* (Paris: J. Guignard, 1690). The authors of these manuals are equally well known as authors of dictionaries (Furetière, Richelet) and general courtesy books (Faret, Ortigue de Vaumorière, Puget de la Serre).

21. See Fumaroli's discussion, 889–93. Erasmus, as Fumaroli points out, was actually elaborating his conception of the letter in opposition to the formal legalism of the medieval *Artes dictaminis*. Erasmus affirms as a fundamental, liberating principle the principle of the "infinite": *res tam multiplex propeque ad infinitum varia.* The letter's infinite metamorphic possibilities come from the unlimited topics that it can treat, the diversity of the correspondents' personalities, and the individual's cultural and spiritual development throughout the ages of life. Erasmus insists on "epistolary freedom" (*illam libertatem epistolarem*), but also on the necessity for a careful pedagogy—of advice, not rules—to develop the personal *ingenium* of the child.

22. This *anthology-manual* hybrid (wherein recognized aristocrats and published authors are held up as models for writing) developed hardy roots in France that persist well beyond the seventeenth century. Consider, for example, Charles Dezobry's *Dictionnaire pratique et critique de l'Art épistolaire français avec des préceptes, et des conseils sur chaque genre. Plus de mille modèles choisis dans les monuments et les documents*

Across the Channel, in England, letter manuals and anthologies evolved in a quite different way. Although British editors, like the French, initially pillaged the Italian courtly writers for epistolary models, locally produced letter manuals in England quickly evolved to include sample letters from servant girls, apprentices, parent-child exchanges, and the like.[23] The English letter books reflect a society where more than one social class is wielding the pen, and they may very well have contributed to the earlier rise in literacy and democratization of literary culture in English society. By way of contrast, it is instructive to look at the kinds of letter collections that were available on the "popular" market in France. If we consult the recently compiled catalogue of titles distributed by the *Bibliothèque Bleue* of Troyes (that is, the inexpensive paperbacks that were sold by peddlars at town fairs and in farmers' markets) what do we find available to workers and peasants in seventeenth- and eighteenth-century France? Although letter manuals appear to have been distributed in greater numbers than other pedagogical handbooks,[24] all of them are simply reprints of handbooks for courtiers, like Puget de la Serre's *Le Secrétaire à la Mode, ou Méthode facile d'escrire selon le temps diverses Lettres de Complimens, Amoureuses & Morales.*[25] In these handbooks, peasants and workers could find models to declare love or break with a mistress, to congratulate someone on his success at court, and to express condolences in proper French. Thus epistolary space, even in manuals designed for

---

(Paris: Delagrave, 1866). This thick volume (1,354 pp.) is a veritable desk encyclopedia of epistolary authors (indexed by name, from Guez de Balzac to Bonaparte, but drawn primarily from the seventeenth- and eighteenth-century courtly epistolarians). It is also a virtual thesaurus of epistolary situations (likewise indexed, according to exactly the same categories as in the seventeenth-century manuals—i.e. letters of congratulation, gratitude, farewell, and comparable social situations). A dedicatory letter places the volume under the patronage of a society lady, and the author considers the broader readership for this letter book to be "lazy or inexperienced" people. Since all of these model letters "come from authors or society people," Dezobry affirms, "our Dictionary has a literary and almost educational stamp." Epistolary *art* (note the title) is still being defined exclusively in terms of the social codes of a particular class; literary and aristocratic values are largely synonymous here.

23. For a detailed listing and description of letter manuals produced during that period, see Katherine Hornbeak's *The Complete Letter Writer in English 1568–1800*, Smith College Studies in Modern Languages, vol. 15, nos. 3–4 (1934).

24. See Robert Mandrou, *De la Culture populaire aux XVIIe et XVIIIe siècles* (Paris: Stock, 1964), 127.

25. See Alfred Morin, *Catalogue descriptif de la Bibliothèque Bleue de Troyes* (Genève: Droz, 1974), 334–37, 358–61, 406–09, for a listing of the letter manuals known to have been distributed. See Geneviève Bollème, *La Bibliothèque bleue* (Paris: Gallimard/Julliard, 1971), 151–56, for some typical extracts.

popular consumption, remains throughout the seventeenth and eighteenth centuries defined by the space of the court and the salon.

If we turn now from the letter manuals to a more arguably literary domain, and scan the letter collections published during the seventeenth century as the compilation of a single author's missive letters (e.g. Guez de Balzac, Costar, Gombauld, Conrart, Maynard, Voiture, Bussy, and others), we note a similar closure of epistolary space in comparison to Renaissance letter books. Although more writers than ever are being admitted to the ranks of published epistolarians, the literary space defined by the published writers and their writing is limited in comparison to the sixteenth century. A bourgeois couple's letters (Gaspar de Saillans), a mother-daughter correspondence (Mesdames des Roches), a woman's defense and illustration of her sex (Hélisenne de Crenne), an autobiographical presentation of personal letters (Pasquier) would find no place among the published letter books of the seventeenth century. Instead we note a striking resemblance among published epistolarians of the seventeenth century: they are almost all men, and most of them are members of the Académie Française, which received its official letters of patent from Richelieu in 1635. Publication of letters has become largely a literary club activity.

Indeed, the period preceding the official founding of the Académie Française can be regarded as a watershed period in the history of French letter books, as well as in the history of French literature in general. As late as 1616 the maverick Renaissance poet D'Aubigné was intending to publish "five books of *Missive Letters,*" as D'Aubigné announced them, "the first being *Familiar Letters,* full of uncommon railleries."[26] D'Aubigné's project is one of the last avatars of the Renaissance vision of the letter book: that is, the book conceived as the commemoration of an individual life, where the tragicomic mix of the "folastre et sage" is still possible. In fact, D'Aubigné's project seems to have aborted, for only one book of letters, the *Lettres touchant quelques poincts de diverses sciences* has come down to us, and these were not published until the end of the nineteenth century.

Meanwhile, during the same period, Malherbe was starting to turn over some of his missive letters to the editor François de Rosset for Rosset's new collection of model letters by contemporary authors (1618), an anthology symptomatically subtitled "lettres des Beaux esprits de ce temps." Nicolas Faret's similar anthology of 1627, dedicated

26. Agrippa D'Aubigné, *Oeuvres,* ed. H. Weber (Paris: Gallimard/Pléiade, 1969), 8.

to Cardinal Richelieu, was also to contain letters by the king's official poet Malherbe, as well as letters by Guez de Balzac, Racan, Boisrobert, Faret, and others who would officially be founding members of the Académie Française eight years later. Both Rosset's and Faret's collections are organized to present letters of compliment, consolation, and the like, which illustrate the new political as well as linguistic turn that published prose is taking during this period.[27] Thus long before publication of the first official grammar or dictionary of the Académie Française, and several years before the notorious quarrel over *Le Cid*, the group of writers anxious to reform and govern language and literary activity in France were exercising their control through letter books.

In 1624 Guez de Balzac published the first volume of his own missive letters (*Lettres du sieur de Balzac*). For both R. Duchêne and A. Viala, Balzac's letters are on a continuum with Pasquier's, as examples of the "lettre érudite," as distinguished from the "lettre mondaine" illustrated subsequently by Voiture.[28] Their distinction between Balzac and Voiture makes sense, insofar as it emphasizes the gravity of tone and topic which Balzac consciously cultivated in his letters (closely linked with the author's own oratory practice) as opposed to the more casual style and frivolity of the topics addressed by Voiture (whose letters are an extension of salon conversation). The "erudition" of Balzac's letters, however, is quite limited in comparison to Pasquier's deep humanist culture and broad spectrum of concerns. Most of Balzac's

27. Raymond Lebègue, in "La Publication des lettres de Malherbe," *RHLF* 22 (1922), 129–64, and *RHLF* 23 (1923), 1–23, gives a detailed account of Malherbe's collaborations with the three editors Rosset, Faret, and Puget de la Serre prior to his death in 1628. Lebègue also carefully teases out of the autograph manuscripts some clear indications of how Malherbe would have revised his letters for the edition of his own letters that appeared posthumously in 1630, in order to "dress [his letters] according to the fashion of the day," as Malherbe put it. In my view, Malherbe is an emblematic and watershed figure: all documentary evidence points to the fact that although he wrote lively, personal, familiar letters on topics that were considered appropriate by Renaissance writers (political, religious, and domestic topics as well as journalistic accounts of events), he did not consider these letters "literary," i.e., worthy of rewriting, keeping, or publishing. Among those letters that Malherbe retained for publication, manuscript indications are that Malherbe eliminated all historical facts and private matters in order to reduce each letter to its principal object, in accord with courtly conventions for letter-writing: expressions of thanks, offers of service, recommendation, consolation, or the like. The 1630 edition of his letters, moreover, was divided into three books, with letters grouped according to the social rank of the addresses, defined in terms of courtly hierarchies: (1) members of court, (2) lesser nobles and colleagues, and (3) mistresses. Letters to his wife, son, and friends Du Vair and Peiresc are absent from this collection.

28. Viala, 168–83, and Duchêne, "Le Lecteur de lettres," 977–83.

letters curry favor, and much of his writing is given over to those courtly compliments to addressees that Pasquier eschewed. By 1624 the compliment and the eulogy had become dominant modes in epistolary writing: letter manuals like Puget de la Serre's even attach a lengthy appendix of set phrases for this new genre of proper French, called "Les Compliments de la langue française." Balzac's often-cited erudition (his use of classical rhetorical turns and quotations and his general reputation as a "sçavant" and "docte" among his contemporaries) is by and large rhetorically subordinated to the politics of eulogy in his letters. Voiture's letters (1650), although stylistically different from Balzac's, are comparably dominated by the complimentary mode.

To appreciate the ideological distance separating Balzac (1624) and Pasquier (1586), it is worth returning retrospectively to Pasquier's letters, in which Pasquier took a strong stand against what he perceived to be a new form of erudition, linguistic practice, and authorship being fostered at the court. When Pasquier speaks to friends about current fashions in language and literature, he waxes particularly indignant. Indeed several of his letters decry a tendency toward short-cut acquisition of courtly speech, manners, and superficial knowledge, which produce servility and mimicry. Pasquier fears that this tendency is coming to dominate all other forms of linguistic expression and inquiry. In letter 2:12 he writes M. de Querquisinere that the court is *not* the best place to go to learn to "speak true French," that the court is the "place where our language is the most corrupted" by "lazy people" who have "turned our language's purity into a Grammar." What Pasquier calls "true" or "pure" French, he insists, is to be found "esparce par toute la France" [scattered throughout France], a product of the soil and the trades as well as of other milieux. Pasquier's vision is profoundly pluralistic: the best speakers should engage in cross-fertilization like bees ("tout ainsi que l'Abeille volette sur unes et autres fleurs") and not hesitate to choose regionalisms, language drawn from tradespeople, manual laborers, and artisans to generate more precise meanings and metaphors (2:12). Pasquier emphasizes that culture is the product of labor and tireless inquiry into diverse milieux. His metaphors for this work of writing and learning are organic, physical, corporal: the mind is a field which must be "cultivated," the writer is a "bee" or a horticulturalist who must make "new grafts, which bear sweet fruit." What Pasquier calls "pure" language, paradoxically, is the product of a good "digestion" of all possible linguistic foods. Pasquier sets a program of readings that include not only Greek and Latin authors but also the oldest medieval French authors—not in order to become antiquarian, he emphasizes, but in order to "transplant" these writings among ourselves, to make them our own (2:12).[29]

In articulating these ideas to his original correspondents and then subsequently readdressing them to the readership of 1586, Pasquier is taking up the Pléiade poets' linguistic project with renewed vigor, in opposition to a courtly vision of authorship which he views as "charlatanism." In a letter to Monseigneur Tiard, bishop of Chalons sur Saulne (317 of 1586 edition), he reports on an argument that he has just had with one of the typical courtisan charlatans who "want to teach us the means to appear erudite without work." Pasquier argues that this "new form of knowledge . . . which one can call courtly" (*courtisan* is Pasquier's word) is just as bad as pedantry: both the courtisan and the pedant seek glory through an authorship that is mimicry (*singerie*). Pasquier decries all of the new cults of reductionist, short-cut approaches to language and literature in this letter, including those editors who "reduce the complete works of others to digest forms."

In the positions that he takes on language and literature, Pasquier speaks as a historian who embraces growth, change, and evolution in the language as a sign of its historical localization, specificity, and vigor. As a linguistic scholar, he takes evolution as a historical given (2:6). In a letter which explores the function and value of translation, he emphasizes the importance of translation to make works generally known; old translations, however, unlike the "originals," must be periodically abandoned for new translations that take into account the way the "mother tongue evolves . . . over time" (2:6). Reading and translation, Pasquier maintains, must be constantly renewed dialogue between past and present idiolects.

The ideological distance separating Pasquier and Balzac, I shall continue to argue, is far greater than the stylistic differences separating Balzac and Voiture. Pasquier's letters present critiques of political institutions and give sympathetic expression to both sides of the civil conflicts that he lived through. Some remarks tucked away in the editor's Postface at the end of the 1624 edition of Balzac's letters, on the other hand, suggest some revealing restrictions on the range of epistolary activity beginning in Balzac's time. The editor makes it clear that two kinds of topics should henceforth be banished from published let-

29. Pasquier was one of the few Renaissance writers who approached medieval vernacular literature and language with the same respectful attention that he accorded to classical Greek and Latin writing.

ters: domestic affairs (which only the "Germans" have the barbarity to speak of) and criticism of the government ("we no longer live in a period when people are accustomed to accuse publicly the State government"). For this editor, like many of the early seventeenth-century writers who hailed Richelieu as the architect of national unity, such restrictions seemed salutary. And so the injunction persisted: in the 1651 reedition of his popular *Secrétaire de la Cour,* Puget de la Serre warns potential letter writers to be careful to avoid writing anything about aristocratic leaders and government affairs ("les Grands et les affaires d'Estat") that could get them into trouble (5). Over a century later, however, Jaucourt would write in the *Encyclopédie* that epistolary art in a nation suffers from lack of participation in the political life of the country, noting that letters by contemporaries are insipid because they discuss petty matters rather than serious interests (see his article "Lettres des modernes," vol. 9 [1765], 413).

The founding of the Académie Française in 1635 institutionalized a Republic of Letters whose dominant and increasingly exclusive concern was the governance of language. Publication of missive letters in the seventeenth century is largely the work of its members, both as original authors and as editors (e.g., Faret, Boisrobert, Conrart, Balzac, Gombauld, Voiture, Maynard, Furetière, Bussy). These officially sanctioned letter books bear clear traces of the alliance between letters and state leaders, showing the extent to which the former depend on the latter.

Symptomatic, for example, is Balzac's volume of *Lettres familières de Monsieur de Balzac à Monsieur Chapelain,* posthumously published by Girard in 1656, two years after Balzac's death. Following Balzac's intentions Girard dedicated the book to the Marquis de Montausier, praising him for his service to the Fatherland ("Patrie") in putting down the Fronde rebels. Such service requires a public profession of fealty, Girard writes, and since poor writers have no riches to offer to their "Divinity," the letter book will serve as his "offering": he will deposit it on the marquis's altar under his "protection." The marquis is sure to approve these letters, moreover, because Balzac had already read them to the marquis, to assure their approval. Girard expresses the hope that other correspondents of Balzac—Chapelain and Conrart [also members of the Académie Française]—will likewise publish their letters, because all of these excellent writers display in their letters the glory of Montausier's patriotism. Like many signataries of published letters in the dominant Republic of Letters of the classical period, Girard closes by affirming himself as the "très-humble, très-obéissant et très-obligé serviteur" of a political figure.

Pinchêne's edition of Voiture's letters in 1650 (*Les Oeuvres de Monsieur de Voiture*) had used exactly the same formulae as Girard's 1656 edition of Balzac: the letter book is the author's and editor's joint "offering" of a shared fealty to the Prince de Condé and the whole Court, testifying to the prince's patriotic actions, all of which are glorified in the letters themselves. The preface affirms in a lengthy argument that the value of the letters derives from Condé's value and that the value of the epistolarian Voiture derives from his social and political connections. Pinchêne lists, according to ascending social rank, all of those "personnes de condition" with whom Voiture was privileged to correspond. Published letter books thus effectively must now bear the portraits of the national leaders who guarantee their value as legal tender.

Etienne Pasquier's son Nicolas had sounded the dissidents' knell against this system of literary value in 1623. In the preface to a book of his own missive letters, Nicolas Pasquier insisted on addressing the reader directly, instead of an aristocratic patron: "Au Lecteur: je n'adresse point ce livre à un Grand." Pasquier does so because a book's "principal recommendation must come from its own depths, and not from the support of the person to whom I would dedicate it." A book, he maintains, is "authorized" ("auctorisé") only by the qualities of its own writing, produced by a "frank, resolute, and bold pen."

In literary correspondences published after Nicolas Pasquier's (1623) both the letter and the letter book are increasingly viewed as a commodity with economic and political exchange value. Letters from officially recognized epistolarians like Balzac are particularly coveted by people anxious to be included in the Republic of Letters forming around him. In his letters Balzac shows pique at persons who maneuver to get a letter out of him (see, for example, *Lettres à Chapelain* 5:23). As a corollary, model writers like Balzac and Ménage are accused of writing letters exclusively as political and economic investments. Chapelain describes Ménage as "being unwilling to lose anything when he writes: he never picks up the pen except with the view of decking himself out in public and enriching some press," so that "if he wrote letters it would only be in order to make a book out of them" (*Lettres familières à Heinsius*, ed. B. Bray, 171, 347–48).

The reflections of writers like Chapelain suggest their rising suspicion of print as a commercialized medium, no longer appropriate for publication of familiar letters. Throughout his correspondence Chapelain elaborated a complex poetics of the familiar letter which owes much to Renaissance humanist thought, as Bernard Bray has so skillfully shown.[30] Indeed, Chapelain shares Pasquier's vision of the letter as a space for unlimited personal and artistic growth through familiar dialogue with correspondents who are close friends. Unlike Pasquier, however, Chapelain did not publish his own letters, and he expressly opposed publication in his testament. In a letter to Heinsius, Chapelain contrasts printers of the Renaissance, who were known humanists, to contemporary publishers, "simple ink and paper merchants," 14 June 1652. Authorship, for Chapelain, should be disinterested; publication of letters under current conditions borders on prostitution.[31] In a stronger vein, Mme de Sévigné will express her repulsion for appearing in print: "Etre dans les mains de tout le monde, se trouver imprimée . . . " [to be in everyone's hands, to find oneself in print . . .], 26 July 1668, to Bussy.

In the Renaissance vision of the familiar letter—as a space for personal and artistic growth—there is relatively little conflict or even distinction between the writer's public and private persona. Publication conventions allow both to appear in the letter book, conceived as the commemorative record of an individual life. By the seventeenth century, however, public space will have been narrowly codified to exclude the domestic, personal, politically dissident, and familiar, which are henceforth relegated to the margins of discourse. Published letters—even posthumously published ones—reinforce this definition of a public space where all activity—literary, social, and erotic—is conducted according to prescribed codes and under the surveillance of recognized social, literary, and political leaders. When private epistolary space exists—as it does for Chapelain and Sévigné—it must be defended *against* publication. Readdressing of truly familiar letters, when it occurs is limited to a known circle of friends and family.[32]

---

30. See Bray's edition of the letters to Heinsius (1966), 64–72, 87–88.

31. For a pioneering account by social historians of the change that Chapelain is lamenting, see Lucien Febvre and Henri-Jean Martin, *L'Apparition du livre* (Paris: Albin Michel, 1958), 217–55. Febvre and Martin carefully delineate the ideological changes in printing practice that occur at the end of the sixteenth century when Counter-Reformation printers replace humanist printers under changed economic and political conditions. The situation will not shift significantly again until the end of the seventeenth century, when the Revocation of the Edict of Nantes forces a new generation of persecuted printers to flee beyond France's borders. Febvre and Martin link the rise of new generations of philosophical printers in the eighteenth century with the rise of a new type of printer, "l'imprimeur journaliste," at the end of the seventeenth century (238) and also with a shift toward economic conditions that are similar to those of the Renaissance (242). For a more detailed account of publishing in the seventeenth century, see H.-J. Martin's *Livre, pouvoirs et société à Paris au XVIIe siècle*, 2 vols. (Geneva: Droz, 1969).

32. See R. Duchêne, "Texte public, texte privé: le cas des lettres de Mme de

We have noted that the publication of missive letters in the seventeenth century is largely the work of members of the Académie Française, an institution that was at the time—as until quite recently—exclusively a men's club. Women's literary clubs, as it is well known, arose quite visibly at about the same time: Molière's *Les Femmes savantes* satirizes the public literary space staked out by women who wanted to share in the power of official literary academies. Curiously, although the learned and literary women of seventeenth-century France wrote numerous letters—lively and interesting ones, in fact—their correspondences were not published until much later. Publication of the letters of Mme de Lafayette, Mme de Sablé, Mme de Maintenon, Mlle de Scudéry and others is largely the work of nineteenth- and twentieth-century editors.

Publication of women's missive letters in the seventeenth century was rare, and took place under circumstances quite different from those of the Renaissance. When the letters of Hélisenne de Crenne, Mesdames des Roches, and Madame de Saillans were published, they appeared with no particular attention called to their gender. These women enter the world of publication through the same doors as men: Gaspar's frontispiece displays a poem by his wife alongside one of his own, with equal division of space between them, as will be the case for their letter exchange in the volume itself. The letters of Mesdames des Roches are printed by the same publisher as Pasquier's, a few months before Pasquier's. Hélisenne de Crenne's defense of women is embedded within her letters as part of a personal experience rather than as a gender-defined generic frame. In the seventeenth century, however, women's letters begin to be published and marketed as such, as emanating from a space that is separate from that of men and even more narrowly confined.

To rediscover this space, we must begin by looking at some of the few women's correspondences that were actually published in the seventeenth century.[33] I shall resurrect four of these little-known letter

Sévigné," *Papers on French Seventeenth Century Literature* (1981), 31–69, and Catherine M. Howard, *Les Fortunes de Madame de Sévigné* (Paris: J.-M. Place, 1982), 14–31, for an account of the few instances in which a limited number of Mme de Sévigné's letters were publicly read prior to her death. Duchêne and Howard both show, contrary to widely held opinion, how rarely Sévigné's letters were ready by anyone other than the original addressee. Chapelain's letters likewise did not circulate broadly and were not published until the nineteenth century. Bray, in the introduction to his edition of Chapelain's letters, discusses the circulation of letters among Chapelain's humanist friends, 60–61.

33. The most complete bibliography of letter collections published prior to the

books, which are not discussed in existing histories of the epistolary genre in the seventeenth century. They are particularly suggestive when compared to the published correspondences of their better-known contemporaries.

In 1666 a collection of fairly general and courtly letters entitled *Les Lettres et poésies de Madame la Comtesse de B.* appeared. The author (now known to be the Comtesse de Brégy) remains anonymous in this book, as do many of her correspondents (mostly women), likewise identified by initial only, although enough real historical names are given to persuade the reader that this is an authentic correspondence. The editor, moreover, assures us that "those who have frequented the Court of France, however little" will recognize the epistolarian. The editor is publishing her letters in order to prove that "If you are often given works by men, it is not because ladies are not capable of producing them, but because this adorable sex has so many amusements [*divertissements*] that they cannot find the time to write. This collection, however, shows that they are able to find a few hours for writing letters and poetry" ("Au Lecteur"). Although ostensibly the publisher is claiming a place for women in the Republic of Letters, that place is anonymous and intermittent; women's letters are presented as a product of leisure hours stolen from other leisurely activities that are more entertaining.

The Comtesse de B.'s letter book may seem an isolated example. In fact, it follows conventions established by the anthology editor Du Boscq, who published a *Nouveau Recueil de lettres des dames de ce temps* in 1635. In his preface Du Boscq likewise ostensibly invokes the equal-time-for-women principle: since so many letters by "hommes d'esprit" have appeared, Du Boscq writes, we ought to publish ladies' courtly letters. The resemblance between Du Boscq's anthology and the preceding anthologies of men's letters by Rosset (1618), Faret (1627), and others stops there, however. Du Boscq's collection identifies no authors or addressees. (It is, moreover, in very large print, for unexplained reasons.)

At least two women, however, had their missive letters published under their own names in the seventeenth century. One was a recognized and published author at the time, Mlle Desjardins (also known as Mme de Villedieu), primarily a novelist but also one of the very few seventeenth-century women to write for the theater, that most public of

---

eighteenth century, to my knowledge, is that compiled by Fritz Nies, in the appendix to his book on Mme de Sévigné, *Gattungspoetik . . . ,* 243–60. Although Nies's list mixes fictional with nonfictional correspondences, it nonetheless reveals how few collections of nonfictional women's letters were published in the seventeenth century.

literary spaces which has rarely been penetrated by women writers. In 1668 the publisher Barbin brought out two different editions of Mlle Desjardins's letters. The first edition, called *Lettres et billets galants*, circulated clandestinely; it contained 186 pages of a woman's passionate letters to her lover. Very few copies of this edition survived. Thanks to the work of the scholar Micheline Cuénin, however, we now have a critical edition of this volume, which gives the curious history of its publication.[34] According to Cuénin's research, these letters were sold by Mlle Desjardins's lover, M. de Villedieu, to the editor Barbin, at a time when Villedieu was in financial straits. Even the writing of the letters was the result of a bargain struck by Villedieu, who bartered his attentions to the smitten author for her letters, requiring, moreover, that they be of a certain type—witty and gallant. Micheline Cuénin's close textual analysis of these letters shows the difficulty that Mlle Desjardins had harnessing her mute passion to meet such a literary contract.[35]

This first edition revealed Mlle Desjardin's name only in the fine print of the king's imprimatur (the "Privilège du Roy"), not on the title page. Another edition, which Barbin brought out after Mlle Desjardins strongly objected to the first edition, contained a less passionate group of letters but capitalized on the author's name in the title: *Recueil de Quelques Lettres ou Relations galantes. Par Mlle des-Jardins* (1668). In this edition Barbin is again publishing without the author's permission. His "Bookseller's Preface" apologizes for the lack of an Author's Preface, since, as he acknowledges, this is the first time Mlle Desjardins has not addressed the reader herself in her published works. The fact that these letters entertained their original readers privately, however, is sufficient in Barbin's view to authorize publication without the author's permission, as he writes in the prefatory "Le Libraire au Lecteur." Barbin's dedicatory letter places this collection under the protection of Mlle de Sévigny [sic] and her mother and identifies these letters generically in opposition to "Academic" literature: "ces sortes d'Ouvrages sont d'un Caractère à dépendre du jugement d'une Ruelle galante, plutôt que de celui de l'Académie" [these kinds of work are of a type which depends on the judgment of gallant society rather than Academicians]. Barbin thus opposes two literary spaces—the Academy and the "Ruelle" (literally the bedside space where gallant society received

34. Catherine Hortense Desjardins, *Lettres et billets galants*, ed. M. Cuénin (Paris: Société d'Etude du XVIIe siècle, 1975).
35. See pp. 19 and 20 of Cuénin edition.

their guests to discuss amorous and literary questions in a public sort of privacy), locating the women in the "Ruelle."

The narrow corridor of the bedside "ruelle" is precisely where most women's published letters of the seventeenth century will be effectively confined. The publication of the *Lettres portugaises* in 1669—by the same printer Barbin who had published Mlle Desjardin's letters a year earlier—consecrated a literature that increasingly limited women's acknowledged epistolary activity to erotic response to men. The passionate love monologue, revived in imitation of Ovid's *Letters from Heroines*, appears to be *the* woman's epistolary genre in the classical period.[36] It is a genre, however, where both authorship and authenticity are dubious, since typically the woman's letters are purloined letters, published anonymously (and even frequently authored) by a male editor.

On those rare occasions when women's letters are turned into letter books in the seventeenth century, then, their authors enter the publication world anonymously and against their wills. The situation has changed significantly from the days when Renaissance women unabashedly published their own letter books and broached the same range of topics as men. Authorship in the seventeenth century has become a male-dominated institution, deeply imbricated, moreover, in political hierarchies. Publicly recognized epistolarians whose letter books are held up as models for prose style are all members of the same sex, share similar political persuasions and social codes, and are situated in clear positions of subordination to ruling class patrons.

One letter book stands out as an anomaly in this world of courtly letter books that clearly monopolize epistolary production after 1623. In 1644, the missive letters of an abbess who had worked closely with François de Sales were published by the nuns of the convent she founded, as the *Epistres Spirituelles de la Mère Ianne Françoise Fremiot, Baronne de Chantal, Fondatrice et première supérieure de l'ordre de la Visitation Sainte-Marie, Fidellement recueillies par les religieuses du premier monastère d'Annessy.* Here are a woman's missive letters published by women, under their own initiative (albeit with the acknowledged approval of their male superiors), carefully gathered and edited over a seven-month period as a communal enterprise. The "Epistre

36. See Susan Lee Carrell, *Le Soliloque de la passion féminine* (Paris: Laplace, 1982) for a full and subtle description of this type of women's correspondence. See my review essay on Carrell's book, "Portuguese Writing and Women's Consciousness," *Degré Second: Studies in French Literature* 7 (1983), 163–75, for a further probe into the relationship between genre and gender in this type of epistolary writing.

Dédicatoire" is written by a nun and is addressed to her sister nuns
under the aegis of sororal affection. Here the letter book is not presented
as an offering of fealty from a "very humble and obedient servant" to a
political superior, nor is it a theft offered by a bookseller to the general
public. This edition of Mother Chantal's missive letters is presented as
the product of communal labor and as a gift for the community—most
immediately for the nuns of the convent who were the original recipients of most of the letters, and, ultimately, for the wider spiritual
community. A second preface, deemed necessary for the general reader
("Avant-Propos tres-necessaire au Lecteur, pour auoir la parfaicte con-
noissance de l'excellence de ces Epistres") stresses the importance of
this book as a freely given gift, which "all people have the right to
inherit." This second preface, moreover, develops a detailed poetics of
the letter as the "Lieutenants of the Person," the "mirror of an interior
life," and an equally lengthy poetics of the letter book as an instrument
for creating spiritual community: free circulation of letter books imi-
tates "that great Communion of the Church, through communication
of the letters of all its Communities."

The two prefaces of the book (the "Epistre dédicatoire" addressed to
the convent sisters and the "Avant-Propos" addressed to the general
reader) frame Mother Chantal's letters as emanating from an interior
spiritual space, originally addressed to intimate friends and relations,
but potentially readdressable to all who might want to learn more of her
exemplary life. Publication is not a comfortable activity for the writers
of either preface. The nun's dedicatory epistle opens with a confession
of "having felt some repugnance at having to write this letter"; she has
overcome her self-consciousness in the public arena by concentrating
on the friends to whom she is writing (1). Her letter is necessary, moreover, to testify to the authenticity of the letters, to guarantee that the
printed letters were faithfully copied from the manuscripts. As the one
who was closest to Mother Chantal while she wrote, she takes her
public testimony very seriously.

It is easy to recognize the Christian and Platonic inspiration behind
this communication model, in which transcription and dissemination
of Mother Chantal's Word, through widening circles of readership, is
valorized by reference to a central Logos; indeed, Mother Chantal is at
one point described as the "Secretary of the thoughts of the Spouse." A
suspicious reader, moreover, might question the disinterestedness of
this publication, much as Fielding satirized Richardson's saintly Pamela as a Shamela out for Mr. B's money. A skeptical reader could thus
read the publication of Mother Chantal's letter book as the first act in a

drama staged with the ultimate end of canonization in mind. In any event, we must recognize that the publication of this letter book is inseparable from Christian institutions. Mother Chantal's epistolary activity is compared to that of the early church fathers inspired by the same Spirit; and her letter book, which contains religious instruction, will serve as the constitution for the convent she has founded, to be reread, interpreted, and followed by the nuns.[37] Mother Chantal's letter book thus affirms and extends an essentially Christian republic of letters.

Doubtless largely because Mother Chantal's letters fall within a certain Christian tradition of letter writing, they publicly resurrect the vision of the letter as a personal diary.[38] In this respect Mother Chantal's letter book stands out rather singularly among seventeenth-century letter books as a throwback to the Renaissance and Erasmian vision of the letter book. Indeed, in its organization and design, the lengthy quarto volume which encloses Mother Chantal's collected letters (904 pages) harks back to Pasquier's book of letter books and anticipates Rousseau's *La Nouvelle Héloïse.* It encompasses an adult lifetime and is organized chronologically; the autobiographical framing of the letter collection is reinforced by the Table of Contents which summarizes the content of each letter in terms of the *writing subject's action,* seen as constituting the writer's personal history (typical, for example, would be the summary of Chantal's Letter 72: "She tells him about some family business").[39] Great care, moreover, is given to the visual design of the volume; like the Renaissance letter books it is richly

37. Over a hundred years later, in *Pamela, Clarissa,* and *La Nouvelle Héloïse,* Richardson and Rousseau will project a similar, albeit secularized, vision of the value of the letter book as the documentary record of an exemplary life, to be reread and imitated by a community inspired by the saintly model.

38. Mother Chantal's correspondence is one of the few published letter books in seventeenth-century France that can be so characterized. However, we can still find the poetics of the letter as a personal diary in some of the *unpublished* correspondences of the seventeenth century. Hercule Audittret, for example, imposed upon himself the discipline of daily letter writing, taking subjects in random order "as they come to me" (Letter 70), as a kind of personal monologue ("je m'entretiens ainsi moy même"—L. 7) and self-portrait ("en un mot, qui fait une lettre fait son portrait"—p. 6). I take the quotes from his letters to Conrart, as they appear in *Lettres à Philandre/le père Hercule,* ed. B. Couton and Y. Giraud (Fribourg: Editions Universitaires, 1975). Hercule Audittret's defense of this form of letter writing, moreover, is closely related to his *anti-mondain* polemics.

39. Compare a summary from Pasquier's table of contents: "he rejoices in the birth of a son" (2:9). Rousseau's table of contents for *La Nouvelle Héloïse* similarly imposes an editor's summary of the principal events, recorded as landmarks in his pilgrims' progress.

engraved, with borders reminiscent of manuscript display.[40] The aesthetic attention that is lavished on the preparation of the book suggests the same desire to produce a perdurable record of a lived experience that we noted in Renaissance letter books.

In Mother Chantal's letter book, domestic affairs are not considered inappropriate topics; the abbess writes to members of her blood family as well as her convent family. Spiritual concerns, however, are primary in her writing, and the letters addressed to spiritual directors are intimately confessional. Seen from a broad historical perspective, her letter book publicly stakes out and maintains a space for the autobiographical and confessional impulse behind letter writing, an impulse which otherwise is largely repressed in the courtly letters which the seventeenth-century print world favors.

When Mother Chantal's *Epistres spirituelles* appeared in 1644, her granddaughter Marie de Rabutin-Chantal was about to marry the Marquis de Sévigné. As Roger Duchêne and others have shown, there was very little contact between grandmother and granddaughter before the abbess's death, and she is rarely mentioned in Mme de Sévigné's letters. It would therefore be difficult to insist overly on an affinity between the letters of the pious abbess and those of her witty, worldly granddaughter. And yet, if we compare these two women's letter books to other published letters of the seventeenth century, we perceive a common hallmark: for each of them the letter was an essentially intimate communication, opening up on an interior space where a highly personal self evolves over time in interaction with close relations. For them the letter is not a political maneuver or a public exercise, an extension of salon- and court-approved conversation.

Even more specifically, if we compare Mother Chantal's and Sévigné's letters to those of another published epistolarian in the family, Bussy-Rabutin, we note this significant difference: much of Bussy's epistolary activity is aimed at winning back his king's favor. As Elizabeth Goldsmith has shown by a recent reading of Bussy's correspondence, the exiled courtier slowly put together his own letter book in order to readdress it to Louis XIV, offering the entire collection as a monument to Louis's reign and hoping for a pardon in return.[41] Bussy's correspondence was published for the first time in 1697, four years after his death, as a kind of appeal to posterity for his rightful place in court

40. Rousseau will also be concerned to engrave perdurable images on his readers' minds, as he carefully oversees preparation of the illustrations to accompany *La Nouvelle Héloïse.*
41. See E. Goldsmith, 237–40.

history. It is well known that this publication, which included letters from Bussy's cousin Mme de Sévigné, ultimately led to publication of Sévigné's letters to her daughter in 1725–26, both letter books owing a great deal to the editorial activity of Bussy's son Amé-Nicolas. However when we look beyond this publishing link toward subsequent developments in the eighteenth century, we perceive that the publication of Mme de Sévigné's letters ushered in a new kind of writing, significantly different from Bussy's, more independent of court and salon, more intimately tied to personal and private history. When Mme de Sévigné's attention turns toward the court and the salon, it is to make grist for the narratives that she addresses to Mme de Grignan, narratives that are always discursively subordinated to the mother-daughter relationship.[42] She writes to amuse close relations and to strengthen private bonds, not to please the public readership of court, salon, and academy. Within the circle of this more private readership, she writes with a mercurial freedom that surpasses even the "negligent" style cultivated by other literary authors of her period. She passes over a radically broader range of topics than any of the previously published epistolarians and in so doing vigorously revives the Renaissance poetics of the familiar letter as elaborated by Erasmus and illustrated by Pasquier, writing conceived as open to the infinite variety of the individual self's evolving vision of its relationship to the world.

It is perhaps only coincidental that the compilation manuscript of the letters to Grignan, prepared by Sévigné's survivors for a wider private readership, was undertaken between 1715–19,[43] i.e., precisely during the period immediately following Louis XIV's death, a death felt as a political and social liberation in many literary circles. Yet I should like to insist on the extent to which publication of the Sévigné correspondence—which began twenty-nine years after her death, much later than most previous posthumous publications of letters—is profoundly an eighteenth-century phenomenon, historically linked to changes in the topography and politics of literary space between 1670 and 1770. Indeed, it seems to me that the delay in posthumous publication of other collections of personal letters—such as La Fontaine's letters to his wife, which were published four years after Mme de Sévigné's let-

---

42. See L. Horowitz, "The Correspondence of Mme de Sévigné . . . ," for a subtle discussion of the relationship between Sévigné's journalism and her affective rhetoric.

43. See R. Duchêne, "Du destinataire au public . . . ," 41–43, for a discussion of this manuscript and Amé-Nicolas's editorial work in preparing it.

ters to her daughter—can be better understood when we look more broadly at shifts in the poetics and politics of literary space at the beginning of the eighteenth century.[44]

Those who study the history of the French novel have long recognized the influx of a new vision of narrative forms and content during the period after 1670, when the novel began to take historical writing as its model. From the *nouvelle historique* to the rapid rise of the memoir novel and the epistolary novel, fictional narrative began to take an intense interest in the private life of recent historical figures first and then in the private life of more ordinary citizens in a subsequent development of novelistic writing. What began as an impulse to see the private life behind the public life will wind up as an increasingly sustained interest in diaristic narratives of private life per se. With the impact of Richardson, Mme de Graffigny, Mme Riccoboni, and Rousseau in the 1740s through 1760s, the representation of domestic interiors and the daily dramas of individuals far removed from the court and salons will bring about the bourgeois revolution in the novel.

Within the history of published literary correspondences, we can discern a comparable influx (or rather return) of personal historical consciousness in the same period. Whereas Malherbe, one of the last literary epistolarians to write chronicle letters, did not consider his journalistic reports to Peiresc as worthy of publication (these were not published until the nineteenth century), toward the end of the seventeenth century missive letters with memorialist value, like those of

---

44. The debate that has polarized Sévigné scholarship has an echo in earlier scholarship devoted to La Fontaine's *Lettres à sa femme*, a travel account written in 1663 (while La Fontaine accompanied an uncle who had been exiled after Fouquet's fall) but not published until 1729. The debate between those who consider La Fontaine's letters to be strictly personal or "intimes" (Emile Faguet and his partisans) and those who consider them to be literary works intended for publication (Gustave Michaut and others) is aptly summarized in the Abbé Caudal's critical edition of the letters (Paris: CDU, 1966), 10–19, which argues for Michaut's position. As with the Sévigné letters, literary critics have devoted their primary attention to an ontological question, "Are these letters 'literary' (defined as 'written with publication in mind') or 'personal' (defined as 'written for a single and unique reader')?" Beyond the obvious difficulties posed by this limited definition of "literary," and the necessity it imposes of deducing an author's global intention from a few casual remarks within isolated letters, the concept of "publication" implied by this binary opposition is even more slippery: does the oral reading or the circulation of parts of letters constitute a "publication"? Moreover, such an essentialist atemporal approach (*is* the letter "literary" or "personal") discourages careful consideration of the broader discursive horizons and value systems that condition the writing and publication of letters at particular historical moments. In my own work I have found it more instructive to focus on the discursive contexts surrounding those moments when letters are actually turned into published books, as a more coherent way of investigating the conditions determining the constitution of the letter as literature.

Guy Patin, are published posthumously: *Lettres choisies de feu Mr Guy Patin. Docteur en médicine de la Faculté de Paris . . . dans lesquelles sont contenuës Plusieurs Particularitez Historiques sur la Vie & la Mort des Scavans de ce Siècle, sur leurs Ecrits & plusieurs autres choses curieuses depuis l'an 1645 jusqu'en 1672*, first published in Frankfurt in 1683. Although Patin's letters were initially published outside of France in countries that were hostile to Louis XIV's hegemony (Frankfurt 1683, Rotterdam 1689), they ultimately were reissued in Paris (1692) and were frequently reprinted. What I should like to emphasize is that Patin is not a professional historian like Pelisson, the royal historiographer whose letters to Mlle de Scudéry were to be published as *Lettres historiques* in 1729. Long before Patin and Pelisson, history writing had occasionally taken epistolary form, just as news reporting in the early gazettes and newspapers of the seventeenth and eighteenth centuries would frequently borrow the discourse of the letter; these letters, however, are embedded within institutions that can still properly be called journalism and historiography, whose discourse has to be examined primarily as such, insofar as the writer and the writer's audience are institutionally conceived in those terms. Guy Patin, however, is a medical doctor and scholar who also happened to write detailed missive letters on the Fronde events. The prefatory material that ushers a reader into his published letters justifies publication by presenting Patin as a member of the "Republic of Letters," hailing the *literary* value of this publication. The book thus is embraced within the prevailing literary institution that publishes letter books as a model form of writing.

The primary value of Patin's letters, as the title makes clear, however, is their historical interest. Accordingly, the author is presented— not through eulogy (the heretofore dominant mode of presentation) but through biography. The reader posited by Patin's letter book is assumed to be as curious about the author's life as about the events that the author lived through.

I would like to stress that the reader clearly implied by the title and preface to Patin's letters—this "curious" reader interested in historical "particularities"—is a significant newcomer among the readers posited by letter books throughout the seventeenth century and is the product of complex cultural shifts in modes of printed discourse that took place in the second half of the seventeenth century—including, most especially, the rise of journalism and developments in novel writing. Toward the end of the seventeenth century there is a symptomatic shift in the rhetorical framing of letter books, which we can discern in the manuals and anthologies as well as in the published correspondences of single authors. The dominant mode of guaranteeing the letter book's value throughout the seventeenth century had been the courtly eulogy—essentially a system of letters of recommendation, in which the value of the letters was guaranteed by the aristocratic status of the writer's correspondents and patron. The typical prefatory presentation of the author took the form of a laudatory portrait, and a great deal of fan mail was included in the collection. Toward the end of the seventeenth century a new, historical, form of presentation appears—biography—which will progressively replace eulogy.

Even the letter manuals which are the organs of court- and academy-approved epistolary discourse will reflect this shift toward biography, albeit belatedly, in the eighteenth century. In his first edition (1689) of *Les Plus Belles Lettres des meilleurs auteurs français* Pierre Richelet merely lists the names of authors at the beginning of the book, with no further indication of who had written which particular letter in the respective chapters devoted to letters of congratulation, counsel, and so forth; the celebrated authors' names are simply presented as a frontispiece to reinforce the value of the prescribed forms of epistolary intercourse. A half century later, however, the 1747 edition of Richelet's anthology attributes authorship more carefully and presents, additionally, a lengthy sequence of biographical notices on each of the epistolarians, entitled "French Authors who wrote Letters." Although in Richelet these notices suggest an effort to shore up the traditional seventeenth-century courtly epistolary art by giving it a history, the appeal to historical continuity and to biography reflects a significant shift in assumptions about reader interest.

The presentation and organization of Bussy's and Sévigné's letters in the early eighteenth-century editions likewise reveals a profound shift toward historical narrativity as a primary value. The letters are carefully dated and organized chronologically to tell as complete a story as possible; responses are given whenever available after appropriate letters to convey a sense of dialogue; newly discovered letters are chronologically melded with previous ones in subsequent editions. The author's personal history has become the organizing principle for the letter collection.

In their prefaces, the early editors of Bussy's and Sévigné's letters call attention to this chronological ordering as an innovation which is necessary to help the reader "understand" the letters.[45] Indeed, Mme de

<hr>

45. See, for example, the "Avertissement" to the 1714 edition of Bussy's letters, where the editor explains that chronological ordering "will greatly serve to make them

Simiane worries in her preface to the 1726 edition of Sévigné's letters that there are too many narrative gaps between letters for the reader to understand all of the references within the letters, but concludes confidently that "an intelligent and attentive Reader will remedy all that, and find enough meaning to be satisfied." The "intelligent and attentive reader" whom Mme de Simiane is positing in 1726—this reader who is interested in filling in narrative blanks and making connections independently—is not much different from the reader posited by Montesquieu five years earlier in 1721 for his epistolary novel *Les Lettres persanes:* the subtle reader who would understand Montesquieu's "secret chain" linking the novel's letters. My point here is to suggest that the new readership solicited by Bussy's and Sévigné's letter books is one whose expectations and interests have been profoundly altered by new developments in narrative forms between 1670 and 1735, particularly in the novel, which make it once again possible to conceive of the epistolary document as the trace of a personal history.

Bussy's and Sévigné's first editors, like Voiture's nephew Pinchêne, are family members who have inherited the treasure of a relative who was an accomplished epistolarian. Pinchêne has little difficulty readdressing his uncle's letters according to the publicly established conventions of courtly letter books; we have already noted the formulaic similarity of his work to that of Balzac's editor.[46] The edition that Pinchêne published in 1650, only two years after his uncle's death, will remain essentially the same throughout subsequent printings and editions. The 1734 edition of Voiture's letters contains exactly the same 198 letters and prefatory material as the seventeenth-century editions, and a 1779 edition of *Lettres choisies* by Voiture will still stress the value of the collection as an exemplary handbook for the art of praising rulers.[47] The courtisan's letter book thus persists, alongside newer varieties of the letter book, as a remarkably stable genre throughout the eighteenth century.

---

better understood, and consequently to let them be read with greater utility and pleasure." The reader's pleasure and interest is thus now conceived as deriving from narrative meaning.

46. Duchêne, in seeking to establish Voiture as a predecessor for Sévigné, picks up on Pinchêne's prefatory statement that Voiture's letters were not written for publication but for a private group and are therefore potentially obscure. But although Pinchêne claims to have provided annotations to furnish keys for the reader, in fact his edition contains hardly any such notes and is nevertheless not particularly obscure for it, since the letters remain essentially within general, courtly conventions.

47. *Lettres choisies de M. de Voiture dans lesquelles ce célèbre écrivain a répandu le plus d'agrémens, par sa manière fine et délicate de louer les Grands et par son galant badinage* (Madrid et Paris: Vve Duchesne, 1779).

Bussy's son Amé-Nicolas, however, was faced with a slightly more delicate problem than Voiture's epistolary heir: whereas Voiture's place in the sun was secure, and indeed already secured by his letters (which, as we have seen, carefully positioned him within the social hierarchy revolving around Louis XIV), Bussy's relations with the Sun King were problematic, and his letters bear obsessive traces of his personal political problems. Bussy himself hesitates to publish a correspondence which is, as one of his correspondents writes him, "a diary of your life, which interests only you and your family, and which therefore would not entertain people who are interested only in great events." This letter, from M. de C*** to Bussy, dated 24 December 1692, is the last chronological letter of the 1697 edition. It reveals a great deal about the shift in value assigned to letter books at the dawn of the eighteenth century. M. de C***'s statement suggests that the ban on publishing the personal still persists, but his letter also reveals that the letter book now has a potentially new model—memoirs, albeit memoirs that are still centered on "great events." M. de C*** tries to persuade Bussy that "most of the Memoirs that are read with pleasure at Court and in town, like those of Monluc and Basompierre" are not better written or full of greater subjects than Bussy's letters:

> and even though you deal only with the events of the life of a private individual [*un particulier*], Sir, I maintain that in all of the estates one can make useful application of this reading, either concerning the fidelity that one owes the King, or on the manner to conduct oneself at Court with Ministers, and at war with Generals. [24 December 1692]

Thus C*** overrules Bussy's objection that readers would "treat as minutiae" most of the concerns in his letters that are important for Bussy and his children.

With the publication of Bussy's correspondence, personal history rides in on the wings of a history that is still court-centered and courtly: the presentation of personal "minutiae" is still ultimately justified as part of a courtly system of fealty, in terms not unlike the dominant practice in courtly letter books. With Mme de Sévigné's letters, however, the editors will have even more difficulty conforming to established conventions for letter books.

As Sévigné's heirs and editors struggled with the work of redressing and readdressing her letters, they had to face constantly one unbending phenomenon: the Marquise's *singularity*. Both her linguistic style and her excessive maternal love simply did not conform to epistolary conventions. The very first edition of her letters takes the simplest and most conventional solution: it is a slim volume (seventy-five pages),

with no prefatory material, containing essentially her narratives of major historical events from 1670 to 1676, appropriately titled to anchor
these events in court life, *Lettres choisies de Madame la Marquise de
Sévigné à Madame de Grignan sa fille. Qui contiennent beaucoup de
particularitez de l'Histoire de Louis XIV* (1725). The first letter in this
1725 edition, however, is an anomaly: it is a brief note from Mme de
Grignan to her husband announcing the birth of their daughter. This
family-history fissure in the wall of courtly history is the hole in the
dike of epistolary conventions that have repressed personal history for a
century. Subsequent editions, which will bring out more and more of
Sévigné's letters to her daughter, will have to deal with the overwhelming importance of the familial and the familiar in Sévigné's writing.
Amé-Nicolas Bussy-Rabutin, in the preface to the 1726 edition, appears
fairly comfortable with the family history frame: he gladly supplies a
brief biography explaining who Sévigné was (in terms of the Rabutin
family tree, of course) and spins a story out of her personal life (marriage,
love for husband and children, separation from her daughter) as an explanation for the genesis of the letters: "this separation which was cruel
for such a tender mother gave rise to all the Letters that you will see
hereafter." (One could hardly expect less from the son of a man reputed
for his *Amorous History of the Gauls*.) The professional editor Denis-
Marius Perrin, however, who was asked by Mme de Simiane to prepare
the voluminous 1734–37 edition of Sévigné's letters, was more aware of
the anomaly that Sévigné's letter book represented within traditional
literary institutions. His preface begins, "the Letters of a mother to her
daughter, however perfect they may be, appear destined for oblivion. . . ." To salvage what he can of conventional decorum in publishing
these letters, Perrin has tried "to omit some details which were purely
domestic and not very interesting for the Public." But Sévigné's personal life plays such a formative role that

> I did not dare permit myself to eliminate any of the maternal love
> feelings, which reappear so often; because that is precisely what deter-
> mines Madame de Sévigné's basic character; and the noble, delicate,
> and varied expressions that she uses to express her affection are no less
> a part of her than the affection itself.

One could hardly come up with a clearer articulation, twenty years
before Buffon's *Discours sur le style* (1753), of the principle that *le style
est l'homme* [sic] *même*. Sévigné's style is inseparable from her character, and both are perceived as problematically "singular" by Perrin in
1734:

> It is true that one has difficulty recovering from the surprise that this

sort of singularity causes, but are such feelings [Sévigné's affection for
her daughter] unnatural for being so uncommon? Cannot one conceive, without too great effort, the characteristics of such an empathy?
Or rather, is it not one of the effects of the corruption of the human
heart to appreciate excess sensibility only in the maddest of passions?

If Sévigné's maternal affection is disturbingly unconventional, the
originality of her style appears less problematic to Perrin. Indeed, he
proposes it as a new epistolary model but confesses that he unfortunately cannot describe it with any preexisting language. In his preface
he resorts instead to quotation, borrowing Sévigné's descriptions of her
own style as the best way of presenting it. He concludes, however, that
the letters themselves must be read in order to appreciate "a style
which can be described only very imperfectly and which is rightfully
regarded as a model for the epistolary genre." Likewise, after lamenting
the lack of documentation on Sévigné's life, he gives as detailed a biography as he can, but asserts that the reader's pleasure will come from
reading the way in which Sévigné articulates her life herself in the full
letter collection. In sum, Mme de Sévigné's "singular" letters force the
rediscovery of the value of the idiolect and respect for the particular
autobiographical experience that it conveys.

As I reread the early prefaces that readdress Sévigné's letters to an
early eighteenth-century readership, I am struck by the joyful independence and freedom with which they are offered to a general readership as
the book of an individual life. Sévigné's granddaughter Simiane seems
aware of the institutional differences between Sévigné's letter book and
other published correspondences when she insistently substitutes a
familiar letter to her cousin Bussy for the conventional preface, in the
1726 edition. She notes that she is not assuming the typical pose of an
author "genuflecting" before a reader. Instead she expects Bussy's and
the eventual reader's thanks for this gift. Simiane stresses the commu-
nicational freedom that presided over the writing of these letters, which
explains their frankness, negligence, and occasional disjointedness:

> Since these Letters were written only for these two dear people [her
> mother and grandmother] they did not disguise through any initials or
> other borrowed names what they wanted to tell each other; and since
> they found in all the words and actions of the defunct King only gran-
> deur and justice, they spoke of him with complete freedom, without
> fearing that their Letters would be intercepted.

Simiane is clearly aware of the constraints which restrict epistolary
communication around the court.[48] She celebrates the "complete free-

48. One of the first concerns of the Constituent Assembly under the Revolution
was to create laws to protect the inviolable secrecy of correspondences.

dom" that her mother and grandmother enjoyed as private correspondents who were relatively independent of the courtly system of rewards and punishments. The correspondents' candor, even in their admiration of Louis XIV, is guaranteed by their disinterest.

Sévigné's freedom of speech erupts upon the eighteenth-century scene as a singular phenomenon at precisely the time when other, more explicitly intellectual and political movements were beginning to propound their own alternatives to the existing monarchic courtly system. Sévigné's freedom is politically less subversive than other ideas and practices that were to undermine courtly authority more corrosively. And yet, if we follow the history of Sévigné's appropriation into letter anthologies in the eighteenth century we note a clear ideological division: alongside the courtly letter manuals, which still promote Voiture and other recognized courtly Academicians as chief exemplars of the epistolary art, there arises a different kind of anthology-manual, which proposes Voltaire and Sévigné as the only epistolarians worth reading and emulating.

Particularly symptomatic is Philipon de la Madeleine's *Modèles de lettres sur différents sujets* (Lyon: chez Pierre Brysot Ponthus, 1761). In 1761 this book was published anonymously, with only a "tacit permission," not a "privilège du Roi." It was to be reprinted after the Revolution with the author's name, but otherwise virtually unchanged, under the title *Manuel épistolaire à l'usage de la jeunesse . . .* (Paris: Capelle et Renand, An II) by a printer whose address, symbolically, is "rue J-J Rousseau." Significant, and appropriately highlighted by Philipon de la Madeleine's second title, is the new readership to whom this work is addressed: youth. Erasmus's program of epistolary apprenticeship had also focussed on the child. Pasquier and Sévigné had each brought up their own children to be accomplished epistolarians. Letter manuals throughout the seventeenth century, on the other hand, posit an exclusively adult readership. With the first editions of Sévigné's letters, however, the child returns as a possible reader and beneficiary of published correspondences: Mme de Simiane notes in her prefaces that her grandmother's letters, because they are so full of "judicious reasoning . . . can be very useful to youth and to everyone."

What then is Philipon de la Madeleine's program? His letter manual emphatically rejects Guez de Balzac, Voiture, and Boursault as epistolary models, promoting instead Mme de Maintenon, Swift, Pope, Voltaire, but most especially Mme de Sévigné, who is now praised unreservedly for all of her "singular" qualities. Philipon's lengthy "Réflexions sur le style épistolaire" explicitly oppose codification of the language by Rhetorics. His preface offers a history of the "natural" development of language which cites Mme de Graffigny and is clearly sympathetic with Rousseau's thought. A long section cites the havoc that writing for and to "les Grands" wreaks, because most of them "want only flatterers or slaves, never friends" as correspondents. Citing D'Alembert's *Essai sur les gens de lettres*, Philipon de la Madeleine's parting advice is to "repel them [les Grands] respectfully." Interestingly, Madame de Sévigné's letters are wholeheartedly embraced as "almost the only model that one can cite" in 1761 (19). The Rousseauist Philipon attributes the special qualities of Sévigné's personal style to her assumption of political independence from the aristocratic linguistic system. Linguistically, Sévigné is seen as functioning within the nonhierarchical space established by friendship, which permits infinite development of the idiolect. Sévigné is praised for precisely the qualities that Pasquier and his son argued for and tried to maintain in their writing during their losing battle against what they perceived to be the rising hegemony of a courtly system of literature over a century earlier.

The cult of the idiolect, of personal style, has traditionally been seen as erupting with Romanticism. Recently Roland Mortier has carefully studied the history of the concept of "originality" in the eighteenth century and concluded that between 1740 and 1770 the theory of classical imitation (*mimesis*) was abandoned in the literary field in favor of an aesthetics of originality, which preceded—rather than followed—the Revolution.[49] Correspondences are not one of the obvious vehicles for elaborating this literary aesthetics, and yet it can be argued that they are one of the important terrains in which it grew. For those epistolarians who held, consciously or not, to the Erasmian vision of the letter as a space for personal and artistic growth, for development of personal *ingenium*, letter writing remained open to the infinite plurality and specificity of individual experiences. I have tried to suggest that this vision went underground in the seventeenth century, when it was repressed from the public arena by a courtly ideology which attempted to subordinate the Republic of Letters to a feudal monarchy. With the emergence of the writer as an increasingly independent political figure in the eighteenth century, epistolary space expands with comparable freedom. In the wake of Mme de Sévigné's publication, Diderot, Voltaire, Rousseau, Mme Du Deffand, Mme de Graffigny, Mirabeau, and countless others will write and bequeath us voluminous correspon-

---

49. Roland Mortier, *L'Originalité. Une nouvelle catégorie esthétique au siècle des lumières* (Genève: Droz, 1982). Mortier stresses that this aesthetic category of "originality" cannot be understood simply as "Preromantic."

dences which reflect and develop the individual personality and world view of the epistolarian.

Indeed, for militant writers like Voltaire, Diderot, and Rousseau, epistolary activity was a privileged means to form and expand the ranks of enlightened cofighters. Voltaire's legacy of over 20,000 letters to 1,200 diverse correspondents all over Europe is doubtless the most remarkable testimony to this activity. By the 1760s Diderot and Rousseau, as well as Voltaire, will be receiving voluminous mail from admirers who seek their intellectual, artistic, and personal advice. Such is the personality cult surrounding Voltaire and Rousseau that before their deaths letter books will be published that purport to document their lives through authentic letters.

The titles of these books indicate their autobiographical pretentions:

> *Recueil de lettres de M. J-J Rousseau et autres pièces relatives à sa persécution et à sa defence.* Londres: T. Becket, 1766.
> *Lettres secrettes de M. de Voltaire, publiées par Mr L. B.* Genève, 1765.
> *Monsieur de Voltaire peint par lui-même, ou Lettres de cet écrivain, dans lesquelles on verra l'Histoire de sa Vie, de ses Ouvrages, de ses Querelles, de ses Correspondances, et les principaux Traits de son Caractère, avec un grand nombre d'Anecdotes, de Remarques et de Jugements Littéraires.* Lausanne: Compagnie des Libraires, 1766.
> *Lettres de M. de Voltaire à ses amis du Parnasse; avec des Notes historiques et critiques.* Genève: Cramer, 1766.

The "Voltaire peint par lui-même" letter book is a particularly interesting prototype for the twentieth-century "par lui-même" series on writers. Its lengthy title, moreover, lists rather comprehensively most of the interests that will attract readers to literary correspondences from the eighteenth century on: the expectation that correspondences reveal in a special "self-portrayed" way the "Story of the Life and Works," the quarrels and notorious relationships, the writer's personality and character, and the writer's reflections on literary questions. Seen as a group, these books not only demonstrate the extent to which Voltaire and Rousseau were literary legends in their own time; they also reveal the extent to which the personal history of these militant writers is deemed already in the mid-1760s to be best represented by their own letters.

The above-cited letter books, composed of purloined and often wholly fabricated letters, introduce a new issue into the world of printed correspondences: the issue of the letter's authenticity and the editor's or publisher's authority. Already the editors of Bussy's and Sévigné's correspondences in the 1720s and 1730s had been sensitive to discrepancies between versions of the same letter in previously published editions and had appealed to the authority of manuscript "originals." In the eighteenth century we begin to see a clear functional split between author and editor, and an incipient professionalization of the work of editorship. A new type of editorial preface appears: one which narrates the work of editing and accounts for the editorial principles applied. Editors, like authors, however, have to deal with literary institutions that they increasingly perceive as undermining their authority: censorship, lack of copyright laws, and finally—crucial for letters—the nature of print itself, which many epistolarians and editors come to realize conveys a quite different authority from the autograph letter.

The history of letter books during and after the eighteenth century is marked by that age's deepened awareness of the relational differences between oral conversation, handwriting, and print as modes of interpersonal communication, as representations of temporally specific experience, and as conveyors of social values. Autograph letters will become the object of a veritable cult, significantly intensified and commercialized after the Revolution by the dispersion of manuscript collections and by the technology of facsimile printing, which enabled collectors to identify authentic originals more readily.

In the nineteenth century, the history of letter books is bound up with the history of other new literary institutions: the rise of the professional literary critic (Sainte-Beuve, whose *Causeries du lundi* are largely based on epistolary documents); the literary historian (Gustave Lanson, who elaborates around the letter a much more complex notion of literary history than Sainte-Beuve's essentially biographical conception); and the pedagogical institutions of the early Third Republic, when epistolary literature officially enters the canon of literary genres taught (in which Crépet's and Lanson's letter anthologies, as well as Merlet and Lentilhac's textbooks play their role). By the nineteenth century, moreover, the letter of the living writer has effectively become private property, with the advent of copyright laws and other measures to protect writers: the interval between posting of the missive letter and publication of an author's collected letters during the nineteenth century is typically extended by a long posthumous protection period.

In the twentieth century, however, many writers will break with this latter practice, enter into a new collaboration with editors, and even publish their own missive letters. The distinction between private and public epistolary space has thus been increasingly blurred in our century in ways that are reminiscent of Renaissance epistolary publication practice. For many contemporary authors, letters are a form of auto-biography that they prefer to publish themselves. Some bookstores, recognizing this, now have a special section which groups correspondences with autobiography.

Letter books by twentieth-century epistolarians, moreover, have often taken the form of the duologue, particularly the published correspondences emerging from writer networks around journals like the *Nouvelle Revue Française*. For these writers (e.g. Gide, Claudel, Copeau, Proust, Rivière, Rolland, and Valéry in the early part of the century), the epistolary duologue has been an important means of exploring intellectual, artistic, and ethical questions. Critical editions of a writer's total correspondence have also assumed a new importance in our era, particularly since 1950, when foundation funding has helped defray the immense cost involved in their careful preparation. In recent years, moreover, the preparation of critical editions has been marked by the general internationalization of the literary profession. Critical editions have become multinational productions, involving scholars from several countries. Major colloquia held in France, Germany, Canada, and other nations have attracted editors from all over the world to discuss methodological questions. The books on editing correspondences that have resulted from these colloquia articulate a veritable poetics of the critical edition.[50] Correspondences, in turn, are increasingly being included as part of the "Complete Works" of published literary authors, whenever feasible.

In dealing with published literary correspondences, I have not found it productive to address the question that has dominated previous critical debates—that is, the question of whether correspondences are—ontologically—literary works. Instead, I have tried to follow the historical metamorphoses of epistolary space as it gets turned into literary space within a specific culture over a period of time. The "literarity" of letters, I would argue, must be described as the system of values attributed to letters (implicitly or explicitly) in any interpretive act that preserves those letters as art for posterity. The literary history that I have traced suggests how important it is to acknowledge that these values change dialectically over time and are conditioned by all of the

50. See, for example, Société d'histoire littéraire de la France, *Les Editions de Correspondance* (Paris: Colin, 1969); "Les Correspondances," *Revue de Synthèse* 97 (1976), 1–189; *Probleme der Brief-Edition* (Boppard: Herald Bolt, 1977); *Editing Correspondence,* ed. J. A. Dainard (N.Y. and London: Garland, 1979).

discursive models and political constraints on writing that obtain within specific cultures at particular historical moments. I have deliberately ranged over three centuries in order to point out the development of an important stratum of personal writing in Renaissance epistolary poetics and practice, a stratum which is obscured primarily by the *publication* practices of the seventeenth century, and whose reemergence in the eighteenth century is more than the product of aesthetic theories of writers traditionally called Preromantic.[51]

The "art" of letter writing under the Old Regime in France clearly implies an ethics as well as an aesthetics, a politics as well as a poetics. Letters published as "art" under Classicism are always transformed into illustrations of the "art" of writing letters, typically construed to position the writing subject as a loyal (male) servant of an aristocratic order revolving around an absolute monarch; this writer serves the monarch through public speech acts that constitute a predictable and universally imitable model of courtesy.[52] The countercurrent to this dominant Classical model, which coexists with it from the outset, is epistolary "art" interpreted as inimitable but inspiring emulation, because it is understood to emanate from differing, private literary spaces that articulate the particularities of historical contingency. The latter concept of epistolary art generates discourses of cultural difference, which will assume a renewed ascendancy in the eighteenth century. These discourses of difference will position writers in a reconfigured, politically powerful Republic of Letters during that period, while constituting the seedbed and battleground for the founding ideologies that will govern literary institutions in subsequent centuries, in ways that I have only been able to sketch. I offer this telescoped history as an indication that correspondences—in particular the correspondences of writers who have an acute sense of the place of writing in society—have a great deal to tell us about the ways in which a culture's linguistic choices have promoted its social values and constructed the social identity of its citizens.

51. Martha Wordmansee's otherwise excellent account of "The Genius and the Copyright: Economic and Legal Conditions of the Emergence of the 'Author'" unfortunately also assumes the view that the Preromantic writers whom she is describing "depart sharply from the older Renaissance and neoclassical conception of the writer" by introducing a "radically new conception of the book as an imprint or record of the intellection of a unique individual," *Eighteenth Century Studies* 17 (1984), 447.

52. Orest Ranum has convincingly argued that even the seemingly trivial aspects of the courtesy system were an integral and instrumental part of the creation of absolute monarchy in France. For his analysis, which offers rich detail on gestural conventions, see his "Courtesy, Absolutism, and the Rise of the French State, 1630–1660," *Journal of Modern History* 52 (1980), 426–51.

MIREILLE BOSSIS

Methodological Journeys Through Correspondences

An expedition into the uncharted territory of literary correspondences is not as easily carried out as one might suppose. There are volumes and volumes of letters waiting to bury the unwitting reader under the sheer mass of their usually very heterogeneous contents.

How then are we to find a way through this epistolary labyrinth?

I do not claim to hold Ariadne's thread; nevertheless, using as a point of departure various questions which were recently addressed at a four-day colloquium on this theme, I should like to try to articulate some of the different approaches taken and to map out the boundaries of epistolary writings in a manner as rigorous and methodical as possible.[1]

The temptation is great to trace the letter back to its original expression, however utopian such an attempt might appear to be.

What is a letter in its simplest form? It is a message written by one individual to another individual who is far away. This writing—a substitute for direct speech, which distance has made impossible—has a utilitarian value, directly linked to daily life, and it is enclosed in a rigid form whose parameters are immutable: signature   address   date and place of inscription   date and place of receipt.

In meeting these requirements, the letter has always been and remains unique: it cannot be assimilated to any other type of writing. In this sense it is legitimate to speak of an "epistolary genre." Whether or

1. The "Colloque international: 'Les Correspondances'" took place at Nantes in October, 1982. The proceedings are reproduced in a publication compiled under the direction of Jean-Louis Bonnat and Mireille Bossis and entitled *Ecrire. Publier. Lire. Les Correspondances (Problématique et économie d'un "genre littéraire")* (hereafter referred to in the Notes as *Les Correspondances*). This publication is available from the Université de Nantes, Département de Psychologie, B. P. 1015, 44036 Nantes Cedex.

not this genre is to be considered literary is another type of question which will be addressed later in this paper.

Without going into a detailed historical study of the letter, I would merely note that it came into being very early, probably in Mesopotamia, for the purpose of transacting business.[2] Letters pertaining to trade, commerce, travel, written first on parchment and later on sheets of paper, also allowed people to express and convey feelings which they considered important—particularly (of course) love. In other words, there were many types of letters, but they all strove for the same thing: to overcome the distance or the absence which was separating two individuals in order to reestablish an exchange.

The letter's function as primarily performative implies a return action (*effet en retour*), which is characterized by its inevitable displacement in time. Thus the return message does not necessarily meet the expectations which have been set out, either in business or in love. But in love or friendship this displacement is compounded by the whole business of writing. To express feelings with words alone implies a transformation of affects, and therefore of their return value (*charge de retour*), for the words of a letter have a *real weight* (*poids de réel*) different from that of the words in any other kind of writing. For writer and recipient the letter is above all an extension of daily life. It seems to me that literary critics have too often neglected this point. (I grant that it is not always easy to conceive of methods for apprehending it, and it is even harder to put these methods into practice.)

It is this *real weight* which leads love letters to be treated as sacred objects, even as fetishes.[3] Indeed, the fact that letters from the distant past survive to speak to us in the present is due precisely to the exceptional value which has been placed upon them.[4]

In order to clarify the givens upon which this study is based, I have provided a general outline of the common structural constraints implicit in any epistolary exchange. Within this general structure there are many possible ways of operating depending upon the psyche of the letter-writer, the psyche of the receiver, and the sociocultural pressures each has interiorized. However, since each correspondence is unique it is impossible to list all of these different operations without risking

2. Pierre Dumonceaux, "Le XVIIème siècle: Aux origines de la lettre intime et du genre épistolaire," *Les Correspondances*, 289–302.

3. Jacques Brengues, "La Correspondance amoureuse et le sacré," *Les Correspondances*, 55–73.

4. Maguy de Saint-Laurent, "Cent lieues et dix-huit jours: lettres d'amour en 1844," *Les Correspondances*, 79–89.

reductive generalization.[5] Thus I shall not develop this point despite its interest.

Should we draw a distinction between literary correspondences and "natural" correspondences (those which you or I might write, produce)?[6] Such a distinction is not obvious; both are acts of writing, and it would be hard to say by what criteria one should judge the literary status of these texts. Only the particular interest the reading of each provides can account for their survival. All of these writings belong theoretically in the same category, but all will not give rise to the same exploitation since some of them, as they reflect the personalities and current emotional states of the writers, are richer than others.

Nevertheless the problem becomes more complicated as we turn to the correspondences of "famous people," those known for their actions, especially their literary or artistic productions. The *real weight* of their letters obscures all other aspects, especially the process of the writing itself. An author's correspondence is then treated as a gold mine of biographical information, the correspondence taking on a fixed and univocal referential value which does not necessarily contribute to a better understanding of the author's work although that work was responsible for drawing attention to the correspondence in the first place. This is unfortunately the most frequent use to which letters (and other "personal" writings like diaries and autobiographies) are put.

Because of her tempestuous life George Sand offers a striking example of this exploitation. The twenty volumes of her letters, edited by Georges Lubin, have already supplied the raw material for several biographies in France and other countries, and there will undoubtedly be more. A fascination with the eccentric personality overrides any interest in the artist, a fact detrimental in every respect to all concerned.

The portraits which the biographers propose are simply reconstructions often of erroneous proportions, for the documents are used without having been passed through any critical filter; as such they are taken literally, "by the letter." It is assumed that they "tell the truth"— unlike novels which weave fictions.

Such an attitude may lull one into a feeling of security, but this is the security of the blind, as is obvious from the ease with which one questions that security as soon as one has decided to stop clinging to it as if it were a life raft.

5. Michèle Ramond, "La lettre ou le lien délirant," *Les Correspondances*, 357–71.
6. Simone Lecointre, "Contribution à une théorie du texte des correspondances," *Les Correspondances*, 195–212.

The contribution of the human sciences must not be overlooked. The act of writing, already complex, is now considered as behavior towards another person; thus it is invested with additional responsibilities which further obscure its already doubtful transparency.

As epistolary "truth" is placed on a pedestal and fetishized, two contradictory attitudes arise. For ideological reasons the critic may select a series of elements consistent with his or her subjective interpretation and, through a process of rationalisation, may from them construct a figure which accords with what he or she expects to find. Such a demonstration is specious since one ends up proving the very argument with which one began. An example of this may be found in the relationship of Sand and Musset which gave rise to virulent confrontations between their respective biographers who, although relying on the same documents, read and used the material differently, according to their adopted biases.[7] Strange as it may seem the dispute is scarcely over!

In contrast with the partisan vision, the integrating vision, having nothing to repudiate, focuses on facets of personality.[8] In this case one is lured into giving credence to everything, truths and countertruths, completely ignoring that hierarchy or organizing logic within the psyche of each individual which insures his or her difference from all others.

This is another aspect of Sand criticism: George Sand had a large number of correspondents and her letters reflect the way in which she adapted herself to each one. She "touched up" her self-portrait, sometimes more, sometimes less, but from one adjustment to the next, one can easily go astray.

Still in the area of the truth of the epistolary document I should like to draw attention to some practices which although currently applied nevertheless constitute methodological errors that we should strive to eliminate.

I shall use as an example the recent edition of a "natural" correspondence, that of Madame de Marèse, associate of the industrialist Oberkampf. This correspondence, *Une femme d'affaires au XVIIIe siècle*, was selected and edited by the historian Serge Chassagne.[9] First of all, we do not know what criteria were used for selecting the letters included in this volume. Further, the letters are offered not in chrono-

7. Charles Maurras, *Les Amants de Venise* (Paris: Flammarion, 1937); Henri Guillemin, *La Liaison Musset-Sand* (Paris: Gallimard, 1972).
8. Kristina Wingard, "Correspondance et littérature épistolaire: George Sand en 1834," *Les Correspondances*, 165–78.
9. Serge Chassagne, ed., *Une Femme d'affaires au XVIIIe siècle* (Toulouse: Editions Privat, 1981).

logical sequence but grouped thematically. Thus the reader or researcher is presented with texts already edited (and therefore deformed) by a prior reading, and he or she has no way of retrieving the original without digging into the archives for the manuscripts.

There are several reasons why such procedures should not be tolerated, reasons which a minimum of reflection on the epistolary genre makes very clear and which I nevertheless think useful to summarize here even at the risk of belaboring the obvious. When a letter which is not addressed to us falls into our hands, we must not forget that this has happened accidentally and that in reading that letter we are trespassers and voyeurs. If, for all kinds of perfectly valid reasons, we assume the right to invade the privacy of another person, then we must do so with the utmost respect for that person's integrity. Even if we do not have all of the letters at our disposal—and we can never be sure of having the entire collection—the order in which they were written cannot be ignored, for one must take into account the *return action* which, even if it is not discernible, for lack of documents or other traces, nevertheless exists.

Editors are generally very conscious of this problem.[10] When they find an undated letter they follow any and every lead which might permit them to fit it into chronological order with the others. In using a letter, the critic should be equally scrupulous: what is said in a given context, at a certain time, does not have the same significance in a different context, at another time. The study of recurring patterns which leads to thematic groupings can completely alter the text of correspondences, insofar as it tends often to eliminate those things which diverge. The letter, not unlike the personal diary, characteristically expresses immediate feelings, emotions, desires, with the accompanying ambivalence and contradictions more or less pronounced depending on the writer. The letter expresses itself in the immediacy of the moment. This is all the more the case in that each letter can be interpreted differently, accorded a different status, depending on whether it is question or response.[11] Each of us knows from experience that there are letters which one writes and others in which one merely responds to a letter received. The degree of implication is very different, ranging from offensive to defensive, from opening up to the other person to closing down the channels of communication and taking refuge in complete opacity.

10. Roundtable discussion: "Pourquoi éditer?" *Les Correspondances*, 404–08.
11. Alain Pages, "La communication circulaire," *Les Correspondances*, 344–53.

A correspondence is a joint endeavor in which meaning is the product of collaboration, but this is too often forgotten as one studies an author and assumes that his or her role is predominant, that he or she is the repository of meaning.[12] The latter view is an optical illusion attributable to the fact that one only rarely possesses both sides of the exchange. In the case of Mme de Marèse, it *does* seem that some of Oberkampf's letters indeed still exist; if they had been placed alongside those of Mme de Marèse—at least by way of example—we would have a fairer perspective on the sequence of the letters and on the relations between them. In this respect, as in others, Georges Lubin's edition of George Sand's letters is an exemplary work.

All of these reflections concern a pragmatic approach which accepts the text as a document laden with information which is real, and therefore truthful because often verifiable. Taking into account all of the precautions outlined above, one can and must work on this pragmatic level when dealing with a large number of letters which fall into the category of "natural" correspondences even if they are composed by famous writers. Yet there are other letters both from private citizens and from public figures, which serve another and equally vital function: that of creating illusion and fiction.

This fiction making is possible because the recipient is absent, unable to perceive the entire register of physical expression unleashed by real-life affective experience. Letters then let one avoid the censorship which language spoken in the presence of the other inevitably calls into play. In order to vanquish absence, a letter must call up images and particularly those of oneself for the other, of the other for oneself. Portraits and photos which may be exchanged are not enough; only words have the power to give them an appearance of life and movement. Thus the images which we construct with words are traced over those which we carry in our imagination. The image of self, which often depends upon the other's view of one, rarely coincides with reality; and the image of the other undergoes the same distortion since it is made to respond to the wishes formed by the image of self. Here we find the whole very subtle problematic of identity and narcissism, made still more complex by absence.[13]

12. Jean-Louis Cornille, "L'assignation. Analyse d'un pacte epistolaire," *Les Correspondances*, 25–51.
13. The reader is here referred to psychoanalytic works on the subject of narcissism, especially Heinz Kohut, *Le Soi: la psychanalyse des transferts narcissiques* (Paris: Presses universitaires de France, 1974) and Janine Chasseguet-Smirgel, *L'Idéal du Moi* ([s.1.], Tchou, 1975).

One is familiar with correspondences which can thrive only upon absence (those of Kafka, Kleist, Rilke and others far more numerous than one might guess). Such letters allow two people to share a dream both have woven, as the words bring about the exact coincidence of two fantasy worlds. Strange paradox indeed where the real—that is, the fact of writing, of sending the missive, of receiving it—guarantees the illusion! Face to face the individuals do not know one another.

An episode in the Sand-Musset relationship clearly illustrates this pattern. She was staying in Venice; he had returned to Paris. Letters were exchanged, letters which steadily if imperceptibly built a new love between them on a different and quasi-mystical basis. When George Sand returned to Paris, the mythical world and the actors within it which she and Musset had invented suddenly disintegrated. Nothing remained but two individuals tearing each other to pieces in interminable scenes, trapped by the power of words and pursuing ghosts. It was also absence which allowed Sand's friendship with Flaubert to grow and flourish in an epistolary space based largely upon the illusion of a communion of souls.[14]

We who read these letters can never forget that we are not their destined recipients: what means do we have to detect the illusion, the fiction, since the reality must forever elude us? We must, I believe, have the lucidity to recognize that we, as readers, are nearly totally disarmed. By a sort of affective asceticism, we must avoid the pitfalls of identification (positive or negative) with the author, identification which might lead us indiscriminately to credit everything. We must accept that the writer will always be to a large degree opaque as an individual.

There nevertheless remains one arduous and painstaking approach towards a perspective on the contents of the letters, a perspective close to what one might suppose to have corresponded to the lived experience as real: this is the study of the explicit and implicit "fantasmatics" (as opposed to "thematics") of the correspondence.

In order to avoid the errors exposed earlier one must avoid any dissection of the material. The fields of investigation must be very precisely defined to allow for a series of microanalyses, both synchronic and diachronic. For example, one might consider all of the available correspondence over a period of several months without differentiating the recipients, or one might study all of the letters addressed to a single person during a fixed period of time. As gaps—sometimes extremely

14. Jean Delabroy, "Le Courant de la plume: mythe et vérité de la correspondance," *Les Correspondances*, 375–99.

small—appear, they can allow one to infer the norm in relation to which they are effected and perceived.

Let me repeat that such a study would have to be long and detailed, and could still never be anything but incomplete. The psychocritical method of Charles Mauron, who is no longer enjoying much favor in the critical community, seems to me to be still viable, even if it needs to be adapted or perfected.[15] Using Mauron's techniques the critic may be able to isolate and examine one aspect of the personal myth of an author; I say *one* aspect because correspondences and private personal writings cannot be privileged in this research. We need to abandon the widespread belief that in these writings one finds an authentic expression of the truth, raw, natural, unmarked by any kind of censorship. In attempting to locate the personal myths of writers or artists, we find that their work provides material at least as valuable—and a major point of comparison. This is why one cannot study the correspondence of a writer without relating it to his or her work.[16] There is no direct correlation between them, but the confrontation of the two separate registers—which must above all be kept separate—lets one develop a dialectic between public and private, a dialectic rich with insights, through the very divergence which it reveals.

Let us consider once again George Sand, always a case in point. She was a writer of letters long before she was a novelist, but her novels put her suddenly very much in the public eye as they gave rise to a certain amount of scandal. She surprised everyone—not the least her friends— with her writings; and to her great astonishment and dismay people began to associate her characters, Indiana, Valentine, and especially Lélia, with her *self.* Her personal image was abruptly modified—and she hardly appreciated this assimilation. Denials abounded in her letters of that period, and at the same time she began to emphasize certain of her own personality traits which were diametrically opposed to those of her heroines, in order to make the difference perfectly clear to her friends. She also stressed the concrete, *whole,* realistic aspect of her letters in order to set them clearly apart from her fiction and its ambiguities. Gone were the great romantic scenes expressed with such passion and delirium. Her letters now cultivated the spirit, the simplicity, the util-

15. Charles Mauron, *Des métaphores obsédantes au mythe personnel* (Paris: Corti, 1963).
16. Monique Schneider, "De l'épistolaire au théorique: l'accidentellement vivant," *Les Correspondances,* 108–22; Alan Verjat, "Le Licencieux ès lettres: la correspondance de Sade," ibid., 328–43; and Nicole Treves-Gold, "La Correspondance de Montaigne et les *Essais:* problématique d'une étude intertextuelle," ibid., 268–85.

itarian spontaneity of daily life, even when she was confessing in a playful tone within the circumlocution of a phrase, that she had nearly "croaked" (crever) in the night. Paradoxically the supposedly realistic and spontaneous nature of her letters reflected her defensiveness. She kept her innermost self heavily guarded, tightly controlled, to the point of forgetting perhaps what it was that she had kept there.

Are we to believe her when she disclaims the lucubrations of her stormy years, saying that she can no longer recognize them as hers? Or are we to think that she relentlessly erased everything, true or false, which the public mirror reflected back to her as unpleasant? If so, her letters would represent *a writing of counterbalance, occultation, and interference with the work.*

Writers often feel more at ease within the sheltering confines of fiction. There they can let their imagination run free, as they people their fictional worlds with characters which are not *themselves* (or at least so they and their readers believe). This is verifiable: the personal myth such as it may appear in the text of the correspondences alone *is not identical* to that revealed in the text of the fictional or poetic work.

Again, what is at stake is the divergence to be measured, the transformations undergone. This is why it is essential not to mix up these different kinds of writing but rather to establish, insofar as one can, a clean separation between them, at least for the time it takes to analyze them. My previous work on George Sand's novels and letters allows me to affirm that this division exists for Sand—and there is every reason to believe that such would be the case for other writers as well.[17]

Let me stress however that this divergence is less a question of style than of the elaboration of the contents. Analyses of George Sand's works have revealed that her sentences are constructed in the same way in her novels and in her letters. Notably, Nancy Rogers has described in some detail the famous "snowball" sentences which Sand uses to sweep the reader along.[18]

One might at first be tempted to suggest that the exact opposite was true of Flaubert, but is this so very certain? A comparative study of Flaubert's literary and epistolary styles has yet to be done, but in the letters composed during the writing of L'Education sentimentale and in

17. Mireille Bossis, "La Femme prêtresse dans les romans de George Sand" (delivered at the George Sand Colloquium at San Diego University) and "L'Homme Dieu ou l'Idole brisée," in *George Sand* (Paris: Sedes, 1983).

18. Nancy Wall Rogers, *The Persuasive Style of the Young George Sand* (Ann Arbor: Univ. Microfilms, 1974) and "Style, voix et destinataire dans les lettres de George Sand avant 1837," *Les Correspondances*, 182–93.

that novel itself do we not find the same rhythm, the same structure, the same symbols and abbreviations?[19] And is not the choice of signifiers like the color which one applies to a drawing? It can vary without essentially changing the drawing.

When faced with diverse aspects of the personal myth of an author, how are we to bring them together? Must we at all costs resolve the problematic disunity? Each aspect (and there may be two or more if, for example, one seeks the personal myth through autobiographical writings whose libidinal economy differs from that of the epistolary genre) is as real as the other, but having been produced in different circumstances, each obeys its own particular logic.

One always has the choice of privileging everything which seems to issue from an unconscious region in order to delineate what is to be *The Myth* of the author, that which will incorporate into one *dynamic movement* the elements revealed by the different types of writing. But we find ourselves here involved in a problematic of the individual where the accent is placed entirely upon originality and upon the specificity of the One or the Other. As we have seen, the territory is vast, and the insights gained are extremely interesting and most often unique. Nevertheless one can become cramped in that space. Then it is necessary to find another perspective from which to study correspondences. One must pass from the individual to the collective.

The letter, a strongly coded, instrumental form of writing, does not escape the markings of time, and therefore neither does it avoid the *fashions* of language. Manuals for the accomplished letter-writer used to teach one to "turn" a phrase and "turn out" a letter fitted to the various circumstances of daily life. This meant that the letter could become the *locus* of stereotype and cliché which, in fact, it frequently did to varying degrees.

Though we may be able to discover those stereotyped expressions which make up the rhetoric of good manners and polite speech in our own everyday lives, it is far more difficult to do so as we go back in time. We are not familiar enough with past attitudes to distinguish what belonged to the general code and what was a creative innovation on the part of the individual. In our ignorance we often attribute to the author alone that which was actually true for a certain social milieu, or even for the community as a whole.

In our defense it may perhaps be said that authors themselves are

19. *Correspondance/Gustave Flaubert, George Sand*, ed. Alphonse Jacobs (Paris: Flammarion, 1981).

generally not conscious of the degree to which the "collective" influences their writing. They, too, feel that they are utterly original or at least distinctly individual and yet in time, if one cares to study the matter more closely, one can easily discern coherent styles. Style is here to be understood in its broadest sense, including discursive strategy and collective fantasy.[20]

The letter must be exploited in every conceivable way, its language rendered ordinary, separated from the motivations of its narrator. The voices must flow together in order to produce a single *discourse* which can be studied scientifically through sequential analysis, but which can also be heeded "with fluid attention," abstracting it from any pragmatics of interpersonal communication: *ça parle* [it speaks], it says something about the collective desire.[21] There is no longer any question here of seeking the personal myth but rather of seeking the societal one.[22]

In order to reach this objective, how in practice are we to exploit these private and personal documents while still treating them with the respect they deserve? Can one do greater violence than to cancel the narrating subject?

Dare we affirm that everything is possible once the protocol of research has been clearly expressed and as long as the researcher sticks to that protocol?

Indeed, if one implements such an approach there is no affective, subjective appropriation of a text and thus there is no diverting of meaning. With no fusion/confusion between researcher and narrator, the correspondence remains an object of irreducible alterity. A good program to be sure, but easier to describe than to carry out: one does not always know how to begin to approach these texts which one has purposely set at a distance, especially when one is working alone.

Experience leads me to conclude that one should always begin with the individual, that is, one should start with the particular and make one's way toward the general. In locating stereotypes in an individual, one can often infer their collective origin. Stereotypes and clichés are heavy with implications; they shape the language of the group, but the language of the individual in turn adapts and assimilates them according to its own economy.[23]

20. Mireille Bossis, "La Correspondance comme figure de compromis," *Les Correspondances*, 220–33.
21. M. Claire Grassi, "Un exemple d'analyse sérielle: Les correspondances intimes de la noblesse française," *Les Correspondances*, 239–54.
22. A. Ruffiot, "Fonction mythopoietique de la famille," *Dialogue*, no. 70, 1980.
23. Ruth Amossy and Elisheva Rosen, *Les Discours du cliché* (Paris: Sedes, 1982).

I have found one particularly striking example of this in very diverse correspondences: the language of the suffering body. The other's physical troubles seem to provide a privileged if not unique way for the writer to show attention to and affection for the other's body. The status of illness is thus called into question. There is indeed a strategy to be examined in letters which verbalize illness. One finds this evidence of this strategy in the letters of Mme de Marèse worrying over Oberkampf's slightest cold, as well as in those of George Sand, Musset, Chopin, and in the early twentieth-century correspondence published as *Marthe*.[24]

There is one aspect of correspondances about which I have deliberately avoided speaking: this is the function of the production of letters in the psychic economy of the writing subject. Certain people will claim that this is the essential question. I disagree. Within our Western scholarly circles the letter has been for centuries, and remains today, the first and nearly inevitable stage in the relationship to writing by way of the other.[25] It is said that every letter is a love letter, that every letter is a verbal enactment of the desire of seduction.[26] On the level of broad generalities all of this may be true, and has been brilliantly, even excessively, demonstrated. However, all of these findings, while they may be based on clinical observation and while they may allow a particular theory to be elaborated, can never make that theory apply exactly to any given individual save at the cost of mutilating that individual's specificity, and thus all of the work of putting into perspective and comprehending would still have to be redone for each correspondence.

To know in advance how an exchange is likely to be played out may allow one to perfect an interpretation and in that way to shed light upon the author's creativity. But to know in advance may also obscure the particular meaning of a document, even suppress it completely. To apply a theory is not necessarily to show objectivity, as we know only too well!

This is why a refined and rigorous method of analysis which defines its object and treats it as *Object* and not as a pretext for subjective discourse seems essential to me in order truly to hear and understand what a text is saying.

Furthermore let us not be afraid to limit the range of our subjec-

24. *Marthe* (Paris: Seuil, 1982).
25. Renate Karst-Matausch, "De la lettre aux lettres: Réflexions sur la genèse de l'écriture épistolaire chez George Sand," *Les Correspondances*, 146–61.
26. Paul Mathis, *Le corps et l'écrit* (Paris: Aubier Montaigne, 1981); Daniel Sibony, *L'Amour inconscient* (Paris: Grasset, 1983).

tivity; it is like the Phoenix which is reborn from its own ashes. In literary criticism we will always have enough subjectivity left to heed the basic polysemy of the text, sufficient unto itself, and this includes the text of the letter which must never be taken *at its word*, literally, *au pied de la lettre.*

Translated by Karen McPherson

MARIE-CLAIRE GRASSI

Friends and Lovers
(or The Codification of Intimacy)

This article is part of a larger analysis which deals with nonliterary personal correspondence, that is, handwritten letters sent by members of the French nobility between 1700 and 1860.[1] The archival sources

1. Marie-Claire Grassi, *Correspondances intimes (1700–1860). Etude littéraire, stylistique et historique.* Thesis, University of Nice, 1985, directed by Michel Launay. 2 vols., 538 and 288 pp. The corpus analyzed includes 1,100 letters; "intimacy" is defined as a tacit understanding between two correspondents that is characteristic of the letter between friends or family members, the letter given to spontaneous and open exchange of confidences. The corpus is composed exclusively of manuscript letters from national and departmental archives, and its contents may be characterized in several different ways: By geographical distribution:
    50% originating in Paris or other large towns
    50% originating in rural areas
Or, 10% from western regions of France
    39% from southern regions
    19% from Paris and the surrounding area
    14% from outside France
    1.5% from central, 1.5% from northern, 3% from eastern regions
    12% of unidentified origin
By sex of addresser and addressee:
    48% man to man
    15.5% man to woman
    11% woman to woman
    25.5% woman to man
By social status of the addresser:
    13% military
    37% "idle" nobility
    14% nobility in the administration or in business
    36% women
Or, finally, by type of affective relationship:
    41% nonfamily (lovers, friends)
    34% family: between children, parents, grandparents
    25% wider family

that have provided this collection of letters are representative of all of France, necessarily including letters of foreign origin or arriving from overseas territories.

An analysis such as this offers points of interest from both a synchronic and a diachronic perspective. Firstly, we seek to define and appreciate an epistolary thematic, the ensemble of subjects of "a long-distance conversation." Secondly, the research provides an insight into a certain level of language through the materiality of writing—the graphic dimensions of handwriting and the dimensions of orthography and style. Finally, the analysis constitutes an investigation of the expression of the emotional life of the past, through the norm illustrated by letters, which is a reflection of the social norm. It is this last aspect that we would like to present here. For indeed, the letter is not only a language in itself, but also a creative source of language; the letter is the written speech of a communication between absent parties, and as such assumes from the social code the ensemble of rules that cast its form; the letter cannot be studied independently of the wider social norm. In its capacity as parturient of language, and constituting a circular emotional structure (for the letter has a beginning, a middle, and an end), the letter is a privileged system of communication.

From the perspective of a diachronic analysis, a sequential approach is well suited to the study of an evolution. The objective here is to circumscribe the developing use of certain key vocables that expressed the emotions of a bygone age throughout the totality of their semantic fields: *aimer* [to love], *embrasser* [to embrace/to hold/to kiss], *amour* [love], *amitié* [friendship]. This analysis is carried out with respect to two major types of relationship between emitters and receivers. Firstly, we look at relationships that fall within the parameters—no matter how large—of the family (that is, between cousins, parents and children, husbands and wives, or siblings), and secondly, at nonfamilial relationships, including all relationships of friendship or love, and any affective rapport within the boundaries of a more or less conventional propriety (e.g., letters between friends, letters between lovers). In addition, the analysis must take into account the gender of both the emitter and the receiver.

In a previous article, we have remarked the overall gender-specific usage of two fundamental affective vocables of the eighteenth century: "attachment" and "friendship."[2] "Attachment" is a specifically femi-

2. The semantic field of *amitié* cannot be rendered by a single English word and exceeds the scope of the mechanical translation chosen here for reasons of clarity. *Amitié* includes resonances of affection, kindness, favor, etc. (Trans.)

nine vocable, uniting in its semantic field submission, obedience, veneration, and both the worthiness and the expectation of reciprocity of the sentiment it expresses; "friendship," on the other hand, is essentially used by men, expressing reciprocity of affection. It is due to the strong affective charge of the word that women use it little, or with infinite precaution.[3]

What becomes of these key vocables in the nineteenth century? The present collection of eleven hundred letters of the French nobility, both Parisian and provincial, represents an equal number of specific relationships, which we classify according to three chronological periods:

I: 1700–1770
II: 1771–1820
III: 1821–1860

Throughout these three periods we propose to analyse the formal constructions of the openings and closings of the letters, the forms of address, and the affective vocables in the body of the texts themselves.

I: 1700–1770

In the familial relationship, the almost total absence of the noun "love" is remarkable. One rare mention is in a letter between husband and wife, which mentions "*l'amour dont je suis embrasée*" [the burning love by which I am consumed], but this is a verbal excess characteristic of this type of relationship. On the other hand, the verb "to love" is the vocable par excellence. We encounter it in the present indicative and the imperative, for an observation or for an injunction. Parallel to this usage of the verb "to love," the standard complimentary close for this type of relationship is "*je vous embrasse de tout mon coeur*" [I embrace you with all my heart].[4] To give "all," "from the bottom of the heart," is the ever present desire:

Je suis à vous de tout mon coeur.
I am yours, with all my heart.

3. Marie-Claire Grassi, "Un révélateur de l'éducation au XVIIIᵉ siècle: expressions de la vie affective et correspondances intimes," *Revue d'Histoire moderne et contemporaine*, 28 (1981), 174–84.

4. Like *amitié* the range of meanings of *embrasser*—from the informal *Je vous embrasse* ["Hugs and kisses"] to the emotional force of the above example—are impossible to capture in a single English word. (Trans.)

Je suis de tout mon coeur à vous.
With all my heart, I am utterly yours.

Je suis toute à vous.
I am all yours.

Je vous embrasse au plus profond de mon coeur (ou du meilleur de mon coeur).
I embrace you from the bottom of my heart (or, with the best of my heart).

For the amalgam of "I love you" and "I embrace you," the following constructions are encountered.

Je vous aime beaucoup.
I love you very much.

Je vous aime de tout mon coeur.
I love you with all my heart.

Je vous embrasse et je vous aime de tout mon coeur.
I embrace you and I love you with all my heart.

The imperative, which characterizes the affective enjoinder, goes hand in hand with a demand for reciprocity. "Love me as well as I love you" is a common construction, but the insistence on reciprocity is not the perquisite of the imperative, for the same insistence is to be found in the present tense, e.g., "I love you as well as you deserve to be loved," or "I embrace you with all my heart and beseech you to love me as much as I love you." In the family, however, "love" is replaced by "tender friendship," which can also be characterized as "true" or "sincere." "Tender" and "tenderness" are specific to the family as qualifiers of "friendship," but "tender attachment" is also used in the same case.

"Friendship" goes by the sign of the "humble and obedient servant," and this formal construction, although it is privileged for this type of relationship, is also very often found between husband and wife, between cousins or between children and parents. "Sincere attachment" and "perfect esteem" accompany this construction, as does "friendship." The intimacy of friendship, then, although purposefully avoiding the stereotypes of formulaic constructions, still gives rise to the same expressions as the family relationship. However, there is an important qualification to be made: this is only true of letters between men, or between lovers. Women "friends" never use the verb "to love"; they speak of friendship rarely, and then only in a very well established relationship.

Between men:

> Peu de personnes sont capables d'aimer, je suis de ce nombre.
> I am one of the few that are truly capable of loving.

> Aimez-moi autant que je vous aime et ce ne sera pas peu.
> Love me as well as I do you, and you will love me well indeed.

> Je suis entièrement à toi.
> I am entirely yours.

Between lovers:

> Je vous aime toujours de même.
> I love you as much as ever.

> Je t'embrasse mille fois et t'aimerai toute ma vie.
> I send you a thousand kisses, I will love you all my life.

Indicating equality or familiarity, the second person singular is used only exceptionally in the eighteenth-century letters of this corpus. It is found only in a very few letters, such as parent to child, between husband and wife, between men, between lovers. After 1800, the familiar "tu" will be, increasingly, in common usage.

II: 1771–1820

"Love," the noun, is still fairly rare in letters within the family. We encounter it, however, in three identical verbal excesses, coupled with the verb "to love."

Between Husband and Wife:

> Il faut souffrir et t'aimer d'un amour qui ne finira qu'avec la vie.
> One must suffer and love you with a love that will die only with the end of life.

Daughter to Father:

> Il serait impossible de retrouver un papa plus tendre et plus complaisant que le mien aussi ma reconnaissance et mon amour pour lui n'ont point de borne.
> No one could ever find a daddy more tender and obliging than mine, and so my gratitude is infinite, as is my love.

Uncle to niece:

> Je t'aime, je t'aime beaucoup, je ne désire rien que te voir et il faut que
> l'amour que j'ai de mes devoirs soit bien puissant pour que je résiste à
> l'envie d'aller visiter une nouvelle débutante dans le monde.
> I love you, I adore you, my only desire is to see you, and my love of my
> duties must be very strong indeed for me to resist the desire to go and
> visit such a newcomer to this world.

If the constructions "I love you" and "I embrace you with all my
heart" remain the stock phrases, this second period is characterized by
two particular aspects. First of all, there is the increasingly generalized
usage of verbal excesses, particularly within the family. Hand in hand
with the increasing use of the familiar second-person singular address,
this tendency contributes to a growing liberation from the use of stereotyped phrases, which, while they by no means disappear, are less frequent. The amalgam of "I love you" and "I embrace you" is retained in
the following forms of hyperbole.

Between children or parent and child:

> Je vous aime mieux que je ne pourrai jamais vous dire.
> I love you better than I could ever say.

> Je t'aime et t'embrasse de tout mon coeur et de toute mon âme, je suis
> ton ami et ton père.
> I love you and embrace you with all my heart and all my soul, I am
> your father and your friend.

Between husband and wife:

> On ne peut aimer plus que je ne fais, on ne peut être plus de toi que je le
> suis.
> No one could love more than I do, no one could be more entirely yours
> than I am.

Son to father:

> Je n'ai pas besoin de vous dire combien je vous aime.
> I need hardly tell you how much I love you.

Daughter to father:

> Je vous aime comme je vous embrasse.
> I love you with all the force of my tight embrace.

Aunt to niece:

> Je t'aime de tout mon coeur et t'embrasse mille fois.
> I love you with all my heart, a thousand kisses.

The enjoinder to love, with its characteristic imperative, is as always in evidence, for example: "Love me as I love you," "Keep loving me a little bit, my dear brother."

This second period is characterized, moreover, by the appearance of what we might describe as intermediate constructions, mediating between the two extremes of "the humble and obedient servant" and "I embrace you" or "I love you with all my heart." With a nice exactitude, these constructions tie a number of elements of each extreme to the verbs "to love" and "to embrace."

> Je vous embrasse de tout mon coeur, votre obéissant et affectionné fils.
> I embrace you with all my heart, your obedient and affectionate son.

> Je vous embrasse de tout mon coeur et vous aime de même, je suis avec respect votre obéissant serviteur.
> I embrace you and love you with all my heart, I am, with great respect, your obedient servant.

These intermediate constructions, as hybrids of a number of variants, bear witness to a very clear evolution in the expression of affection within the family. Friendship is as always centered within the semantic field of either a declaration or the assurance of reciprocity of the sentiment. For the most part, friendship is characterized as "tender and respectful":

> le témoignage de l'amitié et de l'attachement qu'un mari doit à sa femme, principalement quand il est assez heureux d'en avoir une aussi méritante.
> the proof of the friendship and the attachment that a husband owes his wife, particularly when he is so lucky as to have such a deserving one.

> Je réclamerai sans cesse votre amitié et je n'ose dire la mériter.
> Without daring to claim any right to it, I never cease to lay claim to your friendship.

The relationship of "friendship" maintains the earlier characteristics. The parallel that we noted above, the fact of "loving beyond all expression," is again found between men and between lovers, in constructions reflecting on the uniqueness of the person loved.

Between men:

> Tu m'as dit que l'amitié était plus forte que l'amour, donne m'en des preuves. . . . Je suis plus tendre en amitié qu'en amour.

You have said that friendship is more ardent than love, can you prove this? . . . for I am a tenderer friend than a lover.

Adieu mon cher ami, je suis doublement heureux de penser à toi car tu es le seul.
Farewell, dear friend, the thought of you is a twice happy thought, for you are the one and only.

At the same time, the second period is profoundly marked by the emotional engagement of women who dare to liberate themselves from "attachments" in favor of "friendship" and say, when the rapport permits, "I love you" or "I embrace you." A certain number of formulas which had hitherto been the exclusive domain of the rapport between men are now encountered between men and women:

Je suis toute à vous.
I am all yours.

Attachement sincère avec lequel je suis pour la vie toute à vous.
The sincere attachment that makes me, for all my life, entirely yours.

Sentiments que je vous ai voués à jamais, la plus ancienne et la plus sincère de vos amis.
Feelings that I have vowed to you for ever, from the oldest and the most sincere of your friends.

Je vous aime de tout mon coeur et pour toujours.
I love you with all my heart, and forever.

Je vous embrasse autant que je vous aime.
I embrace you with all the strength of my love.

Pour la vie votre fidèle.
Your faithful friend for life.

Je te renouvelle l'assurance de ma vieille et tendre amitié.
I assure you once again of my old and tender friendship.

III: 1821–1860

The noun "love" is, as always, conspicuous in its absence from correspondence between family members, even in evolving forms of address. Remaining, however, is the hyperbole surrounding the usage of the verb "to love":

Celle qui t'aime jusqu'à la mort (ou jusqu'au fond de l'âme).
She who loves you unto death (or, from the bottom of her soul).

Je vous aime tendrement au-delà de toute expression.
I love you with a tenderness that surpasses all expression.

Between husband and wife, one rare form of address is noteworthy: "Mon cher amour" [My dear love].

The apparition of "chérir" [to cherish] and "bien-aimé" [beloved] is specific both to the period and to the relationship. Between parents and children, "cherish" serves exclusively to reinforce either "to love" or "to embrace," but as the following examples demonstrate, the appelation "ma chérie" or "mon chéri" [my dear] is never found.

Je te serre sur mon coeur et me dis pour la vie ton bien-aimé et affectionné fils.
I press you to my heart, and swear to remain, for life, your beloved and affectionate son.

Les embrassements d'un fils qui t'aime et te chérit.
The embraces of a son who loves and cherishes you.

C'est ta mère, rien que ta mère qui t'aime et te chérit.
Your mother, just your mother who loves you and cherishes you.

Adieu mère chérie, je vous embrasse tendrement.
Good-bye, dearest mother, I embrace you tenderly.

"Beloved" is also peculiar to parents and children, thus: "beloved father [or son]," "beloved mommy." "*Maman*" [mommy] and "*papa*" [daddy] are seen in correspondence addressed to parents from the eighteenth century onwards, as are several affective enjoinders, such as the following, in which a son writes to his mother "Love me as I love you, I embrace you with my whole heart."

The body, in this period, occupies an increasingly preponderant place in the family embrace:

Je t'embrasse dans mes deux bras.
I hold you in my arms.

Je me jette dans tes bras.
Let me throw myself into your arms.

Je te serre bien tendrement sur mon coeur.
I clasp you tenderly to my heart.

The embrace appears also, during this period, between friends and between men. Beginning of letter:

Je suis votre ami dévoué, je l'ai toujours été, je vous le jure, ouvrez vos bras je vous embrasse.

I swear to you that I am your devoted friend, as I have always been. Open your arms that I may embrace you.

Adieu, jusqu'au jour où j'aurai le bonheur de vous serrer dans mes bras. Farewell, until the day when I can hope to have the pleasure of holding you in my arms.

Ma femme et moi nous vous pressons sur notre coeur. My wife and I would clasp you to our breast.

Is the central position accorded to the body in the expression of emotion within the family to be considered as associated with the growing usage of two adjectives that qualify emotions, "good" and "tender"? Both adjectives certainly conjure up gustatory images of physical contact; an appreciative body is present in the two terms. In this manner they are to be distinguished from "affectionate" or "devoted," which, referring to a less intimate relationship, have no physical connotation.

"Tender," "tenderness," "tenderly": all are vocables of a parent's vocabulary from the eighteenth century onwards. In 1694 the dictionary of the Académie mentions "the tenderness of a father for his children." In the nineteenth century there is still only the example of "tender friendship" that is synonymous with both parental and filial love. For this period the following examples come from a parent's hand:

C'est toujours avec toute la tendresse et l'amitié possible que je vous embrasse. As always, I embrace you with all the tenderness and friendship possible.

Je vous embrasse, votre tendre mère. I embrace you, your tender mother.

Recevez ma tendre et sincère amitié. Accept my tender and sincere friendship.

Croyez à ma tendresse et à mon amitié. Believe in my tenderness and in my friendship.

These examples demonstrate the connotative field of the word "friendship," which is tied to "tender," "tenderness," or to "I embrace you." "Friendship" has a very strong emotional power in this sort of semivisceral relationship: it establishes an almost physical contact. For children two usages of "tender" and "tenderness" distinguish themselves after 1820. On the one hand, in the constructions of the preceding century that are perpetuated in modified form, "tenderness" is associated with "respect":

Mon cher papa, à vous les plus tendres respects.
My dear daddy, I send you my most tender respect.

Agréez le tendre et respectueux attachement de votre petit fils.
Please recognise the tender and respectful attachment of your grandson.

Recevez l'assurance de mon tendre attachement et de mon profond respect.
Please accept the assurance of my tender attachment and my profound respect.

les témoignages de la vive tendresse de votre affectionné fils.
the proofs of the heartfelt tenderness of your affectionate son.

As soon as a construction becomes stereotyped, the vocable "attachment" makes its appearance. On the other hand, the different usages of "tenderness" and its derivatives constitute an ensemble of sentiments addressed by children to their parents, sometimes unaccompanied by any other vocable.[5] Thus:

Je vous adresse mille tendresses (ou ma bien vive tendresse).
I send you a thousand tender kisses (or, my devoted tenderness).

Toute la tendresse de votre fille.
All the tenderness of your daughter.

Recevez mes vives tendresses.
Accept this pledge of my devoted tenderness.

For a final example, a sister asks her brother to send "un million de tendresses" [a million tender kisses] to father and mother.

"Tender" and "tenderness" come into their own in either an extended family relationship or between friends, in examples such as "believe in my brotherly tenderness." In the handwriting of friendship, and in the form of a superlative, the adjective graces the sentiment it expresses with the sweetness of physical contact.

Between men:

Conservez-moi toujours un peu d'amitié, et soyez assuré du plus tendre retour, mille tendresses.

5. The plural *tendresses* is a nondescriptive, unspecific reference to "tokens of affection," with approximately the intimacy and strength of affection implied by present-day American "Love" (as a standard close) or "Hugs and kisses." (Ed.)

Keep for me always a bit of friendship, and be sure of the most tender return, one thousand kisses from. . . .

Between women:

Chère amie que j'aime et embrasse du plus tendre amour.
My dear friend, whom I love and embrace with the most tender love. . . .

This rare usage by a woman of the word "love," which here becomes a synonym of "friendship," is noteworthy.

"Good," a word infrequently used at the end of the eighteenth century, comes into its own during this period. More so than "tender" and its derivatives, it is par excellence the parental qualifier: it is parents who qualify both themselves and their children as "good." Sometimes this adjective goes hand in hand with "tender":

Parents to children:

Mon cher bon ange, mon bon fils.
My dear good angel, my good son.

La véritable amitié de votre bon et tendre papa.
Your good and tender daddy sends you his true friendship.

J'attends trois bons enfants instruits, capables de se suffire à eux-mêmes.
I expect to find three good children, well behaved and self-sufficient.

Ton vieux bon père.
Your good old father.

Adieu ma fille, au revoir, ta bonne mère Augustine.
Farewell my daughter, till the next time, from your good mother Augustine.

Ton bon père qui t'aime de tout son coeur.
Your good old father who loves you with all his heart.

Recevez l'amitié de votre bon père.
Accept the friendship of your good father.

The form of address, "ma chère et bonne maman" [my dear and good mommy], is very frequent; "good" is the qualifier properly addressed to parents.

Je réitère à la bonne maman mon respect et mon amour filial.
I reassure my good mommy of the love and respect of her son.

Until 1860, filial love, parental love, and conjugal love are all included in the single rubric of "friendship."

This "friendship," from the eighteenth century onwards, is increasingly qualified by the two adjectives that are proper to the expression of parental affection: "good" and "tender." Likewise, in correspondence, brothers and sisters, cousins, parents and children, all accord themselves, with ever-growing frequency, the status of "friends." The form of address "mon cher ami" [my dear friend] comes into common usage between children, as do the ancillary constructions: "brother and friend," "good father and friend," "your good cousin and friend."

In the rapport of friendship, the first decades of the century bring about a "desexualization" of formal epistolary phrases. We find a tendency towards one single formula, used more according to the particular epistolary situation than with respect to the sex of the sender, and fixed by usage and propriety. This tendency has led by 1850–1860 to the formulation of the phrases we still use today. At the end of this period we witness the dawn of the twentieth century, and 1820–1860 sees the emergence of nongender-specific formulas like the following conventional closings:[6]

l'expression de mes sentiments les plus dévoués.
the expression of my great devotion.

l'assurance de ma parfaite considération.
the assurance of my perfect consideration.

l'hommage de mes sentiments respectueux et dévoués.
the token of my devotion and respect.

For women, "friendship" is quite close to "I love you" or "I embrace you with all my heart." Between men, the embrace undergoes a "masculinization" in its replacement by the handshake, which, whether in writing or in person, marks masculine fraternity more often than the embrace.

En vous remerciant avec effusion, je vous serre la main dans les deux miennes, et je suis toujours vôtre, par la reconnaissance et l'amitié.
Thanking you effusively, I shake your hand between both of mine, in gratitude and in friendship. I am yours truly. . . .

6. These three constructions are, either in identical or slightly modified forms, in current usage today in formal correspondence, taking roughly the place of the American "yours truly" or "sincerely yours." (Trans.)

> Je te serre la main de bien bonne amitié.
> In the best friendship, I shake your hand.

The handshake exists in the extended family as well; for example between brothers-in-law:

> Je te serre cordialement les mains.
> I cordially shake your hand.

The effective vocables of epistolary discourse have, in fact, a proxemic value: they are born of and refer to the usage that man makes of space and for this reason reflect the code of social propriety. Of the four spatial categories defined by Edward T. Hall,[7] intimate, personal, social, and public distances, two are pertinent to us here: social and intimate distances. For it is possible to translate the degree of affection reflected by a given vocable into proxemic terms. From the intimacy of "I embrace you" or "I throw myself into your arms" to the social distancing of the "humble and obedient servant," all the intermediate constructions that come into being at the turning point of the nineteenth century show that, in the verbal exchange of emotion, the place accorded to the body grows in proportion to the extent to which the rules of social propriety relax their hold. Although intimacy remains codified in communication, the body speaks with a louder and clearer voice. And yet, this presence of the body, whether experienced at a distance or seen as an effort to abolish distance, must not lead us to overlook the almost complete absence, or the very specific usage, of two vocables in the lexicon of affection: "caresses" [caresses] and "baisers" [kisses]. The former concerns children; it is they who caress or who are caressed; the latter concerns lovers.

In 1860, the "humble and obedient servant," that ultimate sign of respectful social distancing, filial or otherwise, has not completely disappeared. The construction tends to blend in with those asexual "distinguished sentiments" or with a "consideration" that wills itself to be "perfect" or "sincere." In this manner, devotion has come to take the place of servitude.

Friends and lovers, love or friendship: the ambivalence of *l'amitié-amour* is a reality of the emotional life of a bygone era. This emotional reality expresses itself in the formalized epistolary act through a certain number of vocables which have evolved over a century and a half.

7. Edward T. Hall, *The Hidden Dimension* (Garden City, New York: Doubleday & Company, Inc., 1966).

"Friendship" was said in speaking nevertheless of "love," and the verb "to love" was conjugated, like "to embrace," within an ensemble of phrases that illustrate the intensity of the emotion they express and its proxemic value. "Love," however, belongs to the language of passion, but, in the emotions of family life or the life of a friendship, to say "I embrace you with all my heart" is to eradicate social distance, it is to speak with the body, to speak love without pronouncing "love."

To demonstrate the degree to which the word "love" was in general taboo in the context of family or friendship, we take an example from the epistolary manuals of the period. *Le Secrétaire universel* [*The Universal Writing Guide*], published in 1860 by P. Persan and again in 1890 by H. Delaroche,[8] is a general manual which contains model letters for a variety of epistolary situations. Chapter 3, entitled "Letters to Friends," defines "friendship" as "a tender feeling of the soul which leads us to share with someone complete and honest intimacy, stemming from a conformity of thought, opinion, affections, intentions." The author offers seventeen model letters written by a young man—"whose avowals must always be in conformity with his honorable intentions"—either to a young woman or to her parents. In either case, the letters declare a tender, sincere, or true friendship, or give voice to "the sweet avowals of friendship." Conspicuously, the noun "love" is absent; in fact, it is found only in one of the seventeen letters: "a vow of tender, honest, respectful love, which you have always inspired in me." However, the verbs "to love" and "to adore" are present: "I love you, mademoiselle," "I love you with my soul's whole strength."

Is it solely by chance that, at the turn of the century, 1880–1920, there appear a number of manuals for the writing of love letters, even though numerous popular anthologies of "the most beautiful love letters of our best authors" had long since been printed and reprinted? Several evocative titles serve as examples of these manuals.

> 1886 Anon. *Le Petit secrétaire des amants* [*The Lovers' Little Manual*]
> 1893 Anon. *Nouveau secrétaire-guide des amoureux, Encyclopédie de l'amour* [*The New Writing Guide for Lovers, The Encyclopedia of Love*]
> 1899 E Ducret, *Le Secrétaire des coeurs aimants* [*The Manual for Loving Hearts*]

8. Henri Delaroche, *Le Secrétaire universel contenant des lettres de bonne année et de fêtes, de compliments, de condoléances, de félicitations . . . d'amitié et de mariage* (Paris, 1890).

1904 L. Joliet, *Le Secrétaire galant* [*The Galant Writer's Manual*]
1909 M. Fischer, *La Correspondance amoureuse ou le petit secrétaire pratique à l'usage des gens pressés* [*Love Letters, or a Practical
Manual for Those in a Hurry*]

The analysis is still to be extended to the turn of the twentieth
century in order to circumscribe the final avatars of the vocables of
affection. For it is in the fashion of a bygone age to say "I love you and
embrace you with all my heart" in order to speak love without saying
"love." A final example well demonstrates this, in the end of a letter
from a wife to her husband, written in 1828:

> Je t'embrasse, c'est toujours comme ça que je finis mes lettres, mais
> quelle différence pour moi, je ne t'embrasse que d'intention, te rap-
> pelles-tu comme je jouissais de sa réalité? Enfin, nous ne serons pas
> toujours à deux cents lieues l'un de l'autre, adieu cher ami.
>
> I embrace you, so do I always end my letters, but for me, what a
> difference there is! For I only express, here, my desire to embrace you,
> but do you remember the pleasure I took in that embrace's reality?
> Well, it's not forever that we are 200 leagues from one another; adieu
> my dear friend.

Translated by Neil Gordon

DEIDRE DAWSON

In Search of the Real Pangloss: The Correspondence of Voltaire with the Duchess of Saxe-Gotha

La meilleure de toutes les demeures possibles est certainement celle de
Gotha, et je sçai bien quelle est la meilleure des princesses possibles.
—Voltaire to the Duchesse of Saxe-Gotha, 11 October 1756[1]

Pangloss enseignait la métaphysico-théologo-cosmolonigologie. Il
prouvait admirablement qu'il n'y a point d'effet sans cause, et que,
dans ce meilleur des mondes possibles, le château de monseigneur le
baron était le plus beau des châteaux, et madame la meilleure des
baronnes possibles.

—Candide[2]

For scholars interested in the eighteenth century, there is hardly a richer
or more diverse document to be found than the massive correspondence
of Voltaire, a work which is surpassed in voluminosity only by the
Encyclopédie launched by Diderot and d'Alembert in 1751. Though it
may seem odd to speak of the *Correspondance* and the *Encyclopédie* in
the same breath, the comparison is not entirely gratuitous, for the

1. "The best of all possible abodes is certainly that of Gotha, and I know who is the
best of all possible princesses." Voltaire, *Correspondance and Related Documents*, definitive edition by Theodore Besterman (Geneva, Banbury, Oxford: The Voltaire Foundation, 1968–1977), Best. D7023. All future references to the *Correspondance* will be
indicated by the Besterman code number immediately following the quotation. English
translations are mine.
2. "Pangloss taught metaphysic-theologo-cosmolonigology. He proved admirably
that there is no effect without a cause, and that in this best of all possible worlds, the
castle of Monseigneur the baron was the most beautiful of all castles and Madam the
best of all possible baronesses." Voltaire, *Candide,* critical edition by René Pomeau, *The
Complete Works of Voltaire,* No. 48 (Oxford: The Voltaire Foundation, 1980), 119.
English translations are mine.

20,000 or so letters of Voltaire span the larger part of the century (1704–1778) and contain literally thousands of references to the literary, scientific, philosophical, and political developments of the Age of Enlightenment, not to mention the innumerable judgments and anecdotes concerning the patriarch's contemporaries, which make up in humor and irony what they lack in accuracy. Add to these intriguing elements the meticulous attention that Voltaire paid to every detail of his material existence, from wigs and wine to bidets and bookcases, and the modern reader becomes so completely immersed in Voltaire's world that, gazing momentarily out the window, he may find himself mistaking his own garden for the orchards of Les Délices, so carefully nurtured and cultivated by the author of *Candide*. In reading the *Correspondance* we are at once involved in the preoccupations and obsessions of Voltaire. This is not to say however that the primary significance of these letters lies in their historical value or anecdotal quality. The *Correspondance* is in itself a literary work, containing countless examples of the sardonic humor, polemical rhetoric, and philosophical dialogues which came to be recognized as the trademark of the "style voltairien" in the more widely read publications of the author, such as the *Contes* and the *Lettres philosophiques*. And yet, hundreds of pages of criticism have been written on the latter two works alone, while the surface of the *Correspondance* has hardly been scratched.

One reason for the relative neglect that the *Correspondance* has suffered is of a purely material nature: up until the publication of the first Besterman edition, compiled and edited between 1953–1965, there simply was no accessible, chronologically accurate collection of the letters to which one could refer. The second Besterman edition, although described as "definitive," is nevertheless not complete, as indeed no edition of the *Correspondance* ever could be; every year researchers discover hitherto unknown letters of Voltaire in places ranging from national archives to family attics, making the *Correspondance* a sort of posthumous "work in progress." To attempt any sort of comprehensive study of the *Correspondance* would be a herculean task indeed: Voltaire corresponded with hundreds of people during his long and eventful life and continued to dictate letters even from his deathbed. The duration and the tone of the individual correspondences vary greatly. While Voltaire maintained some epistolary relationships for years on end, other correspondents never received more than one or two hastily written notes from the philosopher, dealing with such mundane affairs as business or financial matters. The most interesting and revealing letters by far are those addressed to close friends and associates of

Voltaire, such as Madame Denis or the Tronchin family, or to his numerous royal correspondents, among whom can be counted Frederick of
Prussia, Catherine the Great, and Princess Ulrika of Sweden.

Louisa Dorothea von Meiningen, duchess of Saxe-Gotha, may not
have enjoyed the military power and prestige of the royalty mentioned
above, but the relations that developed between this princess passionately fond of literature and philosophy and the philosopher lured by the
luxury of courtly life put their correspondence in a category all of its
own. Born in 1710, the duchess maintained all through her life a vivid
interest in everything the new philosophical and political currents were
sweeping through the intellectual circles of Europe. The tiny duchy of
Gotha was a stage for works newly published by popular playwrights
and a forum for the teachings of Christian Wolff, the famous philosopher and personal mentor of the duchess. Having already acquired a
reputation as a protectress of literary personalities, it was perfectly
normal that she extend an invitation to Voltaire, who was looking for a
place of refuge after his expulsion from Frederick the Great's court at
Berlin. Voltaire had previously attempted to establish a friendly rapport
with the duchess in his letter of 23 May 1751 signed "the Chamberlain
of the King of Prussia." Always the diplomat, not forgetting for a moment that he was dealing with the first cousin of Frederick, Voltaire sent
Louisa Dorothea a collection of his works that had been published in
Dresden, accompanied by a missive underlining the rare and valuable
nature of this gift: "Il y a plus de deux cent pages corrigées par ma
main. . . . Il n'y a que trois exemplaires au monde de cette espèce" (Best.
D4474). [There are more than two hundred pages personally corrected
by me. . . . There are only three copies in the world of this kind.] The
duchess responded enthusiastically, and hardly a year later she received
yet another shipment of books, this one containing *Le Siècle de Louis
XIV*. The tactic worked as Voltaire had planned: Louisa Dorothea was
flattered by the attention the former historiographer of Louis XV was
paying her and warmly renewed her invitation, hoping to be able to
express to him in person her gratitude and esteem.

This occasion finally presented itself in May of 1753, shortly after
the infamous quarrel between Voltaire and Frederick. Without soliciting a more formal invitation, Voltaire stopped his carriage in front of the
castle of Gotha and descended upon the court completely unannounced.
The arrival of such a well-known personality in what was relatively
unimportant royal territory was taken as a great honor for the small
village, and Voltaire received a welcome worthy of a nobleman. During
his one-month stay, he succeeded in winning the duchess' friendship

and protection, and he left the forest of Thuringia knowing that he had
in her a devoted admirer. His departure by no means marked the end of
Voltaire's relations with the court of Gotha: on the contrary, he renewed his correspondence with the duchess almost immediately, and
the two continued to write each other until Dorothea's death in 1767,
exchanging more than 250 letters over a span of approximately fifteen
years. Their correspondence reached its apogee during the Seven Years'
War; as battles were raging around the castle of Gotha, Voltaire was
preparing to launch his own bombshell on the world, one that was to
prove as destructive to dogma as cannonballs were to cow pastures: in
February of 1759, the publication of *Candide* struck and stunned the
intellectuals of Europe, not the least of whom was the Duchess of Saxe-
Gotha herself.

What role did the duchess actually play in the genesis of the famous
tale? For years scholars have wondered if the mild-mannered Dorothea
could have been the model for Pangloss, the celebrated character
through whom Voltaire succeeded in ridiculing the doctrine of Divine
Providence almost to the point of destroying its philosophical validity.
Their curiosity has been aroused even further by the fact that Voltaire
does not seem to have written a first draft of *Candide*, which could lead
to the conclusion that he used his correspondence with the duchess as a
sketch board for developing the polemical argumentation against philosophical optimism that runs throughout the structure of the story. Certainly everything we know about the duchess points us in this direction: a self-avowed Leibnitzian, she was greatly influenced by the
philosophy lessons given her by Christian Wolff, himself a disciple of
Leibnitz. Voltaire, though violently opposed to this school of thought,
respected the intellectual capacities of the duchess and took neither her
opinions nor her criticism lightly. Many critics agree that it was because
of her influence that Voltaire modified the ending of his "Poème sur le
Désastre de Lisbonne," which she found to be too pessimistic in tone. In
her letter of 17 January 1756 she admired the moving and realistic
images of suffering evoked in the pòem but regretted the note of despera-
tion on which it concluded. ". . . la seule chose que j'eusse souhaité y
voir encor dans cet admirable tableau, c'est les voyes de la Divine et Sage
Providence rétab(l)ies et décelées" (Best. D6693). [. . . the one thing I
would have liked to see in this admirable description are the ways of
Divine, Wise Providence reestablished and revealed.] Ira Wade points
out that after having received a second letter dated 20 February of the
same year, in which the duchess once again extolled "La Divine Providence," Voltaire rewrote the last lines of the poem, sending a second

version to his optimistic friend, who subsequently responded with great enthusiasm.[3]

Whether or not Voltaire substituted the verb "to hope" for the verb "to adore" out of deference for the duchess or out of fear of being condemned in religious circles as an atheist, this concession by no means put an end to the debate on Divine Providence. On the contrary, from November of 1755 until the end of 1759 the correspondence between Voltaire and the duchess is filled with reflections, remarks, and arguments for or against Leibnitz's theory that in spite of the existence of evil and injustice on the face of the earth, it is nonetheless "the best of all possible worlds." Voltaire completed the final version of *Candide* around October of 1758, and though it would be erroneous to suggest that the letters of the duchess constituted a source for the tale, a careful comparison of her correspondence with certain passages from *Candide*, particularly those in which Candide or Pangloss are speaking, reveals striking similarities in attitude and in tone. In this sense one can discern a certain persona of a stubborn, "one-eyed" philosopher emerging through Louisa Dorothea's letters. Likewise the sarcastic reflections uttered by Martin the pessimist in his efforts to disillusion Candide seem to echo remarks made by Voltaire in his battle to open the duchess' eyes to the philosophical implications of the horrible events occurring all over Europe. Indeed, the more closely the reader of Candide examines the *Correspondance*, the more likely it seems that Voltaire used his epistolary dialogues with the duchess as a structural model for the philosophical polemic between Martin and Pangloss. This thesis is supported in a recent article by H. A. Stavan, who remarks that in following the argumentation of Voltaire and the duchess, one has the impression of listening to Martin and Pangloss, though in a less caricatural form.[4] Our aim is to carry this thesis even further, by suggesting that though the characters of Candide, Pangloss, and Martin were unique creations springing from Voltaire's own imagination and experience, the type of relationship that develops between them in the story would not have been the same as we know it without the duchess' influence.

Before delving more deeply into the actual exchange of opposing ideas that transpired between Voltaire and his royal correspondent, it must be stressed that the tactic of setting up a dialogue between charac-

3. Ira Wade, *Voltaire and Candide* (Princeton: Princeton University Press, 1959), 105.
4. H. A. Stavan, "Voltaire et la duchesse de Gotha," *Studies on Voltaire and the Eighteenth Century*, 85 (1980), 44.

ters of contradictory beliefs had long been a favorite polemical and narratological technique of the philosopher. From all accounts of his contemporaries, Voltaire himself was a brilliant conversationalist, and so it is not surprising that he would choose the dialogue as a privileged mode of expression in his writings. This in itself was not a new concept, nor one particular to the eighteenth century. Shaftesbury, in his *Advice to an Author* published in 1710, refers back to the Greeks to support his theory that dialogue is the best literary mode for communicating ideas of a moral or philosophical nature. Through the creation of a distance between the author and the reader, the dialogue permits the reader to assume the role of an objective spectator witnessing the dramatization of different points of view. Thus the dialogue form, used so effectively by Voltaire in the *Contes* as well as in the *Lettres philosophiques*, allowed him to express his views without appearing to moralize or preach directly to the reader. His secret skill lay in constructing the dialogue in such a way that the reader would tend to favor the characters expressing the author's own beliefs, since these characters invariably present the strongest arguments. A good example of this strategy can be found in the first of the *Lettres philosophiques*, "Sur les Quakers," in which Voltaire constructs a dialogue between a Frenchmen entrenched in Catholic dogma and an English Quaker. In reading the dialogue the reader is left to judge for himself the soundness of the arguments presented respectively by each character, which is precisely what Voltaire had in mind. As Voltaire pointed out in the preface to the 1765 edition of the *Dictionnaire philosophique*, "The most useful books are those of which the readers themselves do half of the composing: they hear the germ of the thoughts presented to them; they correct that which they consider defective and strengthen that which they consider weak."[5]

The impact of the *Lettres philosophiques* was explosive. When the French edition finally appeared in 1733 (the first edition had been published in English in London), it was condemned by the French parliament as a threat to political and religious authority and burned at the foot of the palace steps. The sentence, though it forced Voltaire into exile, guaranteed great success for the book. Having developed such an effective mode of argumentation, Voltaire continued to use the dialogue in his other polemical works. In the *Contes*, however, the dialogue took on a more metaphysical dimension and became a means for Voltaire to work out for himself philosophical problems regarding Good and Evil,

5. Voltaire, *Dictionnaire philosophique* (Paris: Garnier-Flammarion, 1964), 20 (my translation).

Fate and Providence. The questions raised by *Zadig* (1747) reveal that Voltaire was already struggling with the puzzling dilemma of calamity befalling the just. Zadig, the righteous prince with the wisdom of Solomon, is persecuted and exiled precisely because of his insight and moral integrity. At certain points in the story, when Zadig feels most acutely the cruelty of Fate, his reflections seem to foreshadow those of the Manichean Martin of *Candide:* "Everything that I have done has always been a curse to me, and I was raised in the height of grandeur only to fall in the most horrible precipice of misfortune. If I had been evil like so many others, I would be happy as they are."[6] But unlike Martin, Zadig does not let his moments of cynicism undermine his faith in the ultimate wisdom of the Supreme Being. His attitude is one of philosophical inquisitiveness, as he struggles to understand better the Divine reasoning behind the structure of the universe. In one of the final chapters Voltaire sets up a dialogue in question and answer form between Zadig and the angel Jesrad, in which the hero demands an explanation for the injustice that has befallen him at the hands of Divine Providence. The response of the angel seems to paraphrase directly Leibnitz's conception of the world, in which even Evil has its place: ". . . there is no such thing as chance: everything is either trial, punishment, compensation, or precaution." Zadig is on the verge of making one more objection, but even as he articulates his last question, the angel vanishes, and Zadig falls to his knees in total submission to Providence. " 'But' said Zadig . . . . As he was saying 'but,' the angel was already flying off to the tenth sphere. Zadig, on his knees, adored Providence, and submitted" (83).

The ending of the story is sufficiently ambiguous to leave room for philosophical doubt. True, Zadig prostrates himself before the mysterious ways of Divine Providence, but his final utterance, "but," is one of resistance, not of acquiescence. In the dialogue between Zadig and the angel, Voltaire was dramatizing the inner dialogue going on within himself concerning the existence of Evil in the world. He was evidently still torn between a spiritual tendency to revere and adore the Creator, and a more worldly attitude of unacceptance and revolt. Stimulated by the reflections of the Duchess of Saxe-Gotha, Voltaire was later able to clarify his stand against Providentialism, and to make the dialogue opposing optimistic passivism with pessimistic activism the central focus of *Candide.*

6. Voltaire, *Romans et Contes* (Paris: Garnier-Flammarion, 1966), 51 (my translation).

Any residual proclivity Voltaire may have had for Providentialism was quelled by the Lisbon earthquake of 1755. Even adamant Leibnitzians were hard-pressed to rationalize this natural disaster as an act of Divine wrath. Ironically, the earthquake occurred on a Sunday morning, and so the devout who were attending Mass in urban areas perished instantly beneath the rubble of the caved-in churches. The senseless death of so many innocents could not be easily explained. Voltaire's immediate reaction was one of horror and outrage. In a letter to Jean-Robert Tronchin, his banker and financial adviser in Lyons, he decried the injustice and cruelty of this mass extermination of his fellow-men: "A hundred thousand ants, our fellow creatures, crushed suddenly in our anthill, and half of them perishing no doubt in unspeakable anguish in the middle of debris from which they cannot be extracted" (Best. D6597). Though it cannot be denied that Voltaire was considerably worried about the effect the disaster would have on his own personal fortune, ". . . families ruined all over Europe, the fortune of a hundred merchants of your country [France] destroyed in the ruins of Lisbon . . . ," the *Correspondance* reveals unequivocally that his primary concern was of an altruistic and humanitarian nature. The vivid descriptions of suffering contained in the "Poème sur le Désastre de Lisbonne" also bear witness to Voltaire's great capacity for empathy and compassion, disproving the fallacious image created by his adversaries and perpetuated throughout the nineteenth century that tends to present the philosopher as a callous, unemotional cynic. It is nonetheless true that the Lisbon earthquake marked a turning point in the philosopher's outlook on the world, which grew increasingly pessimistic as the decade progressed. "Plus je réfléchis sur le mal qui inonde la terre, et plus je retombe dans ma triste ignorance" (Best. D6726). [The more I reflect on the evil that is inundating the earth, the more I fall back on my sad ignorance.] So begin his letter of 10 February 1756 addressed to the Duchess of Saxe-Gotha.

It was precisely at this time that the tone of many of the remarks of Voltaire and Louisa Dorothea changed from that of a friendly exchange of ideas to a veritable epistolary debate on the question of philosophical Optimism. The two correspondents had long held different views on the subject, but the aftermath of Lisbon and the increasing militarism of the European monarchies only served to harden them in their positions. In the duchess' comments immediately following the earthquake, the figure of a kindhearted, somewhat naive character gaily accepting what Fate ordains for him was already beginning to take form. After having read the revised version of the "Poème Sur le Désastre de Lisbonne,"

Louisa Dorothea rejoiced at what she interpreted as a victory of optimism over skepticism and doubt, declaring to Voltaire, "j'avoue ingénument et sans rougir que j'ai le tic d'aimer, d'idolâtrer la providence" (Best D.6860). [I admit ingenuously and without blushing that I'm in the habit of loving and idolizing Providence.] Her reasoning is similar to that of Candide, who also reveals a tendency to forget the ills of the world and revere Providence each time the events turn in his favor. A few months after the great earthquake in Portugal, the duchess informed Voltaire of a slight seism that had been felt in Gotha. ". . . il n'a pas eu de suite, notre frayeur s'est changée en joye, en ravissement; n'ai je pas lieu de m'écrier que tout est bien?" (Best. D6744). [. . . there were no aftereffects, our fright changed into joy, into rapture: have I not reason to exclaim that all is well?] Voltaire's reaction was to remind his correspondent that the fortuitous sparing of Gotha was not sufficient grounds for declaring that all was well around the globe. Referring to Frederick of Prussia's imminent plans to declare war, he wrote, "Le *tout est bien* recevrait un terrible souflet, si les nouvelles qui se débitent touchant une cour de votre voisinage avaient la moindre vraisemblance" (Best. D6772). [The "all is well" would receive a terrible slap in the face if the rumors concerning your neighboring court had the slightest truth to them.] The duchess' contented existence in her peaceful court blinded her to the disasters that were occurring on an international scale, and Voltaire attempted to open her eyes to the truth. A second letter followed, in which he reiterated his views: "Le *tout est bien* est un peu dérangé en Amerique, en Europe et en Afrique. . . . Jugez madame s'il est doux de vivre à Gotha" (Best. D6848). [The "all is well" is a little deranged in America, in Europe, and in Africa. . . . Judge, Madame, if it is sweet to live in Gotha.]

The manner in which Voltaire repeatedly forced the duchess to come to grips with reality is reproduced in the numerous exchanges between Candide and Martin, which follow the same pattern as that of the letters. As the two travellers approach Venice, Candide's initial optimism returns, and all he has previously suffered is swept from his memory. "Dieu soit loué, dit Candide. . . . c'est ici que je reverrai la belle Cunégonde. Je compte sur Cacambo comme sur moi-même. Tout est bien, tout va bien, tout va le mieux qu'il soit possible" [God be praised! said Candide. It is here that I will see again the beautiful Cunégonde. I count on Cacambo as I count on myself. All is well, all is going well, all is going as well as possible].[7] The Manichean Martin, who

7. Voltaire, *Candide*, ed. Pomeau, 224.

is much more of a realist, reacts to Candide's exuberant exclamations in much the same way as Voltaire responds to the duchess, refusing to let his protégé believe in an illusion, preferring to foresee the worst rather than hope for the best. "Il la prendra pour lui, s'il la trouve. S'il ne la trouve pas, il en prendra une autre. Je vous conseille d'oublier votre valet Cacambo et votre maîtresse Cunégonde." [He'll take her for himself, if he finds her. If he doesn't find her, he'll take another. I advise you to forget your valet Cacambo and your mistress Cunégonde.] Martin, like Voltaire, may not have been very "consoling," but his analytical assessment of the situation is presented as much more logical than the optimistic expectations of Candide.

Though a remarkable similarity in the tone of the dialogues and in the relationship between the interlocutors can be noticed in the two passages we have just compared, the first, from the correspondence of Voltaire and the duchess in the year 1756, the second, from chapter 24 of *Candide*, Voltaire, at least initially, proved to be more indulgent towards Louisa Dorothea than Martin towards Candide. Her optimism, more easily explainable than that of Candide, was partly the result of the sheltered life she led at Gotha, safe from physical suffering and political disturbances. In fact, there are sufficient grounds for supposing that Voltaire may have based the fairy-tale castle of Thunder-ten-tronckh on the court of Gotha. In several of his letters the philosopher described Gotha as a sort of earthly paradise in which evil and unhappiness could never find a foothold. In his letter of 10 February 1756, after having reflected upon the series of disasters occurring throughout the world, he congratulated the duchess on her enviable position. "Vous régnez paisiblement sur des états où vous êtes adorée, et V[otre] a[ltesse] s[érénissime] ajoute la considération personnelle la plus distinguée aux respects que sa naissance et son rang luy attirent. . . . Enfin, le nouvau proverbe tout est bien, est vray à Gotha" (Best. D6726). [You reign peaceably over states where you are adored, and Your Serene Highness adds the most distinguished personal consideration to the respect that your birth and rank bring you. . . . In short, the new proverb "all is well" is true in Gotha.] We must, however, go beyond the gratuitous syntagmatic parallel between the two courts. The fact that the duchess possessed many of the character traits that make Candide such a sympathetic hero is just as noteworthy. Her compassion, sensitivity, and highly emotional nature can be discerned in her letters, particularly those written during the Seven Years' War. One is reminded of the innocent, naive Candide, who had never experienced hardship before the invasion of his beloved château, when one reads the following lines, written to Voltaire in January of 1757. ". . . que d'événemens inouis n'avons-nous pas vus arriver depuis, que de torents de sang et de larmes n'a t'ons pas vus couler! J'en suis toute ébaubie" (Best. D7582). [. . . what unheard-of events have we not seen arrive since then, what torrents of blood and tears have we not seen flow! It has left me completely stunned.]

As Candide sought a companion who had suffered sufficiently to be able to understand and console him, the duchess opened her heart to Voltaire, who shared her hatred of war and misery, albeit with more objectivity, like Martin, in the face of troubling situations. The final lines of the opening chapter of *Candide*, ". . . et tout fut consterné dans le plus beau . . . des châteaux possibles," (121), [. . . and all was in an upheaval in the most beautiful . . . of all possible castles] range true for the court of Gotha as well as for Thunder-ten-Tronck. The year 1756 brought with it two tragic events that affected the duchess directly: the premature death of her eldest son, and the outbreak of the Seven Years' War. She turned to Voltaire repeatedly for advice and consolation and was often astounded by the grim accuracy with which her correspondent was able to predict the outcome of military and political events. Voltaire may never have set foot on a battlefield, but he foresaw long before the duchess the dreadful global consequences that would result from territorial disputes. His letter of 23 May 1756 bears testimony to the fact that all was not well in Europe. "L'optimisme et le tout est bien, reçoivent en Suede de terribles échecs. On se bat sur mer, on se menace sur terre" (Best. D6978). [Optimism and 'all is well' are suffering terrible defeats in Sweden. There are battles at sea, and threats on land.] The duchess, who was horrified at the prospect of her peaceful territory being transformed into a bloody battlefield, could only marvel at the cool, detached attitude of Voltaire: "Que Vous être digne d'envie de voir dans le lointain de sang froid tous ses altercations!" (Best. D7086). [How worthy you are of envy to be able to see calmly all these distant altercations!] This remark brings to mind the Manichean philosopher in *Candide*, who maintains his capacity to judge events impartially even as the world crumbles around him. In Chapter 26, Candide and Martin join six other dinner guests at a banquet given during the carnival of Venice. As our hero takes his seat with mixed emotions, "partagé entre la joie et la douleur . . . étonné . . . le coeur agité, l'esprit bouleversé" [. . . torn between joy and pain . . . astonished . . . his heart a-flutter, his mind confused], his travelling companion looks on as a calm, aloof spectator. "Martin . . . voyait de sang-froid toutes ces aventures" (238). [Martin-. . . saw all these adventures with composure.] One cannot fail to be impressed by Voltaire's aloofness as a writer, as he recollected so calmly his own reactions towards the war and parodied so accurately the duchess' emotivity.

The exchange of letters between Gotha and Les Délices reached its peak during the Seven Years' War, and this escalation in the *Correspondance* corresponds chronologically with a significant aspect of the genesis of *Candide*. Although Voltaire had not yet begun to write the tale, René Pomeau emphasizes in his preface to *Candide* that the "paysage" that would serve as the backdrop for the action of the first chapters was already taking shape in the author's mind between 1756 and 1757. During this crucial period the Duchess was of far more service to her correspondent that she realized; by sending Voltaire frequent updates on military operations in Germany, she became a major source of information for him throughout the war. Though the Seven Years' War pales in comparison with the international conflicts that have taken millions of lives in the past two centuries, it must be remembered that it was at the time the bloodiest and cruelest war that Europe had ever seen. Thousands of soldiers fell in the battles, and the carnage that had started in foreign territories finally arrived at the doorstep of the charming castle of Gotha. The duchess' letters are filled with detailed and moving descriptions of the suffering endured by the victims of military ambition. Voltaire, whose sensitivity was so acute, must have trembled in horror as he read the firsthand accounts of senseless slaughter sent to him regularly from Gotha. In her letter of 16 December 1758 Louisa Dorothea provides the following report on a victory won by Frederick the Second over the Russian army: ". . . c'étoit une journée bien meurterière, un carnage affreu, un combat des plus opiniâtre qui a duré du matin au soir. Quel tableau! l'humanité en frémit. Les jours suivants les Russes ont brûlés plus de dix villages et ont comis selon les gazettes de Berlin des cruautés incroyables" (Best. D7863). [. . . it was a murderous day, a hideous carnage, a most relentless combat that lasted from morning to night. What a scene! All humanity is trembling. In the days that followed the Russians burned more than ten villages and committed, according to the newspapers of Berlin, incredible acts of cruelty.] In another missive, the poor duchess, who was of too sensitive a nature to bear the sight of such bloodshed, exclaimed, ". . . les gémissements de tant d'expirants me font horreur!" (Best. D7283). [. . . the moaning of so many dying people horrifies me.] Voltaire retained most vividly the image of the expiring victims left in the wake of the plundering and burning of the villages, for the duchess's description is reproduced almost verbatim in Chapter 3 of *Candide*. As the Abares and the Bulgares are waging a merciless battle, Candide tramples over scores of mutilated bodies in a desperate attempt to save his life: "Il passa par-dessus des tas de morts et de mourants, et gagna d'abord un village voisin; il était en cendres" (126). [He traipsed over piles of the dead and dying, and first arrived at a neighboring village; it was in ashes.] In painting such a realistic "tableau" of the battles that were raging daily around her castle, the duchess evoked certain images of war in Voltaire's mind, to which the writer then added his own brushstrokes, "[des] femmes égorgées, qui tenaient leurs enfants à leurs mamelles sanglantes" [women with their throats slit open, clasping their children to their bloody breasts], rendering the final portrait even more pathetic and powerful.

The duchess' contribution to the genesis of *Candide*, however, went far beyond the furnishing of details for Voltaire's satirical battle scenes. Paradoxically, she accompanied her descriptions of cruelty and injustice with apostrophes to the wisdom of Divine Providence and arguments in favor of Optimism. In this manner she not only aided the philosopher in painting a scathing caricature of war but provoked him into ridiculing the erroneous reasoning of philosophical optimists as well. It was not by chance that Voltaire situated the first chapters of his tale in Germany. To be sure, it was the site of a war such as Europe had never seen before, not to mention the home of Frederick the Great, but it was also the native territory of Leibnitz, Wolff, and the Duchess of Saxe-Gotha, incorrigible advocates of the "best of all possible worlds." Voltaire soon lost patience with the duchess' attitude of acceptance and resignation. To his discouraging predictions regarding the disastrous outcome of the war, she responded placidly, "Le vin une fois tiré il faudra bien le boire quelque amer qu'il soit et quelque répugnence qu'il cause" (Best. D6988). [Once the wine is poured, we will have no choice but to drink it, however bitter it may be and whatever repugnance it may cause.] Though the duchess counted on her correspondent to console her with his insightful reflections and divert her with his witticisms, Voltaire found it more and more difficult to restrain his feelings of outrage and indignation. His well-known letter of 24 June 1757 is written in a tone of biting sarcasm worthy of *Candide*, and contains bleak prophecies for the future that rival even the gloomiest predictions of Martin. Voltaire begins by commenting upon the tragedies that had recently upset the globe, taking a stab at Optimism along the way: "Le meilleur des mondes possibles est bien vilain depuis deux ans" [The best of all possible worlds has been quite nasty for the past two years]. Granted, other ages had seen their share of troubles, but if the war continued the eighteenth century would surpass them all. "Mais avec le

temps on poura parvenir à égaler touttes les misères et touttes les hor-
reurs des temps les plus héroïques" [But with time we will be able to
equal all the misery and all the horrors of the most heroic times]. Voltaire was less preoccupied with the immediate material consequences
of the war than with its long-term ramifications: this "grande tragédie"
that was being played out on the scene of Europe was robbing humanity
of all hope for a better future. To be passive and optimistic at such a time
was an affront to reason and an insult to the suffering, as Voltaire pointed out with acerbic irony: "On ne peut pas dire encor *tout est bien*
mais . . . avec le temps l'optimisme sera démontré." (Best. D7297). [We
cannot yet say that all is well, but . . . with time, optimism will be
conclusively proven.]

Louisa Dorothea, however, remained impervious to such remarks
and stood her ground. The more atrocious the war became, the more she
persisted in her optimism. She tried to adopt a "philosophical" attitude,
remarking to Voltaire in February of 1756, "Avoués Monsieur que nous
vivons dans un siècle plein de merveilles, soit pour le phisique, soit pour
le moral, soit pour la politique" (Best. D6744). [Admit, monsieur, that
we are living in a century filled with marvels, whether they be physical,
moral or political.] Voltaire responded with his habitual cynicism, finding little cause for marvel as he analyzed with a critical eye the military
preparations that were already threatening world peace. In the event of a
conflict, he retorted, "Le mal moral serait bien au dessus du mal phisique; et ce serait bien pis qu'un tremblement de terre" (Best. D6772).
[The moral evil would far surpass the physical evil, and it would be
much worse than any earthquake.] But the irate philosopher was not
content to refute the duchess' statement merely in the form of a personal letter; in writing *Candide*, he retained the key words of her reflection
but gave them an ironic twist, contorting the phrase so that the intended
praise of Optimism was transformed into a bitter critique. As Candide
prepares his voyage to Eldorado, he shares his hopes of finding a better
world with his beloved Cunégonde: "Nous allons dans un autre uni-
vers . . . c'est dans celui-là sans doute que tout est bien. Car il faut
avouer qu'on pourrait gémir un peu de ce qui se passe dans le nôtre en
physique et en morale" (151). [We are going to another universe . . . it is
in that one, no doubt, that all is well. For one has to admit that there is
reason to bemoan what is happening in our own, both in the physical
and in the moral spheres.] Little did the duchess know that her innocent
remarks would be perverted by her correspondent's pen and used to
combat the system she so doggedly adhered to.

Voltaire might have let many of the duchess' letters pass without

comment, had he not felt that his position as a writer and as a philosopher was at stake. For years he had been considered the "oracle" of
Saxe-Gotha, but the admiration Louisa Dorothea professed for him did
not prevent this enlightened lady from also appreciating the views of
his adversaries, in particular Jean-Jacques Rousseau. Voltaire's "Poème
Sur le Désastre de Lisbonne" had elicited a personal response from
Rousseau, dated 18 August 1756, which was later published under the
title, "Lettre Sur la Providence." The duchess had undoubtedly read
Rousseau's rebuttal and had found more consolation in the idea that
"le mal particulier . . . contribue au bien general" (Best. D6973) [indi-
vidual ills . . . contribute to the general good] than in Voltaire's dour
judgements concerning the prevalence of Evil in the world. One can
only imagine what Voltaire's reaction must have been when he read
his mail on a bleak day in November of 1757, only to find the arguments of his archenemy paraphrased and commented upon by the
duchess herself, whom he had once counted among his disciples:
". . . l'on devroit à mon avis changer la phrase, et ne plus dire, *tout est
bon* mais le tout est bon. Nous le voyons sans cesse qu'une chose peut
être mauvaise à certains égards, par partie, pour tel ou tel individu et
être boñe dans son ensemble" (Best. D7449). [. . . one should, in my
opinion, change the phrase, and no longer say 'all is well,' but rather,
'the whole is well.' We see again and again that a thing can be bad in
certain respects, for this or that individual, yet be good in its entirety.]
Voltaire must have restrained his anger, for in his response of 24
November no allusion whatsoever is made to Louisa Dorothea's sug-
gestion. Once again, he saved his last word for *Candide,* making Pangloss the spokesman for both Rousseau and the duchess. As Candide
and Jacques the Anabaptist reflect on the corrupt nature of human
beings, exemplified by the preponderance of bayonettes, canons, and
financial fraud, Pangloss states his view: "Tout cela était indispensable, répliquait le docteur borgne, et les malheurs particuliers font le
bien général, de sorte que plus il y a de malheurs particuliers, et plus
tout est bien" (133). [All of this was indispensable, replied the one-eyed
doctor, and individual misfortunes contribute to the general good, so
that the more individual misfortunes there are, the more All is well.]

Whether or not the individual misfortunes that befell Saxe-Gotha
in the following years contributed to the general welfare of Europe
remains unclear, but we can say with a fair amount of certainty that the
individual remarks of the duchess contributed to the general profile of
Doctor Pangloss. In the early stages of her correspondence, Louisa Dorothea seems to foreshadow the character of Candide, for both optimists

share a strong belief in the fundamental goodness of human nature, which reinforces their providentialist conception of a world arranged for the best. As more and more ills befall them, however, their attempts to use isolated acts of benevolence to rationalize the predominance of malice and dishonesty become increasingly tenuous. Candide finally rejects the teachings of his master when his idealistic theories are disproved by the pragmatic experience of reality. The duchess, on the other hand, became more stubborn in her beliefs. Jacques van den Heuvel brings out very clearly the parallel between Louisa Dorothea and Pangloss in his admirable study of *Voltaire dans ses Contes,* where he writes, "With the Duchess of Saxe-Gotha we see taking shape the image of a doctor who sticks stubbornly to his optimistic reasoning, while all around him is crumbling."[8] As Voltaire continued his vain attempts to convert the duchess to his way of thinking, her redundant recitation of her credo only served to add fuel to the fire.

In this manner, the good duchess, wishing sincerely to promote Optimism, contributed unconsciously to its demise. The fact that the Leibnitzian arguments that undergo the most virulent attacks in *Candide* are often the same ones that the duchess had upheld most stubbornly in her letters can hardly be considered coincidental. The belief that misfortunes are an instrument of Divine justice particularly irritated Voltaire, for he rejected a priori all attempts to explain Evil based on a notion of punishment or sanction, including the concept of original sin. The duchess, however, found some comfort in this reasoning, for it coincided with her belief that Providence arranges everything for the general good of Humanity. In October of 1758 she related to Voltaire the results of a conversation she had held with a Hussar officer: "l'orsque je lui adressai mes jérémiades, pour toute réponse il me dit croyés moi dit il, *Dieu veut punir ce monde perver.* Ces parolles prononcées avec emphase par un Colonel Houssard me parurent admirables . . . (Best. D7897). [When I addressed him with my Jeremiads, his only response was, 'Believe me, God wants to punish this perverse world.' These words, pronounced emphatically by a Hussar colonel, appeared admirable to me.] Voltaire parodied this attitude in two separate episodes of *Candide.* In the first, Pangloss prevents Candide from saving the good Anabaptist, for fear of interfering with Divine retribution. He holds his pupil back, "proving all the while that the roadstead of Lisbon had been formed expressly so that the Anabaptist would drown in it" (134). In the

8. Jacques Van den Heuvel, *Voltaire dans ses Contes* (Paris: Armand Colin, 1967), 246 (my translation).

second episode, involving the sinking of the ship owned by the merchant who absconded with Candide and Martin's treasures, Candide
parrots almost verbatim the earlier reflection of Pangloss, exclaiming,
"Vous voyez . . . que le crime est puni quelquefois; ce coquin de patron
hollandais a eu le sort qu'il méritait" (203) [You see . . . that crime is
sometimes punished; this rascal of a Dutch merchant got what he de-
served]. Just as Voltaire pointed out to the duchess that if the war was a
punishment, it was an unjustifiably long one, ". . . la punition est un
peu longue et n'a pas l'air de finir sitost" (Best. D7910) [. . . the punishment is a bit long and does not look as if it will end soon], Martin
underlines the absurdity and injustice of Pangloss' reasoning: "Oui, dit
Martin; mais fallait-il que les passagers qui étaient sur le vaisseau,
périssent aussi? Dieu a puni ce fripon, le diable a noyé les autres" (204).
[Yes, said Martin, but was it necessary that the passengers who were on
the vessel perish as well? God punished this scoundrel, the devil
drowned the others.] Voltaire's message was clear: the death and suffering of innocent people is never justifiable and cannot be attributed to the
volition of a just and merciful God.

As heated as the polemic on Optimism may have been, it did not
dominate the correspondence between the duchess and Voltaire to the
point of eliminating all other topics of discussion. Indeed Voltaire, even
while working clandestinely to negotiate peace between France and
Prussia, found ample time for cultural amusements, as his letter of 24
February 1758 indicates: "Il est vray madame que pendant qu'on s'é-
gorge dans vos quartiers, nous jouons tout doucement la comédie à
Lauzane" (Best. D7650). [It is true, madame, that while people are slit-
ting each other's throats in your territories, we are gaily performing
comedies in Lausanne.] The letters to the Tronchin family, written at
approximately the same time as those to the duchess, are almost entirely connected with petty material details, such as the number of vats
of wine needed to sustain the household of Les Délices throughout the
winter or the style of chairs required for Voltaire's elegantly furnished
living quarters. "Car que madame la duchesse de Gotha soit mangée et
le roy de Prusse dépouillé, cela ne doit pas m'empêcher d'orner mon
cabinet" (Best. D7436). [For, whether the duchess of Gotha be eaten
alive and the king of Prussia left without a shirt on his back, it should
not prevent me from decorating my study.] Nevertheless, rare were the
letters that did not contain some passing reference to Divine Providence
or Optimism, however slight it may have been. Voltaire often intro-
duced the topic in an insidious manner, incorporating the duchess'
slogans in his opening or closing remarks: "Deux ou trois armées du

meilleur des mondes possibles m'ont privé de la consolation de recevoir des lettres de votre altesse sérénissime" (Best. D7393). [Two or three armies of the best of all possible worlds have deprived me of the consolation of receiving your Highness' letters.] Though the two correspondents frequently lay their differences aside and discussed issues of mutual interest, such as the latest plays being performed in Paris or recently published works of merit, neither Voltaire nor the duchess was prepared to let the other have the last word on the subject.

The greatest paradox in the duchess' attitude, one that Voltaire could not comprehend, lay in the fact that everything she had endured and suffered, from her own poor health and the tragic death of her son to the ruination of her duchy and the extermination of its citizens, was in direct contradiction with her conviction that the world surrounding her was "the best of all possible worlds." In Voltaire's eyes, Louisa Dorothea was living proof of the absurdity of Optimism, for surely no one deserved less such cruel misfortune than this enlightened, kindly monarch who ruled over her subjects with equity and generosity. Her obstinate faith in Providence can be likened to that of Pangloss, who after having been hanged, dissected, and broken on the wheel still maintained that all was well. "After this trying ordeal of sorrow and misfortune," she wrote to Voltaire in November of 1757, "I hate the war a little more than usual and admire no less the decrees of this wise and good Providence" (Best. D7449). Pangloss, too, refuses to undergo any evolution in his thinking. The scarred, bedraggled doctor who continues to expound his world view at the end of the tale is no different from the carefree, happy tutor who once philosophized in the garden of Thunder-ten-Tronck: "Pangloss avouait qu'il avait toujours horriblement souffert; mais ayant soutenu une fois que tout allait à merveille, il le soutenait toujours, en n'en croyait rien" (256). [Pangloss admitted that he had always suffered horribly, but having once maintained that all was going marvelously, he continued to maintain it and believed not a word.] It was precisely this immutability on the part of the duchess that so angered and baffled Voltaire.

Our goal has been to demonstrate, through a parallel reading of Voltaire's correspondence with the Duchess of Saxe-Gotha and *Candide*, that this long-ignored princess had a far greater impact on the genesis of the story than has previously been suggested. Her effect on the structure of the tale was in fact twofold. The continuous stream of remarks in favor of Optimism that prevail in practically all of the duchess' letters provoked an equal number of rebukes and responses from Voltaire, who was thus able to develop and strengthen his anti-Leibnitzian arguments in an informal manner, before committing them to posterity in the final draft of *Candide*. Furthermore, the duchess' refusal to back down from her stand even in the face of unspeakable disasters incited the philosopher to create an analogous character in his tale, a ridiculous personage who would incarnate her optimistic absurdity in viewing the world through rose-colored spectacles while half of Europe was being reduced to cinders. Even though *Candide* may not have been composed during the first years of the war, the duchess' comments on the "best of all possible worlds" were not forgotten by Voltaire. They remained fresh in his memory until the moment when, ready to launch his final attack that was to put to rest once and for all Leibnitz and his theories, the powerful polemicist pulled them out of his arsenal. Early in 1758 it seemed as if Voltaire already had his Doctor Pangloss in mind when he wrote the following lines to the duchess: "Il est vray qu'elle est un peu embarassée avec le sistème de Leibnits. Elle ne sait comment faire avec tant de mal phisique et moral pour vous prouver l'optimisme . . ." (Best. D7554) [It is true that she is a bit perplexed by Leibnitz's system. She does not know what to do with so much physical and moral evil to prove Optimism]. Candide makes a similar remark in referring to his master, as he reflects on the misery of humankind: "Ce Pangloss, disait-il, serait bien embarrassé à démontrer son système" (200). [This Pangloss, said he, would be at a loss to demonstrate his system.] Voltaire continued to chide the duchess in his slightly mocking manner, for he knew that she would eventually run out of new arguments, as the old ones were being demolished daily by world events.

On 16 January 1759 Louisa Dorothea finally put an end to this debate, which was growing tiresome and monotonous. Realizing that Voltaire, a far better polemical writer than herself, could reproach her ad infinitum for her optimism, she defended her beliefs one last time in an elegantly written letter summarizing all of the major tenets of the doctrine of Divine Providence. All of Pangloss' arguments are assembled side by side. By this time, Voltaire had already completed *Candide*, so the letter cannot have had any effect on its composition; nonetheless, it is still an interesting object for study, if one keeps Doctor Pangloss in mind. "Il est demontré . . . que les choses ne peuvent être autrement: car tout étant fait pour une fin, tout est nécessairement pour la meilleure fin" (119) [It has been proven . . . that things cannot be otherwise, for everything having been designed for a certain end, everything is necessarily for the best end]. Just as Pangloss "prouvait admirablement qu'il n'y a point d'éffet sans cause" (119) [proved admirably that there is no effect without a cause], the duchess affirms that "tout effet ressemble à sa cause" (Best. D8048) [each effect ressembles its cause] and concludes that therefore "il faut . . . que ce monde soit le meilleur de tous les mondes possibles" [this world must be the best of all possible worlds]. Unfortunately for modern-day partisans of either Pangloss or Martin, we will never know if the duchess ever read *Candide*, or what she thought of it, for she made virtually no reference to it in her future correspondence. How would this staunch defender of Optimism have reacted to this biting satire, in which entire phrases from her letters were often directly parodied? No doubt, she would have stood her ground, as did Pangloss himself: "Je suis toujours de mon premier senti- ment . . . car enfin je suis philosophe, il ne me convient pas de me dédire" (251) [I am still of my first sentiments . . . for after all, I am a philosopher, and it does not suit me to go back on what I have said].

ENGLISH SHOWALTER, JR.

Authorial Self-Consciousness in the Familiar Letter: The Case of Madame de Graffigny

The correspondence of Madame de Sévigné has been regarded as a literary masterpiece almost from the date of the first edition in 1725. In recent years Sévigné scholars have carried on a lively debate about the status of the familiar letter.[1] Roger Duchêne defines a true letter ("une vraie lettre") as "the spontaneous and direct expression of lived reality intended for a particular other person." The writers of such texts he calls "épistoliers" and distinguishes them from "auteurs épistolaires," who use the letter form but with the intention of addressing a wider public. According to Duchêne, Sévigné was an *épistolière,* who wrote with minimal literary awareness. The factors that shape her art emerge from her life.

Bernard Bray, on the other hand, defends the view that Mme de Sévigné deliberately exploited the resources of a recently fashionable genre.[2] For Bray, a correspondence is generated within, and bears the signs of, an "epistolary system." Sévigné does not therefore differ significantly from other authors in the nature of her work. Whereas for Duchêne the meaning of the work is bound up with ("se confond avec") the meaning of the life, for Bray the meaning is inseparable from the social and cultural network that defines the epistolary system.

Duchêne[3] observes that one often confuses the literary value of

1. Bernard Beugnot and Louise K. Horowitz provide good summaries of the debate, with additional references. Beugnot, "Débats autour du genre épistolaire: réalité et écriture," *Revue d'Histoire Littéraire de la France,* 74 (1974), 195–202. Horowitz, "The Correspondence of Madame de Sévigné: Letters or Belles-Lettres?" *French Forum* 6 (1981), 13–27. All translations in this article are my own.

2. Bernard Bray, "L'Epistolier et son public en France au XVIIᵉ siècle," *Travaux de Linguistique et de Littérature* 11 (1973), 7–17.

3. Roger Duchêne, "Réalité vécue et réussite littéraire: le statut particulier de la lettre," *Revue d'Histoire Littéraire de la France,* 71 (1971), 177–94.

113

letters with their value as eyewitness documents. An eminently scholarly editor himself, Duchêne does not disdain historical references, but
he would distinguish between letter writers like Stendhal, whose correspondence interests us only because it gives us information on Stendhal, and others like Flaubert, whose correspondence is an artful work
of literature as well as a source of information on a great novelist.
However when Bray describes a system as a microcosm offering the
complete image of a society, he clearly means more than just a set of
illustrative historical references, but rather some sort of conception
that interprets society and gives it meaning.

In trying to comprehend an entire and vast correspondence, it is fair
and perhaps necessary to privilege one mode of interpretation. This
debate will not settle the question of the literary status of letters, however, if only because most letters contain elements supporting both
perspectives. A correspondence normally contains a much greater degree of historical referentiality than most literary works, and one of the
real pleasures of reading correspondences is the heightened sense of
reality and presence that occurs when a person already known from
other sources enters the epistolary world, or when an event already
encountered in other readings is described by an eyewitness. At the
same time, letters and correspondences belong to a system roughly
comparable to a genre, and this genre encapsulates basic cultural assumptions. The specific functions of a letter, as a message-bearing object delivered from one person to another, contribute to the specificity
of the genre or system; but this situation is not necessarily different
from that of other literary forms, where economic forces, censorship,
the technology of printing, and theater architecture, for example, have
direct effects on literature. Finally, like any author, the letter writer
brings an individual mind, perhaps one of genius, to bear on the problem
of encoding an experience and a set of referents within the forms available. The letter writer normally enjoys unusual freedom, both because
the genre is loosely defined and because the communication is private
and need please (or produce the desired effect upon) only one person,
usually well known to the writer.

In short, common sense enables us to describe the basic characteristics of familiar letters sufficiently to enable a critical discussion of
the genre or of individual correspondences as examples of the genre.
Janet Altman[4] has used the term "epistolarity" to designate the most
distinctive generic properties, as they appear in epistolary novels; there

4. Janet Gurkin Altman, *Epistolarity: Approaches to a Form* (Columbus: Ohio State
University Press, 1982).

is, I think, less epistolarity in many real correspondences than in the novels, but the categories of mediation, confidentiality, reading, closure, patterning, and temporal polyvalence might still serve to organize a discussion of the aesthetics of real correspondences. The case of Sévigné has been debated as if her correspondence were representative, but in fact hers is a unique case in one respect: her letters, or those of her circle, including Bussy, constituted the first such private correspondence to be published, at least in the judgment of eighteenth-century readers. Whether Voiture, or someone else, really deserves the title of creator of the genre, or whether Sévigné was or was not imitating a model, does not really concern me here; I emphasize only the fact that *after* 1725 every literate French man or woman writing a private letter would have been aware of the possibility of publication, intended or not. And the question I want to address is the degree to which this awareness in itself transforms the genre from 1725 onwards, whether after that date there can be any "épistoliers" in Duchêne's sense.

The case I will discuss is the correspondence of Françoise d'Happoncourt, Madame de Graffigny, which I am now editing, with a team of scholars headed by J. A. Dainard of the University of Toronto; the first volume was published by the Voltaire Foundation in 1985, and as far as possible I will draw my examples and quotations from this volume, which contains letters 1–144, through 15 June 1739.[5] Graffigny was born in 1695 and died in 1758. The first letter we have from her dates from about 1716, but the bulk of her roughly twenty-five hundred surviving letters were written between 1738, when she left her native Lorraine for Paris, and 1758, when she died. In those twenty years she had achieved fame as the author of *Lettres d'une Péruvienne* (1747), an epistolary novel, and *Cénie* (1750), a sentimental play, and as the hostess of a much frequented salon. Around 1750 she was certainly one of Europe's foremost women of letters, but her popularity as an author declined rapidly after her death, and she has been known for the past century and a half chiefly for some thirty letters written between December 1738 and February 1739 from Cirey, where she stayed with Voltaire and his mistress, the marquise Du Châtelet.

These letters were published in 1820, apparently on the basis of copies made a few years earlier.[6] They came from a collection of some

5. Mme de Graffigny, *Correspondance,* ed. J. A. Dainard et al. (Oxford: The Voltaire Foundation, 1985–), 1 volume to date: letters 1–144 (1716–1739). See also J. A. Dainard et un collectif, "La Correspondance de Madame de Graffigny," *Dix-huitième Siècle,* 10 (1978), 379–94.

6. *La Vie privée de Voltaire et de Madame Du Châtelet* (Paris: Treuttel et Wurst, 1820).

one hundred volumes or binders, which was acquired by the English bibliophile Sir Thomas Phillipps, probably between 1820 and 1825, and which remained unknown to the scholarly world until it was auctioned in 1965. H. P. Kraus, a well-known publisher and rare book dealer, purchased the largest part of the collection and subsequently gave most of it to Yale University's Beinecke Library. Two volumes were later acquired by the Morgan Library in New York. The Bibliothèque Nationale also bought several volumes from the collection, although they contained few Graffigny letters.[7]

Graffigny's letters resemble Sévigné's in one major respect: the largest number are addressed to one correspondent, François-Antoine Devaux, called "Panpan," who remained in Lorraine when Graffigny went to Paris. Both Sévigné and Graffigny turned their letters into a kind of journal, writing at every post, and therefore not awaiting a reply between letters. For Graffigny's letters we also have most of Devaux's answers, as well as the original manuscript of virtually all her own letters, two major differences from the Sévigné correspondence. A typical Graffigny letter covered three sides of a sheet folded once; the fourth side usually bore the address. The post left for Lorraine three times a week, and under normal conditions a reply would come back within a week. The conversational rhythm thus flowed in three somewhat independent channels, although there were frequent crossings and much confusion. Like Sévigné, at least according to her letters, Graffigny structured her life around the arrivals and departures of the mail. When there was a delay because she or Devaux was in the country, she grew restless and complained; when there was an unexplained delay, she became agitated and fearful. She seems to have been genuinely obsessed with this correspondence, which was only one of many she maintained; but it apparently engaged her interest and satisfied her emotionally far more than her correspondence with her lover, Léopold Desmarest, who was, according to the letters to Panpan, an unreliable correspondent.[8]

With so many letters, there is great variety in form and content, but the basic patterns are repeated. Graffigny wrote something almost every

7. Mme de Graffigny, MSS Papers, Beinecke Rare Book and Manuscript Library, Yale University, uncatalogued; MSS Letters from Cirey, Pierpont Morgan Library. Manuscripts of Graffigny's letters in these collections are quoted with permission. For assistance in finding exact locations of passages cited, see the article by Dainard and others, cited in note 5. Original spellings have been retained in the transcriptions. Translations are my own.

8. No letters from this correspondence are known. Desmarest died in 1747; after his death, Graffigny's several hundred letters to him were returned to her. She read and destroyed them in 1748. The disposition of his letters to her is uncertain.

day, sometimes more than once a day; generally she dated each section. She began typically by narrating what she had done since she last wrote; then she replied article by article to Devaux's most recent letter. As part of her own activities she often inserted long passages on her health, her feelings, her plans, and the like; and she repeated news, gossip, anecdotes, and witticisms that she had heard about. Less often a question or remark in one of Devaux's letters would trigger such a digression. The responses tended to take the form of sympathy for troubles, expressions of joy for good news, advice, criticism, and occasionally anger. At the end of the letter she usually sent greetings to various friends and quite often asked Devaux to run errands.

Such are the general conditions of the correspondence. As with Sévigné, the elements of a loose system are clearly present, yet the variations within it are wide enough to argue that Graffigny does little more than put her life on paper. Even the system seems to grow from her own feelings and private priorities, not from an epistolary code or genre. I would like therefore to look at three exemplary fragments, which illustrate certain problematic aspects of this and, I believe, any correspondence, for each one points simultaneously to the private, ultimately unknowable life that the two correspondents lived, and to the social, cultural, and indeed specifically literary system within which they wrote.

Society, culture, and literature, as systems, are comprised largely if not wholly by public signifiers. After two centuries, some of these signifiers may be lost or obscured, especially if they were transmitted orally. One of the values of a correspondence is surely its yield of such cultural artifacts, in the realm of colloquial language and everyday custom, for example. Even so, however, they tend only to fill gaps in an already familiar repertoire, such as lexicon or an etiquette. A private life, especially one written in letters, can obviously also be treated as such a system. The ways in which Graffigny thinks herself depend on preexisting social codes. There is nonetheless, I would argue, an elusive unique individuality of conceptualization and of lived experience, of which only traces may be glimpsed. Another value of a large correspondence is that it translates some of this individuality into a discourse we understand, and as we immerse ourselves in the correspondence we begin to perceive the traces of what could not be directly written. In a limited, even trivial form, the three fragments will reveal some of this quality. To the twentieth-century reader or scholar, however, each one begins as a puzzle: to what does this refer?

"A propos, si tu avois scû que la signora accoucheroit d'une fille, tu n'aurois pas eté si empressé la veille de ton depart a lui dire bonsoir par la fenêtre." [By the way, if you had known that the signora would give birth to a daughter, you would not have been so eager on the eve of your departure to say good evening to her through the window. 10 August 1735, Graffigny 18: 19.]

"Bonsoir le St, bonsoir le Chien, le Chat, *toutti quanti*. Il me sied bien, croasseuse que [je suis,] de voler des expressions a cette adorable femme." [Good evening Saint, good evening Dog, Cat, *tutti quanti*. I have a lot of nerve, old croaker that I am, stealing expressions from that adorable woman. 1 May 1739, Graffigny 124: 467.]

"Ce seroit une Du Plecy si elle avoit moins de presomption." [She would be a Du Plecy if she had less presumption. 2 June 1739, Graffigny 138: 524.]

The first quotation, from an isolated early letter, obviously refers to the birth of a girl; this clue in fact makes it possible to date the letter with fair certainty. Other details point to the summer of 1735; the Lorraine archives record the birth of a daughter to Graffigny's friend the comtesse de Grandville on Tuesday, 9 August 1735, and this letter is dated "Wednesday." The second quotation is a typical closing formula; the capitalized words are nicknames for friends who are identifiable from other letters: "le Saint" is the marquis d'Adhémar, "le Chien" is Nicolas Liébault, and "le Chat" is Clairon Lebrun. The third quotation is part of a portrait of Mademoiselle Sauveur, daughter of a mathematician and a regular guest of the duc and duchesse de Richelieu in Paris. These, then, are the primary referents of the three fragments.

In the second and third there are obviously other referents, however. Who is "cette adorable femme" and who is "Du Plecy"? Nothing in the immediate context gives any help, and so we must assume that Graffigny expected Devaux to understand these allusions without explanation. They might refer to a previous conversation, to old friends, to people in the public eye, to legendary or literary characters. The first quotation, moreover, contains a provocative term: why is Mme de Grandville, who was not Italian, called "la signora"? This turns out to be, in one sense, the easiest question to answer, because Graffigny is quoting (or, as was her custom, slightly misquoting) a famous line from La Fontaine, a proverbial expression of anticlimax, botched planning, or false expectations: "La signora mit au monde une fille" ("L'Ermite"). At this remove one can hardly say with certainty whether such a glancing allusion reflects the general state of cultural literacy and readerly competence, or whether it depended on a more intimate and specific memory of a poem enjoyed together.

If La Fontaine's line is easy to identify because of its fame, the "adorable femme" is easy to identify because Devaux names her in his reply: Mme de Sévigné, from whom Graffigny had "stolen" the expression "tutti quanti," used in a letter to Grignan on 29 July 1676, "Le maréchal de Lorges m'attaqua sous le nom du chevalier de Grignan, enfin *tutti quanti* . . ." [Pléiade #531, 2:351; The maréchal de Lorges accosted me in the name of the chevalier de Grignan, in fact *tutti quanti*].[9] Here the triviality of the phrase leads to the conclusion that Devaux and Graffigny most likely had savored reading that letter together. Furthermore it happens that Sévigné had cited the line from La Fontaine in another letter (Pléiade #114, 1:113); and a similar indirect quotation had probably occurred in Graffigny's letter of 25 March 1739: "Le calme est venu comme apres le *cos ego*" [Calm returned as after the *quos ego*, Graffigny 108, 401], Virgil's *quos ego* having been used also by Sévigné (Pléiade #203, 1:351). The allusions in Graffigny's letters are by no means all so obscure; to flatter Devaux, she writes of his style, "C'est un tissus de Sevigné rebroché de marivaudage" [It's a tissue of Sévigné interwoven with Marivaudage (incidentally the earliest recorded use of the term "marivaudage"). 12 May 1739, Graffigny 129, 487], and to complain of the irregularity of the mail, she remarks, "Cela fait un dejingandement qui me deplait autant qu'a Md. de Sevigné" [That makes an awkwardness that displeases me as much as Mme de Sévigné. 12 April 1739, Graffigny 116, 432], and so forth. The indirect allusions that we have been fortunate enough to recognize in editing, however, suggest a broad and shared familiarity with Sévigné on the part of Graffigny and Devaux. It was, then, not surprising (although very pleasing when the connection was first made) to discover that Du Plecy was Sévigné's Breton neighbor, Marie-Anne Du Plessis d'Argentré (Pléiade #167, 1:256n4), a comic figure whom Devaux and Graffigny compared to several of their acquaintances.

Graffigny's letters are thus saturated with the awareness of her illustrious predecessor. Even in places where my coeditors and I fail to recognize the allusion, the private communication between the two letter writers may have transmitted hints of an eventual or imaginary public of readers; in any case, identifiable allusions appear regularly. Whatever the status of Sévigné, as *épistolière* or *auteur épistolaire*, after 1725 she was a model whom other correspondents could scarcely help recalling from time to time, but the very terms of the recollection may

9. Mme de Sévigné, *Correspondance*, ed. Roger Duchêne (Paris: Gallimard, Bibliothéque de la Pléiade, 1972–1978), 3 volumes.

betray a profound disregard for the eventual public. Bray argues that already in the seventeenth century the possibility of publication had been recognized, without radically modifying the relations between the letter writer and the addressee. Graffigny's experience seems to support the plausibility of the argument.

The correspondence would not exist today if the two correspondents had not agreed from the start to save each other's letters; Devaux even numbered the ones he received, a care for which I am very grateful. One cannot conclude that they planned publication, however. True, Graffigny sometimes complained of bawdy passages in Devaux's letters and crossed them out, saying that they were unworthy to be preserved, and once in a while we find a statement such as, "Quand tu penses a la posterité, tu ecris comme un Bussi. Je demelle fort bien les jours ou tu lui ecris de prefference a moi" [When you're thinking of posterity, you write like a Bussy. I can easily tell the days when you write for it instead of for me. 22 May 1739, Graffigny 133: 505]. The remark itself, however, emphasizes the rarity of the event, and they gave other, more compelling reasons for keeping and classifying the letters. For example, Devaux wrote to Graffigny on 6 October 1738, less than a month after her departure from Lorraine. "C'est l'histoire de ma vie et de mon ame que je fais en vous ecrivant. C'est pourquoy je vous prie de garder mes lettres, toutes mauvaises qu'elles sont. Je me fais un plaisir de rabacher un jour avec vous en les relisant. Cela me rappellera mille choses qui pour lors seront toutes nouvelles pour moy. Vous concevez bien que je ne perds pas une ligne des votres. Elles se recommendent d'elles-memes, celles-là. Je les numerote pour en retrouver la suite. Faites de meme des miennes" [It's the story of my life and soul I'm telling when I write to you. That's why I ask you to keep my letters no matter how bad they are. I look forward to reminiscing with you some day while rereading them. That will remind me of a thousand things that will seem quite new to me then. You know I never lose a line of yours. They're good enough in themselves to want to keep. I number them to be able to keep them in order. Do the same for mine]. To which Graffigny replied on 11 October, "Belle recommendation que tu me fais de garder tes lettres. Je ne voudrois pas en perdre le cachet. Je les mets en ordre a mesure pour les rabacher un jour" [Some recommendation you make, that I should keep your letters! I wouldn't want to lose the sealing wax. I put them in order to go over them some day. Graffigny 38: 79 and n. 29]. The correspondence contains numerous instances, moreover, when one or the other rereads old letters and relives a past experience.

However persistent the thought of posterity may have been, the

immediate concern for the audience of one and the pressure of circumstances seem to have dominated the composition of the letters. On 19
November 1738, Graffigny wrote to Devaux, "Comment, tu relis tes
lettres? Ah! tu as bon foye. Les mienes vont comme elle vienent, aussi je
crois qu'il y a de belle phrase et une belle ortographe. Ce seroit la mere a
boire que de les relire. Pourvu que je ne rabache pas les memes choses, je
suis bien contente" [What, you reread your letters? Ah! You have a
strong stomach. Mine go as they come, and I'll bet there are some
beautiful sentences and beautiful spelling. It would take forever to read
them over. Provided I don't repeat the same things over and over, I'm
satisfied. Graffigny 53: 160]. Time and privacy were recurrent problems;
the sense of obligation to recount her own activities, to reply to Devaux's letter, and to convey requests for errands prevailed over any
impulse to organize or to write well. Quite often, an event aroused her
verve or her troubles evoked a natural eloquence; but when she set out
in the late 1740s to compose an epistolary novel, the effort proved long
and painful and the result, although immensely popular at the time, did
not survive the test of posterity. By the middle of the nineteenth century, Sainte-Beuve assumed that his audience preferred the spontaneous
letters from Cirey to the carefully composed *Lettres d'une Péruvienne*.

Indeed, the freedom to write without concern for judgment was one
of the charms of the correspondence for Graffigny. She describes the
subjects of their letters as "nos riens" [our nothings]; some years later,
she complained of Devaux's self-deprecating reticence, saying with little exaggeration, "moi qui te dis que j'ai eté pisser" [I who tell you that
I've gone to piss]. Concern over the subjects they write about arises most
often when they suspect that the letters are being intercepted by police
or other spies; the most notorious example occurred during the stay at
Cirey, when Mme Du Châtelet and Voltaire were in fact opening the
correspondence of their guest. Deprived of any alternate method of
communication, Graffigny and Devaux created an almost impenetrable
confusion of coded messages, letters intended to be intercepted, letters
written over many days for posting at a safer time, and ordinary letters
containing ordinary information. Voltaire scholars today are indebted
to Graffigny's willingness to write about the lowliest details and to
Devaux's insatiable appetite for reading these details, for one of the
most vivid and complete accounts of how Voltaire actually lived. The
same wealth of information exists on many other facets of eighteenth-
century life, thanks precisely to their usual disregard for any possible
third reader.

Yet paradoxically the letter is often most interesting to readers other than the addressee. When Mme Du Châtelet opened Devaux's letter to Graffigny, she discovered what she took to be a plot and imagined a drama of ingratitude and betrayal. Police spies and court gossips, real or imaginary, transformed the simple exchange of letters into the pretext for a plot; and from *La Princesse de Clèves* to *Les Liaisons dangereuses*, how large a role do intercepted and misinterpreted letters play! The control of information, the wearing of masks, and the penetration of secrets constituted the keys to power within the aristocratic society of the old regime. Early editions of Sévigné's letters played on the public's appetite for glimpses into the private lives of great figures. The 1725 edition included in its title the phrase, "qui contiennent beaucoup de particularités de l'histoire de Louis XIV" [which contain many details about the history of Louis XIV], and the English translation of 1727 was entitled suggestively *Court Secrets*. In just the same way, the Graffigny's Cirey letters were printed in 1820 with the title *Vie privée de Voltaire et de Madame Du Châtelet*.

While the chronicle of scandals held an undoubted attraction, especially for early readers who had known many of the people mentioned, other qualities soon came to be regarded as equally important. Prefaces to eighteenth-century editions of Sévigné praised the informal style, the wit, the maxims, the instruction in the ways of society, the models for polite letter writing, and the moral value of the actions described; it was not until quite recently that the exceptional quality of Sévigné's love for her daughter has seemed a positive trait rather than a flaw in an otherwise almost perfect example of an "honnête femme," the female version of the seventeenth century's moral ideal. Early editors considered suppressing any mentions of such maternal excess, but did not, or possibly could not, do so. They did, however, cut "quelques détails, ou purement domestiques, ou peu intéressants pour le public," as a 1734 French editor put it, or "a multiplicity of private Domestic Occurrences altogether useless to every Reader," in the words of Edmund Curll, editor of the 1727 English version.

These editors miscalculated. Increasingly, the reading public found those very details to be a major source of reading pleasure. Graffigny, on reading the letters of Mazarin, wrote to Devaux on 19 April 1745, "Il est vray que les letres tant mauvaises soient-elles se font toujours lire et que quand elles ne diroient que l'histoire d'une vie aussi commune que les notres, on liroit qu'on s'est levé, chaussé, vêtu, diné, soupé, etc. Est-ce l'amour de la verité qui nous les rend si amusantes, ou la curiosité de penetrer dans ce qui etoit autrefois des secrets? Le genre n'y fait rien au moins. Nous lirions avec le meme empressement les lettres de nos valets, temoin celles de Pamela" [It is true that letters, no matter how bad they are, are always interesting to read and that if they told only the story of a life as common as ours, people would read how we got up, put on our shoes, dressed, dined, supped, etc. Is it love of the truth that makes them so interesting to us, or the curiosity of penetrating into what used to be secret? The genre makes no difference at least. We would read our valets' letters with the same eagerness, witness the letters of Pamela].

In other words, Graffigny located the interest of letters in an aesthetic principle, which we think of today as particularity, and which can be seen developing in almost all forms of artistic expression in the eighteenth century. No doubt a social and political evolution is at work, too; what one considers important enough to write down depends in part on one's own station in life and one's personal preoccupations, and the ability to write it depends on being literate. Material or technological progress also played a role; without inexpensive paper and a reliable postal service, a correspondence like Graffigny's would have been impossible. Graffigny may not speak for all her contemporaries in praising *Pamela*, but the evidence indicates that her feeling was widely shared. The invention or discovery of correspondences as a genre probably arises from the same causes as the rise of the novel and the development of realism. In any case, Graffigny's conception of herself as author of familiar letters, "auteur épistolaire," need not imply any effort at literariness. The best way to imitate Sévigné would have been to immerse herself so much in the immediacy of her own experience and writing that she felt as free and spontaneous as she did in conversation with Panpan.

In short the internal evidence of the Graffigny letters yields an ambiguous or paradoxical conclusion. The letter writer can simultaneously imitate a literary predecessor and ignore an author's principal literary concerns, such as genre, form, and the public. As I have showed, Graffigny sometimes proclaims in the same phrase, "This alludes to a famous model," and "This alludes to something intelligible only to you, Panpan." Perhaps one could argue that letters are literature only to the degree that the former tendency makes itself felt, thereby situating the letter in a genre, imposing a form, catering to a public; and perhaps also the most engaging letters are those in which the literary impulse most effectively makes accessible the invisible private world of the writer and gives readers the feeling of having grasped secret allusions.

My discussion so far has treated the letter and the correspondence as if they were equivalent. Implicitly, I have assumed a person producing a text which, at a definable moment, becomes a work of literature that undergoes a reading. Although such a model oversimplifies, it works reasonably well for most literature; to rectify the oversimplification, we tend to focus on one complexity at a time and explore the biography, the text, the work, or the reading, trying not to let the others impinge on the one that interests us.

A correspondence poses far greater problems than the usual essay, poem, play, or novel, however. It is not only that "real life" crops up more persistently than in other genres or that the work is less cohesive, both in formal structure and in textual reliability; it is also that the very constitution of the collection raises questions usually left unnoticed. Bray calls attention to the process whereby a correspondence is formed. He describes a sequence in which the community of addressees comes to recognize the unusual quality of a given correspondent's letters; then the thought of eventual publication occurs and people begin to collect letters, copies, notes, and drafts. Under those circumstances a sense of literary authorship enters the minds of the correspondents. Such was no doubt the case with the Bussy-Sévigné circle and also with many famous figures of the eighteenth century, like Voltaire. In Graffigny's case, however, she and Devaux did not wait on any demonstration of their letters' value to begin collecting and organizing their correspondence; and my work in French archives has persuaded me that many eighteenth-century letter writers kept virtually all the letters they received. Heroines of epistolary novels who kept the incriminating documents in their drawer were following social custom, not just setting up a twist in the plot. The constitution of a collected correspondence while the writers are still writing does not by itself prove literary self-consciousness.

By contrast to Bray, Duchêne looks for a structure binding the Sévigné letters into a coherent unity. He argues that Sévigné's letters were a nonliterary text that became literature retrospectively, that Sévigné wrote without authorial self-consciousness and became an author after the fact. As Beugnot points out, however, Duchêne denies the generic classification of epistolary literature, only to redefine the exceptional quality of Sévigné's work as "roman," that is, novel or romance. It is as if she had unwittingly inscribed the traces of a literary style in a subliterary genre or a form of writing with no generic status whatsoever. Duchêne's method produces a fascinating reading of Sévigné but the question seems to me still open what the method's implications are. Has Duchêne merely exposed the unique superiority of one correspondence, unified by the author's maternal obsession? Or should we look retrospectively for the inevitable plot underlying every correspondence? Having performed the heroic labor of editing the most reliable possible text of the Sévigné correspondence, Duchêne attempts the critical move of fixing on that text and making the author disappear; his Sévigné is only a projection of the text. The question of what might happen to her should good fortune restore to us Sévigné's holograph letters or Mme de Grignan's replies is evaded.

A sociological approach is no more helpful. By whatever social or economic definition one uses, Graffigny was an author when she wrote for publication such works as *Lettres d'une Péruvienne, Cénie,* and *La Fille d'Aristide.* Yet she resisted calling herself an author, because she found the role inappropriate for a woman. At the same time many men adopted the role without ever publishing anything; already in the eighteenth century Paris was full of aspiring writers who frequented the cafés, theater lobbies, and salons, while awaiting a call from their muse. In socioeconomic terms, being an author is primarily a matter of self-definition. Where the correspondence is concerned, we have simply returned to the starting point: was Graffigny thinking of herself as an author when she wrote letters to Devaux? At this point we must acknowledge a unique aspect of correspondences as works of literature: the inevitability of an editor.

Despite their significant contributions as editors, Bray and Duchêne do not treat the editor's role as crucial to the literary status of a correspondence. Yet the necessity for editorial intervention is not only an important fact in itself, but also it points to other distinctive traits of a correspondence. The writer's relation to an individual letter falls within the range of ordinary relations of authors to their works. The writer has control of the text, decides what to include or omit, arranges the contents; if the writer chooses, the text can be revised repeatedly, and it becomes a letter only when the writer releases it. Since most letters are not destined for immediate publication, the letter writer has even more freedom and authority than most authors.

Any written text, including a letter, will nevertheless be conditioned in its origin by the writer's assessment of the public; any text that is published will be editorially processed in some fashion. Authors may consult editors before and during the process of publication; in general, changes made under such conditions must be regarded as the author's, even if reluctantly accepted. Changes made without an author's consent are normally trivial and peripheral, or else they are indicated in a preface or by signs in the text. When these principles have not been followed—and until recently editors interpreted their function quite differently—we now regard the text as corrupted, and a contemporary editor would almost certainly attempt, insofar as possible, to return to the author's original intended version.

Such editing is certainly not peculiar to letters, and so taken by itself, a letter is like other texts in the ways it is conceived, produced, and published. But placing the isolated letter into the context of a collected correspondence requires a wholly different mode of conception and production. The author does not decide, or even negotiate, what constitutes the correspondence; an editor does that. The editor must make such fundamental choices as: to include all the letters written by the author, or only a selection, and if only a selection, by what criteria; to include only letters by the author, or also letters to the author; to include only letters to or from the author, or also letters between third parties concerning the author; to include letters only, or also other documents; to include minimal, or maximal annotation; to organize the materials in one chronological sequence, or in some other order. Excellent recent editions could be cited in which each of these possible options had been elected, although the present trend is toward maximum inclusiveness and annotation with a single chronological arrangement and extensive indexing. The key point, however, is that a correspondence does not exist until someone makes those decisions and collects a group of letters accordingly.

Letter writers may, of course, edit their own correspondences, as Bussy did. If they decide to do so while still writing the letters, then obviously the remaining correspondence can be as self-conscious a work of literature as any other. The author may choose to let circumstances and the course of events dictate much of the substance, but the prior intention to shape the accumulating parts into a publishable whole must also influence each individual letter. Moreover, under such conditions, the author would probably feel no compunctions about revising the letters before publication, to strengthen their coherence. But letter writers who decide after the fact to collect and edit already existing letters become editors and cease being authors, even of their own letters.

An illustration may clarify that point. There is a gap in the Graffigny correspondence on 19 December 1738, created when Graffigny burned part of a letter she had sent to Devaux and then had him return to her (see Graffigny 65, text note a, 238). Had she destroyed the pages before sending them, no gap would exist; but once the text was sent and became a letter, Graffigny lost the author's privilege of revision. Traces of the burnt pages survive elsewhere in the correspondence, in Devaux's reply, in the narrative of incidents the letter provoked, in the request for its return, and in the story of its use and destruction. By contrast, there is no gap in Graffigny's novel *Lettres d'une Péruvienne,* even though all the early drafts are lost, no author's manuscript is known, the 1747 edition was revised in 1752, and many critics found the denouement incomplete because the heroine remains unmarried.

The letter uniquely comes into being almost simultaneously as a physical object and as a text. In everything we have traditionally called literature, the usual process of literary creation includes a period of conception, elaboration, drafting, and editing, followed by an appearance in print in a medium accessible to the public. The ways in which these stages are accomplished are infinitely varied, and may hold great interest for the literary historian, but do not constitute an essential quality of the finished, published work. As already noted, the stage of conceiving a letter may also be experienced in widely differing ways, and there are some who write many drafts, by hand, by typewriter, even latterly by word processor. The text becomes a letter, however, when it is placed in the mail, and the manuscript—the piece of paper on which it is written—becomes a part of the life of the correspondents and of the text recording their lives.

We find instances of self-reflexivity in fiction, as when Don Quixote encounters in book 2 people who have read his adventures in book 1; but these cases are exceptional, whereas for the letter writer the reception of the letter and the response to it make up significant elements of the structure of the correspondence. Even in *Don Quixote,* the physical reality of the book is of little consequence; Cervantes plays havoc with the historical plausibility of his narrator, as if to demonstrate how inconsequential the physical origin of the text really is. With letters, the material object and the text inscribed thereon cannot be separated at the origin, and the presence of the original object continues to radiate throughout the correspondence that follows.

We have seen in passages from Graffigny how a letter encodes simultaneously a relationship shared only by the two correspondents, a set of external referents that may be partially intelligible to the outsider, and a social convention governing communication by language and by letter. Moreover, the desire for an immediate and spontaneous expression coexists with an awareness or fear of ever-widening circles of readers, culminating in the thought of publication. The pressure is strong for every individual letter to carry the full range of these ambiguities, although the possibility exists for the writer to purify and organize a single letter. As the single letters accumulate to form a correspondence, however, the mixing of voices becomes inevitable.

Perhaps the surest sign that the most famous epistolary novels are fictions and not real correspondences is the unity of their structure. Even in gigantic and digressive novels like *Clarissa* and *La Nouvelle Héloïse,* no words are wasted. The plots and themes announced in the first letter are developed and resolved by the end. Along the way there are self-contained incidents and essays on barely related topics; but there are no altogether false starts, nothing utterly irrelevant, no lapses that serve only to confuse everyone. The reader can just credit the necessary fiction that an editor has trimmed away the extraneous matter and emended the pointlessly obscure parts. In any real exchange of letters, the main threads of what might pass for a plot are constantly entangled with the accidental circumstances of daily living. To cite a well-known example, the seventeen letters of Sévigné to Pomponne relating the trial of Foucquet form an extraordinarily coherent narrative; no doubt the early copyists and editors did some cutting. Even so, the story is interrupted by accounts of the marquise's other activities, by anecdotes she heard, and by her replies to Pomponne's letters.[10]

The letters Graffigny wrote from Cirey could be turned into a novel, I think. The plot is that a widow arrives at an isolated château as a guest, is accused of betraying her hosts, lives as a prisoner for several weeks, and is finally rescued by her lover. Since the hosts were Voltaire and Mme Du Châtelet, the story is reasonably well known, but not as a sort of Gothic anecdote. Indeed, although the outlines have been retold by dozens of Voltaire scholars and biographers, until recently no one had looked at the events closely enough to see who was telling the truth (Graffigny) and to understand why Mme Du Châtelet was lying (she was opening everyone's mail, including Voltaire's, to try to intercept *La Voltairomanie,* and she did not want Voltaire to know it). The confusion was almost inevitable, because the narration proceeds irregularly, with ups and downs of mood, silences, postponements, and misinterpretations; and at the same time much more space is devoted to peripheral questions (such as the weather, Graffigny's health, her dog, her maid, her debts), to answers to Devaux's letters, and to the rhythm of the correspondence itself than to the narrative center such a story might have in fiction, the feelings of terror and hope in the heroine. To come out right it would have to be retold with hindsight. But that is

10. Pomponne's replies, however, are not known; if they were, the coherent sequence would be disrupted by the alternating flashbacks and interweaving of two separate time frames. It is, moreover, only by chance that no other letters to or from the marquise exist for that period; if they did, the still greater disruptions are easy to imagine.

precisely what the letters' material existence prevents; once posted, each letter entered permanently into the growing structure of the correspondence.

A correspondence is thus a strange genre, in which one of the central prerogatives of the author, that of conceiving and implementing a coherent organization, is denied. Coherence can occur only if the letter writer's vision possesses such unifying power that, despite accidents and the randomness of daily events, it imposes a feeling of destiny on the writer's life. Sévigné's obsessive love for her daughter may have accomplished such a transformation, converting the most tangential circumstance into a pretext for seduction. Such a reading is, however, of our times and not of the eighteenth century. Graffigny and her contemporaries prized the naturalness of the voice, the realism of the details, and the glimpses of secret truths, of which the marquise's passion for Mme de Grignan was only one intermittent example, and not the most interesting. Even raising the question of unity introduces a post-Romantic perspective quite alien to the period. Many genres, such as thoughts, maxims, and anas, were supposed to remain fragmentary and unstructured, while a sense of artfulness pervaded more of life than it generally does today, encompassing dress, gastronomy, etiquette, and conversation, for example. The expense of a quasi-authorial care on an ephemeral activity would not have seemed strange, nor would the possibility of publication have necessarily entailed a quest for coherence.

In short Graffigny and other letter writers could have felt aware of themselves as authors without that awareness having visible effects on the immediate act of writing the letter. This is not, however, to dismiss altogether the importance of their self-consciousness. It functioned more broadly and diffusely than with traditional authors modifying traditional genres. Sévigné's example authorized subsequent generations to observe and relate a more common, more ordinary, more routine, even more vulgar level of experience than had previously been possible, in a style that was neither burlesque nor elevated, but rather characterized by unfailing sureness of taste. To each subject there was a suitable tone, ranging from the grave to the frivolous, from the passionate to the bemused, but constant in its respect for the reader and for the subject. I would argue, in other words, that the letter writers of the era both reflect and amplify a change in sensibility that is equally visible in other genres. Graffigny, whose letters have remained unknown until the present time, cannot be said to have contributed to this evolution with her private letters, even though she participated in it and exercised a strong influence through *Les Lettres d'une Péruvienne* and *Cénie*. Once the letters are widely available, however, I think it will be obvious that she used the freedom of private correspondence to extend still further the range of literature in the simple act of writing her life, day by day.

PIERRE RIBERETTE

On Editing Chateaubriand's Correspondence

While the letters of many other contemporary Romantic writers first began to be assembled shortly after their death, the first volume of a general correspondence of Chateaubriand appeared more than sixty years after his demise. How can such a delay be explained? Less by any indifference of succeeding generations toward one of the "fathers of Romanticism," in our opinion, than by the difficulty of obtaining access to documents of a mostly personal nature—like intimate letters—zealously hidden by families who feared the kinds of revelations they might provide.

It is true that during Chateaubriand's lifetime a few of his letters had already been published separately. Young authors in need of publicity, for instance, tried to promote their work by prefacing it with the encouragements or congratulations that Chateaubriand had condescendingly addressed to them. A lawyer from the *Cour des comptes* had seen fit to bring to Chateaubriand's attention his dealings with the administration, and then took the trouble to insert, at the beginning of the pamphlet he wrote on this subject, his correspondence about it with the author of *Atala*; these letters only confirm what one already suspected about Chateaubriand's total incompetence when it came to money! Do readers still know that his famous letter to M. de la Luzerne about the death of Pauline de Beaumont in Rome (a letter he himself had had copied several times, while still forbidding its publication) appeared, despite his prohibition, as early as 1836, in the literary section of a major newspaper?

His contemporaries should not be accused of indiscretion. Chateaubriand had shown the way himself, by freely inserting into his *Congrès de Vérone* and *Mémoires d'Outre-Tombe* both letters he had sent and letters sent him, without worrying in the least about whether his correspondents or their heirs had authorized such publication. He had even, off-handedly, revealed letters exchanged between other people, which he had come to know only through a particularly dear friend.

Chateaubriand's death was far from putting a stop to this kind of infatuation with the most insignificant lines to flow from his pen. As late as 1869 the author of a tragedy on the combat of the "Thirties" (a Breton episode in the Hundred Years' War) published in the second edition of his work, as his title to fame, the letter of acknowledgment the author of *Moïse* had sent him upon receiving a copy of the first edition. To an article about him in 1851, the Lyonnais writer François-Zénon Collombet did not fail to append some ten letters that Chateaubriand had sent him before his death. On the other hand we shall probably never see the unpublished correspondence whose imminent appearance was vigorously acclaimed about that same time by the newspaper, *L'Ere nouvelle:* a change in the paper's management apparently quashed it definitively.

During the Second Empire interest in Chateaubriand's correspondence did not slow down. Can one fail to mention, in first place, Sainte-Beuve? His *Chateaubriand et son groupe littéraire* is filled with unpublished letters. In 1853 a former diplomat, the count of Marcellus, published his correspondence with the former Minister of Foreign Affairs from the period when he was one of his closest collaborators; but his insistence on presenting himself as one of Chateaubriand's privileged confidants led him to commit what have to be called forgeries. More authenticity can be found in the letters of Chateaubriand to Madame Récamier which the latter's niece and heiress assembled in the second volume of *Souvenirs et Correspondance,* dedicated to her aunt's memory, even though a concern for respectability led the editor to make some cuts in the texts she presented.

Finally at the dawn of the twentieth century everything seemed to be in place for undertaking a collective edition of Chateaubriand's Correspondence, and all the experts, from Edmond Biré to Victor Giraud, agreed that it was needed. Several new publications had shown the way. In his fashion, which was no less unfaithful than Marcellus's, Agénor Bardoux had enriched with unpublished letters his trilogy devoted to the best-known of the Egerias who had peopled Chateaubriand's sentimental life—Pauline de Beaumont, Delphine de Custine, Claire de Duras. The principal contribution, as far as unpublished letters go, came from a clergyman, abbé Pailhès, a tireless discoverer of documents, from which he sometimes drew rather risky conclusions.

It would be an exaggeration to claim that the five-volume edition of Chateaubriand's *Correspondance générale* which Louis Thomas brought out from 1912 to 1924 satisfied all the requirements and met all the needs of a scientific enterprise. First, it was unfinished, since its fifth and last volume stopped on 6 June 1824, the fatal day when Chateaubriand was dismissed from the Ministry of Foreign Affairs with the same brutality, he would later write, as if he "had stolen the king's watch from the mantle." It had inexplicable lacunae, since Louis Thomas had forgotten to include in these volumes letters he had himself previously published in journal articles. Too many misreadings, unwarranted corrections, almost nonexistent notes make his edition both incomplete and faulty as a tool. Must it be added that Louis Thomas's attitude during the German occupation of France does not dispose one to indulgence on his behalf?

Nevertheless despite all its failings his edition had at least one good point, which was simply to be there, providing us with some texts which have since, for various reasons, become inaccessible. Moreover Louis Thomas was conscious of the gaps and imperfections in his work. He tried to fill the first, palliate the others, by means of supplements which terminate almost every volume; their copiousness does not make them easy to use.

The Louis Thomas edition far from exhausted the reserves of unpublished letters held in public and private collections in France and around the world. Nor did it discourage scholars from continuing their investigations and publishing their finds. Thus came to light the correspondence of Chateaubriand with various individuals, for example: Hyde de Neuville, Cordélia de Castellane, Léontine de Castelbajac (the "Occitanienne"), and the extraordinary countess of Pierreclau.

The establishment of the Société Chateaubriand gave a new and decisive impetus to the collecting of the writer's unpublished letters. Founded in 1930 by Dr. Le Savoureux in the former property of the author of *Les Martyrs* at the Vallée-aux-Loups (now in Châtenay-Malabry, just south of Paris near Sceaux), the Society had placed at the head of its objectives the launching of a definitive edition of Chateaubriand's Correspondance (if one can ever say, "definitive," in speaking of publishing a correspondence). Almost every issue of the Society's *Bulletin*, which has appeared annually except during and just after the German occupation, has included discoveries made by its members: for example, a series of fifteen letters from Chateaubriand to Joubert, brought to light by Maurice Chalvet: a contribution of the first magnitude. These discoveries and others of equivalent interest made it apparent that the time for the new edition had arrived.

Since the publication of the first volume in 1977, under the auspices of the Société Chateaubriand and with the collaboration of the Centre national de la Recherche scientifique and the Centre national des lettres, three more volumes, of a projected fifteen, have appeared. In these first four volumes there are 1,529 letters, plus several supplementary ones, as opposed to the 650 published by Louis Thomas for the same years: an increase of almost 200 percent.

Reflections of correspondence editors about their profession rather resemble the stories hunters tell in the evening before the roaring fire, as they tirelessly describe the long pursuit, interminable lying in wait, the thousand dodges used by their elusive prey.

The prey in question is the handwritten document, the original letter: a prey which is getting harder and harder to trap. Seemingly bottomless private archives, generously opened to scholars at the beginning of this century, are today definitively shut. Autograph collectors, until recently willing to communicate their treasure, now lock it up jealously in the safe. Those who consent to let it be seen, imperiously insist on anonymity. Such is one of the perverse results of the inheritance tax laws. If one takes into account the prices autograph letters of certain writers, notably Chateaubriand, have reached at public auction—even though in Chateaubriand's case these prices seem clearly excessive—it is easy to see that a collection of autograph letters of some magnitude can be worth the price of a château in Touraine, and if it is declared part of an inheritance it can occasion a similar tax liability. Thus arises a great temptation for the holders to conceal its very existence, in order to keep open the possibility of selling it clandestinely. Nothing is easier to hide than a collection of letters, unless it's a stamp collection, and nothing, at least in appearance, easier to sell. This is no doubt a false impression, since specialists will hardly mistake the real origin of an important lot of autograph letters that suddenly come up for sale, but it nevertheless incites the owners to respond negatively, if at all, to all requests for consultation they receive.

The solution might be to adopt measures in favor of all who, for whatever reason, possess collections of autographs of private archives: measures analogous to those enjoyed by owners of châteaus of historical significance, to the extent that they permit public access under controlled conditions. However paltry such advantages may appear to those who enjoy them, at least they might constitute an invitation to open collections that are at present protected by almost inviolable hush rules.

Another cause for reticence in the face of the correspondence editor is the fear that the publication of a heretofore unpublished letter will diminish its sale value. Although such a fear may be justified in certain instances, as for example when the revelation found in the letter threatens to overturn completely what had been considered established fact about its author, it is generally far from the truth. The best proof of this is that dealers in autograph letters regularly hold back from indicating whether or not most of the documents in their hands have yet appeared in print. On the contrary: it can happen that the publication of a letter, with the commentary accompanying it which permits the identification of its addressee or describes the circumstances of its writing, adds to its interest for collectors and consequently to its value. Such is the case of a letter which, in the dealers' catalogs in which it was mentioned, was simply described as Chateaubriand's answer to a dinner invitation from a duchess. In fact, as we later demonstrated, it was a letter addressed to the duchess of Broglie, the daughter of Madame de Staël, and the invitation in question was to the famous dinner of 28 May 1817 which Mme de Staël was too ill to attend but which saw the beginning of the love story of Chateaubriand and Mme Récamier. Anyone interested in René's life and loves, who remembers the pages in the *Mémoires d'Outre-Tombe* where this episode is consecrated, cannot fail to be sensitive to the charm and nostalgia that arise from this note which is only a few lines long.

A part of the task of the editor of correspondences, not to say the essential part of that task, can be summed up in two words: *quête* and *enquête*, "search" and "investigation." Seek out the raw document first; then inquire around and about it, in order to make it admit to everything it may be concealing.

When the person is someone like Chateaubriand, who was not only one of the greatest French writers of the nineteenth century but also a public figure who had political responsibilities at the ministerial level, not to mention his journalistic career and his dignity as a peer of the realm, one may presume that there was no political, literary, or society figure of the time with whom he did not have at least the opportunity to engage in correspondence. His letters are today kept by his correspondents' families, or dispersed in public or private collections, or perhaps, while awaiting a purchaser, held by autograph dealers. In the worst case they have been destroyed.

It is necessary therefore to trace the descendants of Chateaubriand's possible correspondents down to the present day. For a number of them, particularly those belonging to noble families, various genealogical studies help in the search, provided that one can get hold of them, since some of these volumes were published in confidential editions, exclusively for kith and kin. For others the disappearance of the family runs us up against a blank wall; only by infinite searching through notarial archives does one stand a chance of learning into whose hands the papers of a now extinct ancient line have passed.

Once the descendants have been found, the editor must proceed to new tasks. The reticence he runs into on the part of some not very cooperative heirs has already been mentioned. As for those letters that have become the prey of collectors, their fate is most uncertain. How many collections of autograph letters there must be, considered piles of uninteresting trash, asleep, covered with dust, under the eaves of an inaccessible attic or at the bottom of the trunk with the unpickable lock! Old autograph catalogs list, right next to those documents that keep showing up on the market, a host of letters of which there is no longer a trace.

Other collections, luckier ones, have found the way to libraries, archives, and even museums. Their fate ought to be suitably assured. Unfortunately that is not always the case. Not all have been properly catalogued, all the more in that some of them, thanks to a collector devoted to his town or region, have ended up in the most unlikely places where no one would ever have the faintest idea of asking for them. To locate them the scholar is well advised to imitate the example of those who preceded him in the hard work of editing correspondences. If one of them has succeeded in following the track of a letter of Voltaire, Balzac, or George Sand to the library of a distant town, why should there not be a letter of Chateaubriand there as well? Beware, however, not of the obligingness, but of the competence of the keepers of these modest—or maybe not so modest—repositories. How many simply do not know the nature of the treasure they are guarding! It surely need not be mentioned that these remarks are in no way directed at the invaluable assistance that qualified librarians and archivists are in a position to render to editors of correspondence.

In any case, whatever kind of repository you intend to visit, write ahead. So many problems can be solved by a simple letter. By writing you have a chance of being answered by the most competent person. If you haven't taken this preliminary step you risk being met on your arrival by subordinates whose knowledge may be less great than their good will.

Some repositories provide photocopies, with or without a fee. Without denying their advantages one must note that nothing is as good as direct contact with the original document. The person doing the copying may have overlooked the address, or the date, or the signature, or a marginal notation, or some other element essential to establishing the correct interpretation of the document. Besides, the consultation of other documents belonging to the same collection may eventually shed light on yours.

There is still another category of letters that is almost as hard to get to as those in libraries or archives not yet thoroughly explored. These are the letters of Chateaubriand which have been published in books or periodicals that are in such little demand that, even in as heavily used an institution as the Bibliothèque Nationale, their pages have not yet been cut. No bibliography has indexed them, and often chance alone brings them to light. This is the case of those innumerable poems of the Romantic period whose authors thought it wise to embellish with letters of appreciation they had received from their elders in literature or talent. It is also the case of certain periodicals deemed of so little interest that no one has ever gone through them: for example, those two Lyonnais reviews edited by so extravagant a personage as Adrien Peladan, the father of Sar Peladan: *Le Feuilleton* and *La France littéraire, artistique, scientifique*. Impelled by a curiosity that must be called perverse we had the surprise of finding in them two important letters of Chateaubriand, both dating from his trip to the Near East, one addressed to Joubert and the other to Madame de Chateaubriand, both unknown to scholars for more than 120 years.

Another example: the *Bulletin périodique de la Société ariégeoise des sciences, lettres et arts et de la Société des études du Couserans*, in its thirteenth volume, published no fewer than three letters of Chateaubriand to the marquise de Casteras-Seignan. We should probably have been forever unaware of their very existence had we not on one occasion, while engaged in research in the Bibliothèque Municipale of Toulouse, gone through the alphabetical subject catalog under "Chateaubriand." The article containing these three letters was listed because there was an offprint of which the Toulouse library (probably the only one) had a copy. That shows how useful library catalogs can be!

There is no miracle recipe for making these forgotten publications come to light. One has sometimes to follow one's instinct. Having found once at a second-hand bookseller's the offprint of an article entitled "Last notes concerning Eustache de Saint-Pierre," and remembering that its author, Hector Piers, had been in communication with Chateaubriand, we purchased it all the more eagerly since its asking price was small. In cutting its pages, for no profane eye had ever sullied the virginity of this pamphlet, we were lucky enough to find mention of no fewer than two letters of Chateaubriand.

Problems of dating ought to arise only when letters are undated or incompletely dated. Calendars and other such charts lead indeed to the resolution of most enigmas arising from the absence of year, month, or day of the month. But, like the rest of us, Chateaubriand occasionally makes a mistake—maybe even more often. Writing late at night he confuses the day with the following one, or even the preceding one. His errors can be fairly easy to resolve if one has the other elements of the date, but if a second element is missing one can be off by a year or more.

When he writes at the end of a letter addressed to one of his cousins, "Monday, 28 July 1811" for "29 July," the correction is easy. It is much less so when, dating two other letters written on the same 29 July he puts simply "Monday 28." So that in the case of Chateaubriand one must always be aware of a possible lack of agreement between the day of the week and the day of the month.

Still one must take care not to make arbitrary corrections under the guidance of an intuition that could be misleading. This has happened to certain editors. During the first years of the Restoration Chateaubriand made two visits to the Norman coast, the first in October 1819 and the second in August 1820. Because he was unaware of the first of these trips Louis Thomas thought he could attribute all the letters concerning it to the 1820 trip, and then since the days of the month no longer agreed with the days of the week, he did not hesitate to change them, printing on his own initiative "Tuesday 22" and "Wednesday 23" (August 1820), instead of "Tuesday 12" and "Wednesday 13" (October 1819), which were the right days—and appeared as such, moreover, in the original. It was an unfortunate initiative, since it helped confuse the chronology of Chateaubriand's travels in 1819 and 1820.

In *Souvenirs et Correspondance de Madame Récamier* her niece, Madame Lenormant, published a letter from Chateaubriand whose manuscript is now lost; she dates it "Tuesday, 8 October 1822." In it he announced his arrival in Verona to Mme Récamier. Correctly observing that this date was unlikely, if one took the ambassador's itinerary into account—on that date he was in Geneva—Louis Thomas changed it, again on his own initiative, to "Saturday, 12 October," basing his correction on a letter to Villèle dated 13 October and published in Villèle's Correspondence. There Chateaubriand also announced his arrival in the city of the congress. For similar reasons the same correction was also adopted by Maurice Levaillant in his edition of the letters of Chateaubriand to Mme Récamier. It appears, however, that the date printed in the Correspondence of Villèle is itself wrong and should, on the basis of the autograph letter we have seen, be corrected to 15 October, which is in fact the only date to retain for Chateaubriand's arrival in Verona. It is also the date to adopt for his letter to Mme Récamier, of which, it must be remembered, we no longer have the autograph. It is to be presumed that the latter had solely for a date, "Tuesday," and that it was Mme Lenormant who took the initiative to complete it arbitrarily with the day of the month, month, and year. But not knowing the exact course of Chateaubriand's travels in Italy she was off by a week and dated "Tuesday 8 October" a letter that had been written on "Tuesday 15."

Such a cascade of errors has perplexed historians of the Congress of Verona, and it is totally the responsibility of ill-considered initiatives by maladroit editors. Considering such a situation one cannot insist too much on the urgency of both noting and justifying every correction or every addition made to the original text. This is of course the principle adopted in all critical editions.

And now for those little notes, undated or incompletely dated, intended to accept or refuse an invitation: nothing in the text permits the identification of the date—not even of the year—of their writing. One is almost sorry that their addressees, like Mme Récamier, did not simply throw them away! They have no interest other than demonstrating the frequency of an epistolary relationship, and they often encumber unprofitably the volumes of a Correspondence that aims to be "general."

The identification of a letter's addressee can also present mysteries worthy of the attention of detective-story readers. When the letter has been kept by the addressee's family, it is relatively easy, even in the absence of any other indication, to determine the identity of the ancestor with whom Chateaubriand corresponded. The problem becomes more complex when, like the prodigal son, the letter has escaped from the family circle and is wandering at the mercy of sales and auctions from one collection to another. Fortunately, during the eighteenth century and still at the beginning of the nineteenth the address was placed ordinarily on the fourth page of the letter which, folded over and sealed, served as the envelope. Still the address can be missing, either because the page on which it appeared has been torn or because the letter, instead of being posted, was hand-delivered and it was deemed unnecessary to place on it the addressee's name. Finally one must take into account the separate envelope, such as we use today; its use starts to spread at the beginning of the nineteenth century. Independent of the body of the letter, it is easy to misplace, if indeed it is not purposely destroyed, since the addressee may well see no reason to keep a document whose only use is to show that he is the one to whom the letter was addressed. Thus the rise of the envelope has ended up by depriving us of one of our most certain and rapid ways of identifying the addressee. One of the earliest examples of Chateaubriand's use of an envelope is a letter of 1811, addressed to one of the *"mainteneurs"* of the Académie des Jeux Floraux, abbé Jean Saint-Jean. Its text (see the facing illustration) is so uncharacteristic that without the envelope it would have been absolutely impossible to attach a name to Chateaubriand's correspondent.

No doubt there are other possibilities of identification: the content of the letter, an answer that has been kept, comparison with other letters addressed to the same individual, or perhaps a marginal comment in the addressee's hand. A whole correspondence can thus find itself personalized if on but one of the letters is an annotation that can be used as a guide. The Bibliothèque Municipale of Orléans owns a series of four letters by Chateaubriand each of which is addressed to a woman whose identity is not otherwise specified. On one of them, however, is found a note in the handwriting of Cordélia de Castellane, which provides the proof that she was its addressee. Cross-checking has led us to the same conclusion for the three other letters. But let us suppose that the group of four had been split up: we should never have been able to identify the addressee of three-fourths of them. Another example: recently a collection of papers originating with a minor Romantic, Saint-Valry, came up for sale. Two of them were letters from Chateaubriand, one bearing an address and the other not. If the two letters are separated no one will ever be able to guess to whom the second was addressed.

It is thus impossible to exaggerate the importance of tracing the history of every letter whose addressee is unknown, that is, of establishing, on the basis of vendors' catalogs, the list of sales in which it has appeared. The oldest catalog may well furnish information about the letter's origin which more recent catalogs have ignored. The Louis Thomas edition gives under the date of 12 September 1820, on the basis of an 1883 autograph catalog, a letter fragment addressed to a lady who, to judge from the context, was a gifted singer. Under the same date the

Monsieur,

J'ai reçu les deux exemplaires de l'Ode que vous avez bien voulu m'envoyer. Je ne reconnais point, Monsieur, mes faibles écrits pour le grand... où vous avez puisé vos belles images : c'est l'Écriture qui a inspiré votre Muse, et David a trouvé en vous un digne interprète.

J'ai l'honneur d'être, avec une haute considération, Monsieur,

Votre très humble et très obéissant serviteur
de Chateaubriand

Paris 30 mai 1811

Lettre de Chateaubriand à l'Abbé Saint Jean.

catalog of the Pixérécourt sale of 4 November 1840 indicates a letter addressed to "Madame Martainville"—without reproducing its text. Since that lady is known as a singer, the letter partially published by L. Thomas and the letter from the Pixérécourt catalog are doubtless identical. This one example can suffice to show the usefulness of autograph catalogs, if they have been carefully edited. In the absence of the complete text of a letter, they provide fragments lengthy enough to give an accurate idea of its contents; they may even contain facsimiles. No doubt it would be naive to trust their accounts blindly, but scholars know how to track down their concealed errors; anyway, these catalogs present the only available recourse for a number of letters which have disappeared.

Consulting them is therefore one of the principal tasks of any editor of correspondences, but it is boring and repetitious and must be begun all over again whenever the publication of any new author's letters is undertaken. To cope with this dispersion—indeed, waste—of effort, the creation of a central bureau charged with the establishment and regular updating of a concordance (eventually computerized) of autograph catalogs has been repeatedly suggested. Unfortunately it seems highly unlikely that at the present time this worthy goal can be attained. In the absence of such a tool it would be desirable to have at one's disposition at least a complete collection of these catalogs, but neither the Bibliothèque Nationale nor any French library has such a collection, these documents not having always been kept with the care their intrinsic interest should have merited. Different in this respect from the catalogs of art auctions, there is not even an exhaustive bibliography of them.

Chateaubriand's handwriting in his letters is more legible than is generally believed, more legible in any case than Stendhal's or Balzac's. Familiarity however with certain of its characteristics can help one avoid misreadings. For example the exaggerated upper loop on capital *C*, that makes it look like an *l*, the similarity of *n* and *u*, a *v* that looks like *w* while *r* often resembles *v*, and so on. Only at the end of his life, when arthritis had weakened his hand, did his handwriting become frankly detestable, but rather than inflicting on his reader the problem of deciphering it, he then preferred to make use of a secretary; less often—we know of only a few instances—Mme de Chateaubriand would write for him.

Mistakes in reading that editors have made usually involve proper names, not always easy to identify; picturesque confusions can result.

One such mistakes a dog for a person. In a letter to Madame de Custine dated 7 June 1804, first published by Chédieu de Robethon, is found this mysterious sentence: "Tresnes did something very naughty, and I'm going to talk to him about it when I get to the country." As a former magistrate named Latresne was a member of Chateaubriand's circle, it was thought that he was the one Chateaubriand was referring to, even if he had cut off the first syllable of his name; but what had the fellow done that was so "naughty"? Study of the manuscript leads to a correction from "Tresnes" to "Trimm": Mme de Custine's dog, whose name Chateaubriand spells with one *m* in immortalizing it in the *Mémoires d'Outre-Tombe*. "Trim, the famous dog who ate up the food that had been brought for the trip." Trim had probably run off in hot pursuit of some bird or other.

In a letter to Mme de Duras, likely on 11 April 1819, are found the names chevalier de Clunoy and duchesse de Vilain. At least that is how abbé Pailhès, the note's first editor, spelled them. Knowing of no one with either surname, we proposed the reading: chevalier de Thuisy and duchesse d'Orléans, and we had the satisfaction of finding our conjecture confirmed in a copy revised according to Chateaubriand's original letter. Other corrections are almost self-imposed, making recourse to the original, itself sometimes inaccessible, unnecessary. Thus in another letter to Mme de Duras dated 4 June 1822 where there is mention of Benvenuto Cellini's Memoirs and (in the Louis Thomas edition) the "prix [prize] de Rome." Clearly the "prise [taking] de Rome" is what should be read, in reference to the action of the imperial forces commanded by the constable of Bourbon in 1527 which is evoked at length in the famous goldsmith's Memoirs. On the other hand we'll never recover from our failure to guess that at the end of a third letter to Mme de Duras, dated 13 March 1818, which is adorned exceptionally with Chateaubriand's signature, one should have read, not (as in the Louis Thomas edition) "I sign because you reign [régnez]," which doesn't make much sense, but rather "I sign because you sign [signez]," which is much more logical.

All the corrections, all the changes that the editor believes he is entitled to make in the text on which he is working, whether it be the author's autograph or a more or less faithful copy, must of course be pointed out in the notes. That brings us to the question of the length of these notes, and here there are two conflicting schools of thought. Should they be short and succinct? or should they instead be expanded to include everything that has been found out about the author, the correspondent, and the society in which they lived?

It is no doubt pointless to reproduce at length information which is readily available in handy reference works, although one must keep in mind the reader's natural disinclination to look elsewhere, all the more if the reference work in question is not at hand. But one would certainly not blame the editor for furnishing information in the footnotes that results from careful investigation aimed at identifying the addressee or a person referred to, elucidating a mysterious allusion, or correcting errors which by dint of repetition have come to be considered truths. Who better than the editor, who has had to accumulate knowledge about the life of the writer and his times, to furnish all the explanations indispensable for a complete understanding of the letter? If he did not do it, he would oblige other scholars to begin all over again, with renewed expenses and perhaps less hope of success than he, the same painstaking and meticulous investigations he has already conducted for himself.

It is clear that the editor himself must know everything about the author, his life, his contemporaries', and the history of their times. To do so he will have had to make use of biographical dictionaries, individual biographies, correspondences, memoirs, newspapers and magazines. He must not only conduct his inquiry through already published texts but also be prepared on occasion to venture into the thicket of unpublished manuscripts. In a letter dated 14 November 1818 Chateaubriand writes to an anonymous correspondent with some corrections for an article concerning him; at the same time he announces his subscription to his "useful work." Nothing would have authorized us to give a name to this addressee had we not in the manuscripts of the Bibliothèque Nationale taken note of the correspondence exchanged for the identical reason and at the same period between the brother of Rivarol and genealogist Nicolas Viton de Saint-Allais, who turned out to be our man.

But let the editor beware of drawing too hasty conclusions from his discoveries. In letters addressed to various correspondents from London, where he was ambassador, Chateaubriand expatiates rather complaisantly upon the great reception at court on the occasion of George IV's birthday, 23 April 1822, during which he had a long conversation with the king. George IV was actually born on 12 August, and 23 April being Saint George's Day it would have been tempting to accuse Chateaubriand of carelessly confusing the monarch's saint's day with his birthday. A look at the English newspapers allows one to clear the French ambassador of any accusations: for reasons of expediency, since high society absented itself from London during the month of August, it had been decided that the king's birthday would be celebrated on Saint George's Day.

There is still one more area in which the discernment of the editor is put to the test: the nature of the relationship between the author and his correspondent. Any exchange of correspondence implies a relationship between sender and receiver and necessarily forms part of a system of symbols that have to be deciphered. The annotator's role is to clarify the nature of that relationship, at least implicitly, and from time to time point out, under the conventionality of the language, a friendship about to form, a nascent romantic attachment, or else a passion about to die out. In Chateaubriand's case the task turns out to be all the harder in that most of the Other's letters no longer exist, since the destruction he ordered in about 1840 of most of the letters he had received. And so to our great disappointment, and with few exceptions, the letters of Mme Récamier or Cordélia de Castellane went up in smoke. Who could ever imagine from the first and the last letters of Chateaubriand to the latter that at one point their relationship had become very intimate? One has to know how to listen to contemporaries' whispers in order to go beyond the words and succeed in reconstituting, under trite formulas, the lived reality of a liaison.

"General correspondence" in a chronological order? or the juxtaposition of particular correspondences, each to a single addressee? Today's editions of correspondences seem to be hesitating between the two modes. For a long while isolated correspondences were considered as only temporary expedients, preliminary but essential stages in the publication of a general correspondence. The new edition of Chateaubriand's correspondence had thus been preceded by the publication of ten or more particular correspondences. Some of them are, frankly, mediocre; others have the advantage of bringing down to us texts that are at present, for various reasons, inaccessible; finally, a few combine a properly edited text with useful commentary. The complete substitution of particular correspondences for general correspondences seems hardly to be justified except when, as in the case of Tocqueville, who carefully kept all the letters he received, the editor has all the addressee's responses at his disposal. The correspondence between Tocqueville and Gobineau finds thus its proper place just as much in the works of the one as of the other. As far as Chateaubriand is concerned the question cannot even be raised, since during his lifetime, as is well known, he had the great majority of his papers destroyed.

Other considerations can of course arise when it is a question of choosing between the two modes. Often they are commercial considerations, skillfully camouflaged under the guise of scientific rigor. Publishing houses, of course, are not patrons of the arts, and one can only deplore the fact that commercial interests may decide the fate of publications whose interest derives not only from their author's personality and character and their own literary value, but also from the essential and most rigorously authentic documentation they furnish as well to the historian, sociologist, moralist, and even psychoanalyst.

What future may one reasonably hope for editions of correspondences? The vogue which this kind of publication appears to have enjoyed for some twenty years can be compared with the taste of today's public for biographies. Correspondence and biography go together. Correspondences nourish and enrich biographies, and biographies make their readers eager to read correspondences. Sometimes the same scholar plays the role of biographer and correspondence editor. What will happen when there are no more fish in the pond and no more major authors whose letters still need to be gathered and published? No doubt the small fry will remain, the *minores,* but since their letters will not have been so carefully saved as their betters', they may well present fragmentary or irregular sequences, good at best for articles in the learned journals. Or should work already finished be begun all over again, with a given author's correspondence the object of successive editions?

Editions of correspondence did not immediately attain the point of development which is theirs today. Those of the first generation appeared as incomplete collections, their texts often mutilated or inaccurately transcribed, without annotation or critical apparatus. The notion of a critical edition came in with the second generation, although not according to any common model, fortunately, since each edition had to respect the character of the writer whose epistolary inheritance it was assembling. The work of editing still has an artisanal flavor, most often with a single editor who is so filled with his author that at times he gets confused with him. One cannot evoke the correspondence of Sainte-Beuve without mentioning Bonnerot, or George Sand without Georges Lubin, to mention only editions still in process. But already a third generation is in the wings, characterized by teamwork, systematic recourse to the computer, and the use of the most modern scientific technology, such as chemical analysis of ink and paper. The end result may not be a publication in book form but the eventual constitution of a data bank giving access to a series of microfiches each corresponding to a document. Mathematical rigor will henceforth take precedence over intuition. But with the disappearance of the artisanal methods, however empirical or archaic they may be, there may be a risk of the charm and fascination of the task simply fading away.

Translated by Charles A. Porter

MARTINE REID

Correspondences: *Stendhal en toutes lettres*

Figurez-vous qu'il y a à Vérone des philosophes sévères, ennemis déclarés des épanchements de l'amitié. Ces messieurs allument leur pipe avec mes lettres. . . . Ce que c'est que d'avoir un nom!
—Stendhal, *Correspondance*, 3, 12

Would you believe there are some severe philosophers in Verona, self-declared enemies of the outpourings of friendship. These gentlemen light up their pipes with my letters. . . . That's what it's like having a famous name!

AU COMMENCEMENT LA POSTE[1]

Writers' letters up to this day—and except for a recent issue devoted to this topic by the *Revue des Sciences Humaines*[2]—have rarely been examined in their "specificity." The question asked is often none other than this: what do a writer's letters contribute to our understanding of him? This was already the gist of a remark made by Stendhal in the context of his own correspondence. On 7 October 1805 he wrote to his sister:

tu n'as qu'à lire les lettres de Voltaire et celles de Rousseau. . . . On ne

---

1. J. Derrida, *La Carte postale* (Paris: Flammarion, 1980), 34. (Part of this work was presented at the colloquium on Stendhal held in Rome in November, 1983.) All English expressions appearing in the text or notes are my own, unless otherwise noted; all French expressions, whether in the text or notes, refer to the original French text. —Translator's note.
2. Cf. number 195 (1984) devoted to writers' letters.

les connaîtra parfaitement que lorsque toutes les lettres qu'ils ont écrites seront publiées.[3]

just read Voltaire's letters or Rousseau's. . . . They will be completely known only when all the letters they wrote are published.

This attitude, inherited from a long-standing tradition, is still prevalent today. In Voltaire's correspondence the critic looks for a commentary on some work in progress, in Rousseau's a confirmation of his views on the state of societies. Writers' letters are thus limited to their *use:* they supply irrefutable facts (dates, places, addressees), are both diary and autobiographical prose, and come merely to double for "the life and works." Correspondence, reduced to a document, and generally published long after all of the author's other texts, is thus marginalized, and as such, its only real status is that of supplementary information. This is also what Victor Del Litto maintains in the preface to his edition of Stendhal's correspondence[4] when he writes: "this correspondence is an inexhaustible source of information and reveals Stendhal's personality to us in greater depth."[5] *To know,* Stendhal had already said. But know whom, and how?

Faced with a corpus which includes some two thousand letters, I intend in turn to pose a question which has two sides, one literary, the other linguistic. The letter is a more or less stereotyped form which belongs to a genre and to the history of that genre. This genre finds its fictional form in the epistolary novel, its literary sanctification in a few great epistolary writers, without the benefit of a painstaking critical reflexion on the aptness of such a categorization, as would be accorded other genres. Are we perhaps dealing with a seemingly more "obvious"

3. *Correspondance,* 1, ed. V. Del Litto and H. Martineau (Paris: Gallimard, Bibliothèque de la Pléiade, 1962), 236. Hereafter the volume number (2: 1967; 3: 1968) and page number will be indicated in parentheses in the text. The same will hold for the two volumes of novels, *Romans* (1 and 2: 1954) cited below. The translations of individual novels referred to in the text will be designated as follows: *Armance,* trans. C. K. Scott Moncrieff (New York: Boni and Liveright, 1928), (*Arm*); *The Charterhouse of Parma,* trans. C. K. Scott Moncrieff, 2 vols. (New York: Liveright, 1925), (*CP 1, CP 2*); *Lucien Leuwen,* trans. Louise Varèse, 2 vols. (New York: New Directions, 1950), (*LL 1, LL 2*); *Red and Black,* trans. Robert M. Adams (New York: W. W. Norton, 1969), (*RB*). All other translations, unless otherwise noted, are the translator's.

4. This edition is incomplete. In fact, a certain number of letters have since been discovered. The reader is referred to the issues of *Stendhal Club* (24, 30, 31, 38, 42, 43, 47, 48, 64, 80, 83, 92, etc.) for the complement of texts.

5. "Cette correspondance est une intarissable source de renseignements et nous fait découvrir plus à fond la personnalité stendhalienne." Preface to the *Correspondance,* 1, ix.

genre than the others, since everyone practices it, and is familiar with it? Are authors' letters merely the marginal manifestation of talent, a kind of *peripheral writing* condemned, moreover, to an a priori veracity which limits them to the role of Exhibit A? This would be to forget strangely enough that before being pinned down as *writers' letters* and belonging to a collection whose primary addressee has been totally supplanted, these letters were, according to the insouciant dictionary, "a piece of writing addressed to someone for the purpose of communicating something to him."[6] The letter is then first of all a practice of a communicative nature and as such is caught up in a complex network of meanings. As a *sign*, it operates on several levels, which can be located and are independent of one another. An examination of the ways letters are used in Stendhal's novels will lead us directly to an appreciation of the extraordinary diversity which Stendhal inscribes at the heart of his own epistolary procedure.

Letter exchanges occupy a large place in the realm of Stendhal's fiction (more often than not in the form of "quotations") when they do not secretly take away the ending (as is the case in *Armance*);[7] they also act as a momentary substitute for the conversations between characters, in a way whose effects are worth analyzing. As they are presented in *Armance, Le Rouge et le noir, Lucien Leuwen, La Chartreuse de Parme*, and, though to a lesser extent, in *Lamiel*, the correspondences not only offer an interesting anchoring place in what has been called Stendhal's "semiotism,"[8] but also enable us better to grasp, by their surprising similarities with the author's own correspondence, and beyond a difficult distinction between the real and the fictive letter, an enormous *textual pleasure* (*plaisir du texte*), in every kind of category. Whether it is a matter of a message devised to be inserted in a work of fiction or of a written meditation addressed to someone close to him, Stendhal handles the letter's semiotic properties like a master and, conscious of its possibilities, offers an interesting typology of the turns taken by correspondence. In so doing, the author favors above all the coded form of the letter which he resolutely unites with countless literary practices and reminiscences. In so doing, he noticeably obfuscates

6. "un écrit que l'on adresse à quelqu'un pour lui communiquer quelque chose." Robert, *Dictionnaire de la langue française* (Paris: Société du Nouveau Littré, 1967), 984. 984.

7. The elucidation of this novel is found in the explanation furnished by Stendhal to Mérimée in his correspondence (*C* 2, 96, letter dated 23 December 1826).

8. This is Derrida's term taken up by M. Anjumbault-Simons in the title of his book: *Sémiotisme de Stendhal* (Geneva: Droz, 1980), in which epistolary exchanges are pointed out.

the business of *telling the truth*, authorship, ownership, and originality—which are the cornerstones of his relationship to language and to his literary development. The epistolary corpus is thus rehabilitated in that it reveals, no more or less than any of his works, Henry Beyle in metamorphosis into an other through the ludic power of writing.

THE EQUIVOCATIONS OF A GENRE

We cannot help but notice that, from the outset, the Stendhalian letter exceeds its boundaries. It turns itself into a message or note, an open letter-lampoon, an anonymous letter which claims to be a denunciation, a letter from Rome which is an absolute "stroll," a letter which is more like hurried annotation, note pad, *marginalia* of novels. "Every letter has the properties of being a diary, of being writing in the present," Jean Rousset observes.[9] This is what specifies a first shift, all the more interesting in that it enables the letter to be allied, indeed confused, with what Michel Foucault has called "self-writing."[10] The Portuguese nun had already remarked: "I write more for myself than for you."[11] Stendhal can widely adopt this affirmation as his own and especially in the letters addressed to his sister Pauline between 1800 and 1815. He decides to give Pauline the same education that he is busy enthusiastically instilling in himself. This allows him to write down—more often than not, to write to himself—everything that makes up his daily instruction. Diary, correspondence, or *filosofia nova*, one form substitutes for another. He writes to his sister:

> voilà, ma chère Pauline, quatre pages de philosophie que je viens d'écrire sur du papier à lettres au lieu de les mettre sur mon cahier. [*C* 1, 143]

> my dear Pauline, here are four pages of philosophy that I've just written on stationery instead of in my notebook.

and conversely:

> j'ai eu l'idée d'écrire mon journal le plus possible. . . , deux avantages: abréviation des lettres et sûreté. [*C* 1, 519]

> I had the idea of writing my diary as much as possible. . . , two advantages: the abbreviation of letters and security.

9. "Toute lettre a la vertu d'un journal, de l'écriture au présent." Cf. *Forme et signification* (Paris: Corti, 1962), 71; see also *Narcisse romancier* (Paris: Corti, 1973), 58 ff.

10. M. Foucault, "L'Ecriture de soi," in *Corps écrit* (Paris: PUF, 1983), 3–23 (in particular on correspondence as an exercise in self-knowledge: 13 ff.).

11. "J'écris plus pour moi que pour vous." Guilleragues, *Les Lettres portugaises* (Paris: Garnier, 1962), 58.

In search of a style and a personality, Stendhal, on whatever paper he comes across, copies out maxims, quotes profusely, "borrows" expressions from his readings, endlessly questions literature, thus finding himself immersed in a complex process of imitation ("to be the Molière of his century"),[12] one whose ultimate, and apparently paradoxical, goal is his metamorphosis into an original author. Pauline is a double ("nous avons le même esprit" C 1, 53 [we are of the same mind]), and *as such* a pretext. Stendhal intends for her to lock herself up with him in the vast universe of his letters, to reread them (C 1, 298), and to make excerpts from them which she can consult more readily ("Tu ne ferais peut-être pas mal de faire un cahier et d'y copier mes lettres, en laissant de la place pour des notes" (C 1, 129) [Maybe it would be a good idea for you to make a notebook and copy my letters into it, leaving room for notes]). From this viewpoint, Pauline anticipates the act of the future publisher and is therefore the first reader of a Henri who claims to be a writer. "Brûle mes lettres" [Burn my letters], he repeats to her incessantly,[13] only to order her immediately thereafter to preserve them carefully, and above all to shun all prying eyes (C 1, 49, 99, 264, etc.). Of course Stendhal dreads once again the *terzo incommodo* who will come and creep between his select addressee and him (the same precautions apply to all those to whom he writes at the time), but all these commands nonetheless resemble the secret hope that a chance reader will read these letters and hail them as a work of genius. What he particularly wants to hide is "toute l'étendue de [son] ambition" (C 1, 542), [the whole extent of (his) ambition]. While he is waiting in this "magasin de bonheur" (C 1, 575) which is made up of great literary works, Henri, together with Pauline, is transformed into the characters of novels or plays. All of the allusions and references, all of the examples are literary: Pauline is, by a stroke of good fortune, "la Pauline de *Polyeucte*" (C 1, 200); in all circumstances Lovelace must be "notre fidèle modèle" (C 1, 801) [our faithful model]. It is necessary to *speak* like Saint-Preux (C 1, 133), to be Delphine rather than Merteuil (C 1, 311), to *feel* like Phèdre (C 2, 221), to *shudder* like Jocaste (C 1, 821).

The questions which have been raised most pertinently regarding Stendhalian autobiography[14] can no doubt be extended to the context of a correspondence which tells how to become an author-narrator-char-

12. *Pensées, Filosofia nova* (Paris: Le Divan, 1931, vol. 2), 33.
13. See C 1, 77, 87, 487, 517, 602. . . . "Garde ce que tu brûles, voilà la demande" ["Save what you burn, that is the request"], Derrida rightly remarks, op. cit., 67.
14. Cf. especially B. Didier, *Stendhal autobiographe* (Paris: PUF, 1983), 6 ff., 55 ff.; and M. Crouzet, *La Poétique de Stendhal* (Paris: Flammarion, 1983), 23 ff.

acter, that is, always and never where anyone says *I*, allowing oneself to
pose as a secondhand bookseller along the banks of the Seine (*C* 2, 9–10);
putting oneself in the shoes of a bishop's secretary in order to address
one's sister as "Madame l'ambassadrice" (*C* 1, 320–22) [Madam ambas-
sadress]; taking up the pen in place of one's brother (*C* 1, 816–18);
inventing a family for oneself ("Ma femme vous dit mille choses" *C* 2,
92 [My wife sends you her regards], "Mes deux enfants se portent bien"
C 2, 123 [My two children are well], etc.); and finally systematically
eluding the only element which authenticates a letter, a signature. "Indeed, how many twists and turns, how many oblique manoeuvers characterize Stendhal's writings!"[15] If the writer, under the known pretext
of foiling Austrian censorship, uses a pseudonym, he also invites his
correspondents to do as much (*C* 1, 1002). He himself gives them on
occasions a "nom en l'air" (*C* 1, 1042) [a pretend name], and in writing
him back they use the pseudonym which he has just given himself (*C* 2,
893, 908). In other words, Stendhal is recognized by his false name,
while he stands waiting in fear as well as eager anticipation for the
moment he will be "épinglé" (*C* 2, 133) [caught].[16] This confusion of
genres begins in Stendhal as soon as he writes because, finally, only the
fact of writing matters. This will to hide without respite while always
pointing oneself out, in short this way of linking together truth and
falsehood (giving the appearance of the greatest casualness because a
text is "un billet de loterie et rien d'autre" [nothing but a lottery ticket]
on which posterity will decide)[17] seems particularly well illustrated by
his correspondence, such as this letter to his cousin Romain Colomb,
dated November, 1834:

> j'ai écrit horriblement vite douze ou quinze volumes in-octavo, que M.
> de Stendhal a imprimés. Tout cela fait qu'à cinquante et un ans j'ai une
> écriture illisible. La vergogne de voir un indiscret lire dans mon âme
> en lisant mes papiers, m'empêche, depuis l'âge de raison, ou plutôt
> pour moi de passion, d'écrire ce que je sens, ou plutôt les aspects sous
> lesquels je vois les choses, *aspects* qui sembleront peut-être amusants
> au lecteur, si, par hasard, il a une âme mélancolique et folle comme la
> mienne.

15. V. Brombert, "Under the Mask of Sincerity," *Times Literary Supplement*, May
27, 1983, 547.
16. Cf. J. Starobinski, *L'Oeil vivant* (Paris: Gallimard, 1961), who insists upon Stendhal's pleasure in utilizing pseudonyms and thus "se sentir vivre à plusieurs exemplaires" [feeling himself live in several copies], 204.
17. *De l'amour* (Paris: Garnier-Flammarion, 1965), 79; *On Love*, trans. H. B. V.
(New York: Grosset and Dunlap, 1967), 62.

L'expérience . . . m'apprend que je ne cours pas le danger d'être compris, pour une troisième raison que je dirais en grec si je savais l'écrire:

comme les Béotiens, je tends mes filets *trop haut* [C 2, 722]

. . . I've written twelve or fifteen volumes in-octavo horribly fast, which M. de Stendhal has printed. All that results in unreadable writing at fifty-one years of age. The shame of seeing a pryer read into my soul while reading my papers has prevented me, ever since the age of reason, or rather for me of passion, from writing what I feel, or rather from writing about my vision of things, a *vision* which will perhaps seem funny to the reader, if, by chance, he happens to have a melancholic and crazed soul like mine.

Experience . . . teaches me that I don't run the risk of being understood, for a third reason that I'd say in Greek if I knew how to write it:

like the Boetians, I set my nets *too high.*

Some major tendencies of Stendhal's thought are to be found here: the perpetual displacement of the name (here the pseudonymous signature is ultimately challenged, M. de Stendhal is now only Beyle's publisher); the fear, constant in the correspondence as in the autobiographical texts, of being surprised by a "pryer" (to which is linked the secret hope of perhaps finding a reader identical to himself, as Pauline had been in his childhood); finally, by way of a paradox ("courir le danger d'être compris" [run the risk of being understood]) a self-condemnation which borrows nonetheless another's voice, since Stendhal resorts to a quotation (a quotation he will put more than once in the mouth of one of his literary doubles, Lucien Leuwen).

The letter thus shows that for the writer there is no literary genre which does not betray its difficult relationship to him and to language. The epistolary genre, a crossbreeding of diverse genres, says nothing different from what Stendhal maintains everywhere else. It remains nonetheless, as a detailed analysis of the mechanics of his correspondence will attempt to show, a unique form of communication in which the Stendhalian voice in turn reveals and hides itself, turning all language into literature.

THE EQUIVOCATIONS OF A SIGN

At the outset there is the gesture of the addresser who creates the letter and of which the paper bears the trace; there is the text which it offers to be read by the addressee; then there is its existence as a sealed letter, a letter-signifier delivered over to the hazards of the mail, presupposing "a relaying or a suspensive time limit, the place of a mailman, the possibility of rerouting and of forgetting."[18] Stendhal's correspondence, in the wider sense that I have proposed to give it, does more than illustrate the semantic importance of these three moments: it exemplifies in a singular way the manipulation, interference, and overloading specific to this communicative venture.

From its stage of composition, the letter signifies (*fait signe*).[19] The paper is of a certain kind, so is the ink; the handwriting is bold or hesitant. The text is marked or is not marked with words crossed out, spelling mistakes ("j'en fais beaucoup et je les aime" *C* 1, 97 [I make a great many and like them], Stendhal declares): so many aspects which on the surface offer a character, a sociology; so many aspects which the addressee first grasps globally, at first glance, a letter-picture signing an intention. While Stendhal traces "lentement des caractères informes avec une plume de poulet" (*C* 1, 13) [slowly ill-formed characters with a chicken quill], Mathilde de la Mole has "une jolie petite écriture anglaise" (*R* 1, 523) [a delicate little English script (*RB*, 260)], Lucien Leuwen forms his letters badly, which would be rather an advantage in politics (*R* 1, 1082, *LL* 2, 20), Octave de Malivert

> a l'enfantillage d'écrire avec son sang qui coulait encore un peu à travers le bandage de son bras droit. [*R* 1, 134–35]

> is so childish as to write with his own blood, which continued to ooze from the bandage on his right arm. [*Arm.*, 189]

Stendhal's heroes write letters to each other which are described more often than not as infinite, and Stendhal rails against his friends:

> je vous écris des lettres superbes, des lettres de quatre pages et vous restez trois mois sans me donner signe de vie. [*C* 1, 59]

> I write you superb letters, four pages long, and you go three months without giving me any sign of life.

Whether the letters are long or short, the addressee reacts immediately to them, like Lucien observing that his father sends him mockingly "une toute petite lettre écrite sur le papier le plus exigu possible" (*R* 1,

18. "un relais ou un délai suspensif, le lieu d'un facteur, la possibilité du détournement et de l'oubli." J. Derrida, op. cit., 73.
19. This is the level T. Todorov calls "connotation" and whose semantic possibilities he describes regarding *Les Liaisons dangereuses* in *Littérature et signification* (Paris: Seuil, 1966).

835)][the briefest possible letter written on the smallest possible piece of paper (*LL* 1, 86)]; or like Bathilde de Chasteller who is enraged by the mere sight of a seven-page letter (*R* 1, 964, *LL* 1, 227). Stendhal's correspondence furnishes numerous echoes of these reactions.[20]

On a fictional level, Stendhal does not hesitate to give the letter's content a decisive role in a novel's plot: a fake letter from Armance drives Octave to suicide; a letter written by Mme de Rênal and dictated by her confessor shatters the career of Julien who is nearing the top. In almost every case, however, the letters which come and inform or fill out the plot are "repeated," quoted at the time, we might say, occasionally with an *etc.* that makes the reader intervene in a form with which he is supposed to be familiar. Stendhal more often than not leaves aside salutations and addresses, platitudes he considers unworthy to reproduce, providing us with only that part of the letter which is felicitously called "narratio" in classical terminology.[21] This effort at synthesis, characteristic of an elliptical style heightened by moments of impatience, recurs explicitly in some of his own letters.[22]

For Stendhal, and as if from the depths of his essence, the necessarily conventional nature of the letter calls for *imitation*. M. de Soubirane will have a "forger of autographs" copy a letter supposedly written by Armance and addressed to her friend Méry de Tersan (*R* 1, 181; *Arm*, 267). This process is repeated in *La Chartreuse de Parme* (*R* 2, 263; *CP* 2, 22). In the same way the fabrication of an anonymous letter is meticulously described in *Le Rouge et le noir*. Mme de Rênal writes to Julien:

> coupe dans un livre les mots que tu vas voir; colle-les ensuite avec de la colle à bouche sur la feuille de papier bleuâtre que je t'envoie. . . . Si tu ne trouves pas les mots tout faits, aie de la patience de les former lettre à lettre. [*R* 1, 330][23]

Cut out of a book the words with which I'll furnish you; then glue

20. See especially *C* 1, 17, 45, 61.
21. L. Versini, *Le Roman épistolaire* (Paris: PUF, 1979), see the comments in chapter 3.
22. See notably *C* 1, 95, 130, 902; *C* 2, 446.
23. We should point out here the texts designating one another: Mme de Rênal gives Julien instructions (first text) for the composition of a denunciation (second text), which is supposed to come about from the mutilation of a book (third text), which itself has served as a sign of the whole undertaking: "la cuisinière . . . lui apporta un livre sur la couverture duquel il lut ces mots écrits en italien: *Guardate alla pagina 130*" (*R* 1, 328) [the cook . . . brought him a book, on the cover of which he read these words in Italian: *Guardate alla pagina 130* (*RB*, 94–95)], the whole being part of the text which makes up the "Chronique de 1830."

them on the sheet of blue notepaper enclosed here. . . . If you don't
find the exact words, take time to form them letter by letter. [*RB, 96*]

This concerns the time of composition. Matters become more complicated when we come to the matter of content. The addresser can send in
his name a message which does not belong to him, like Julien's copying
(for the benefit of Mme de Fervaques) the correspondence, in fifty-three
letters, of a Russian prince madly in love with an English woman (*R* 1,
603; *RB*, 328). This tactic of seduction by letter is one which Stendhal
recommends to his friend Adolphe de Mareste. He does more: he makes
a point of slipping into his missive a declaration of love ("Je sens,
Madame, que la démarche que je fais est ridicule. Il y a plus de deux mois
que je me représente tous les jours combien il est ridicule, et même
inconvenant, à moi inconnu, d'oser écrire à une femme que la gloire
environne et qui . . ." *C* 2, 64–65 [I realize, Madam, that the steps I am
taking are ridiculous. For more than two months I have been thinking
every day how ridiculous, and even improper it is for me, a stranger, to
dare write to a woman surrounded by glory and who . . .]) which the
latter needs only copy; and he promises other ones! But the addresser
can also pretend to copy a message which in reality is his own. This
curious effect of displacing the addresser, where the "real" letter is
inserted in another, "fictive" one, occurs more than once in Stendhal's
correspondence.[24] Thus, for instance, he writes to Schmit on 4 May
1818:

> Cher tyran,
> Enfin hier soir en rentrant jé havé trouvé une *letter* du duc de
> Steindhal; elle est tellement excellente que je crois devoir vous faire
> bien vite cadeau d'une copie d'icelle.
>> le 1 mai 1818
>
> Mon aimable compagnon, que votre longue lettre m'a fait plaisir! Elle
> m'a attendu vingt-quatre heures, parce que j'étais dans nos mon-
> tagnes . . . [*C* 1, 919]

> My dear tyran,
> Finally last night upon arriving at home, I 'ave founded a *lettre* from
> the Duke of Steindhal; it is so excellent that I think I should quickly
> make you a present thereof.
>> 1 May 1818
>
> My lovable companion, how your long letter pleased me! It waited
> twenty-four hours for me, because I was in the mountains . . .

24. Cf. particularly *C* 1, 917–18; *C* 2, 204, 245.

Finally the addressee can in turn resort to copying, out of caution or attachment. Julien has Mathilde de la Mole's declaration of love copied, which he sends to Fouqué, hidden in a Bible (*R* 1, 536; *RB*, 272). As for himself, Stendhal urges Pauline to make a "notebook" out of his letters (*C* 1, 197).

The epistolary process is thus singularly fictionalized, even within a form which is already fictional, as is the case of the novel. As a result the letter loses all of its character *proper*. How can Stendhal's introduction to Schmit guarantee the veracity of the message which follows? Stendhal copies out in his imagination a text of which he claims to be not the addresser but the addressee, and in this gesture obliterates any claim to originality. The same holds for the letter which he prompts Mareste to send to the woman with whom he is enamored. Whose voice states "Je sens, Madame, que . . ." [I realize, Madam, that . . .] which Stendhal signs Edmond de Charency, while the previous note is signed Porcheron? What difference is there between this letter, in the tradition of the amorous letter, and Stendhal's letters to Mathilde Dembovski (*C* 1, 940 ff.) whose style and vocabulary are reminiscent of Valmont's letters to the présidente de Tourvel, to name only the most obvious of literary references, which, moreover, foreshadow the love letters Stendhal attributes to his characters? What status can be given to the famous "Turkish letter" (itself repeated in the *Journal*)[25] which, after reading the *Lettres persanes*, Stendhal sends to his cousin, and which is at one and the same time a declaration of love and a pastiche of Montesquieu? M. de Soubirane, searching for a way to foil the marriage of Octave and Armance, recalls

> un roman vulgaire où le personnage du méchant fait imiter l'écriture des amants et fabrique de fausses lettres. [*R* 1, 180]

> a vulgar novel in which the villain has the lovers' handwriting copied and fabricates forged letters. [*Arm*, 265]

Further on, the *Liaisons dangereuses* is alluded to, but what emerges from the conversation the chevalier and the commandeur have in this connection is that the model is outmoded: "Notre siècle est plus sérieux que cela" (*R* 1, 181), [Our generation is more serious than that *Arm*, 267]. Is it again Laclos that Stendhal has in mind when he has Julien, having just received a note from Mathilde, say: "Il paraît que ceci

25. *Oeuvres intimes*, 1 (Paris: Gallimard, Bibliothèque de la Pléiade, 1981), 698–700; *The Private Diaries of Stendhal*, ed. and trans. Robert Sage (New York: Doubleday, 1955), 384–85.

va être un roman par lettres" (*R* 1, 531), [It looks as if this is going to be an epistolary novel (*RB*, 268)]? At the very least one can assert that the epistolary techniques, tactics, and trickeries that Stendhal stages in his novels are highly reminiscent of the *Liaisons*. That is no doubt what puts us on the track of the author's temptation towards the epistolary novel, particularly when we know to what extent he admired from time immemorial, not only *Les Liaisons dangereuses*, but *Les Lettres portugaises*, *Les Lettres persanes*, and *La Nouvelle Héloïse* as well. Nonetheless this "temptation" readily extends beyond the scope of the novel. While merely developing its potential, Stendhal seems to suggest that the epistolary form welcomes fraud.

As an overall sign of communication, and without considering its meaning or content, the letter can be experienced by the addresser, as well as by the addressee, as something exciting, touching, dangerous. Mathilde sees in the letters she writes the opportunity to defy the proprieties:

> c'était l'imprudence que Mathilde aimait dans ses correspondances. Son plaisir était de jouer son sort. [*R* 1, 510]

> it was imprudence which Mathilde was aiming at in her letter writing. She loved to play with fire. [*RB*, 249]

As for Bathilde, she writes to Lucien without realizing that the danger lies not in the letter's content, but in the very fact of answering;

> hélas . . . elle se trompait elle-même. . . . Elle *répondait:* tout était dans ce mot-là, qu'elle ne voulait pas regarder. [*R* 1, 959]

> Alas . . . she was deceiving herself. . . . [S]he *answered him:* that was the one important thing she failed to realize. [*LL* 1, 221–22]

This last aspect, relatively characteristic of epistolary exchanges between lovers, reveals a somewhat surprising attitude vis-à-vis epistolary practice. It presupposes the primacy of intention over content: the letter's only message is to say *I write you.* Let us recall the Russian prince's correspondence copied by Julien:

> les quarante premières lettres n'étaient destinées qu'à se faire pardonner la hardiesse d'écrire. Il fallait faire contracter à la douce personne . . . l'habitude de recevoir des lettres. [*R* 1, 606–07]

> The first forty letters were intended merely to beg her pardon for his boldness in writing. It was necessary to induce this sweet creature . . . to form the habit of receiving letters. [*RB*, 331]

This motif of the letter's indicating nothing other than a will to communicate is found in *La Chartreuse de Parme* when Mosca begins corresponding with Sanseverina, having no other aim than making her feel his presence (*R* 2, 344; *CP* 2, 129–130). In this sense the présidente de Tourvel wrote to Valmont: "I am beset by the thought of you."[26] If intentionality is thus privileged, and it is in a spectacular fashion in *Armance*, where the whole novel stages "the symbolic journey of a signifier,"[27] and where Octave is seen to keep for a while, in pieces, the letter containing his dreadful secret, it is because writing, and in it the portrayal of feelings, is experienced as an eminently dangerous act. Speaking is "frightful," but writing is even more so, and Stendhal does not hesitate to bring in as a guarantee for this assertion the name, so important to him, of Napoleon (*R* 1, 529, *RB*, 266). For the written word proves to be even more difficult to manage than the spoken word. As soon as it is set down on paper, it takes on an unexpected semantic opacity, loses its hoped-for "transparency," betrays, and is unrecognizable. Thus Lucien who

> croyant bien faire avait suivi sans trop s'en douter les leçons vagues de fatuité et de politesse grossière envers les femmes. [*R* 1, 964]

> thinking he was acting for the best, . . . without realizing it, was following the doubtful lessons in conceit and crude cuning toward women. [*LL* 1, 227]

As for Bathilde, she certainly intends not to lose her ordinary conversational tone by writing,

> mais à son insu des phrases d'un sérieux profond s'étaient glissées dans cette lettre, écho des sentiments, des chagrins et des pressentiments de cette âme agitée. [*R* 1, 964]

> but unknown to herself there had crept into her letter phrases of a profound seriousness that were the echo of her real feelings, the pains and presentiments of a deeply troubled soul. [*LL* 1, 227]

Thus there is an impossibility of mastery reminiscent of the one which arises on the level of spoken language, this will of Stendhal's (and of the

---

26. "Vous m'entourez de votre idée." Choderlos de Laclos, *Les Liaisons dangereuses* (Paris: Garnier-Flammarion, 1964), 117; *Les Liaisons dangereuses*, trans. P. W. K. Stone (New York: Penguin, 1961), 125.

27. "le trajet symbolique d'un signifiant" S. Felman, *La 'Folie' dans l'oeuvre romanesque de Stendhal* (Paris:Corti, 1971), 189. See also P. Bayard's remarks in *Symptômes de Stendhal: Armance et l'aveu* (Paris: Lettres Modernes 186, 1979), 25 ff.

Stendhalian hero) to coincide with his own speech and the painful ac-
knowledgement of its impossibility;[28] a haunting obsession of a perfect
junction between word and thing which makes him prefer music or
painting, "non-constraining languages, whose signs are at the interpret-
er's disposal;"[29] an incapacity behind which is hidden the formidable
danger of forming sentences (*C* 1, 155, 965), of writing a "dull" and
"insipid" letter (*R* 1, 961; *LL* 1, 225). Moreover, the words which recur
most often to describe the epistolary enterprise are *weakness* and
ridiculousness.[30]

A written letter asserts something very different from what the
addresser meant to indicate. Furthermore, the letter happens to be read
by an addressee altogether incapable of seeing anything other than what
he expected. Persuaded in advance that Bathilde's reply would be negative, Lucien

> tomba à bas de son cheval plutôt qu'il n'en descendit . . . il s'assit et se
> plaça bien à son aise comme un homme qui s'apprête à recevoir le coup
> de hache qui doit le dépêcher dans l'autre monde. Leuwen . . . ne dis-
> tinguait point . . . l'idée principale qui eût dû être: "Madame de Chas-
> teller répond!" [*R* 1, 960]

> fell rather than dismounted from his horse . . . sat down and settled
> himself comfortably like a man . . . awaiting the stroke of the axe that
> will dispatch him into the next world. Lucien . . . did not yet receive
> the principal point of the letter which for him should have been:
> "Madame de Chasteller has replied!" [*LL* 1, 222–23]

Likewise, Fabrice receives from the countess Pietranera a letter of
which "un certain tour énigmatique" [a certain enigmatic tone] fright-
ens him. Stendhal specifies:

> C'était un caractère auquel il ne fallait qu'un mot pour prévoir facile-
> ment les plus grands malheurs; son imagination se chargeait ensuite
> de lui peindre ces malheurs avec les détails les plus horribles. [*R* 2, 93]

> His was a character to which a single word was enough to make him
> readily anticipate the greatest misfortunes; his imagination then

---

28. P. Bayard, op cit., rightly remarks that these fantasies of mastery "relèvent de la
névrose obsessionnelle en sémiologie médicale et de l'introspection en littérature" [are a
product of obsessional neurosis in medical terminology and of introspection in liter-
ature], 8.

29. "langages non contraignants, dont les signes sont à la disposition de l'interprète." M. Crouzet, "Stendhal et les signes," *Romantisme*, 3 (1972), 73.

30. Cf. in particular *C* 1, 9, 784; *C* 2, 64 (this word appears twice in the space of three
lines); *R* 1, 134, 960; *Arm* 189; *LL* 1, 224.

stepped in and depicted these misfortunes to him with the most horrible details. [*CP* 1, 92–93]

As for Stendhal, he continually asks "si vous sentez en lisant cette lettre la douce émotion qui me l'inspira" (*C* 1, 85) [if in reading this letter you feel the sweet emotion which inspired me to write it] and replies to Mélanie Guilbert's complaints by writing:

> Mon imagination erre dans tous les accidents possibles depuis que je sais que vous n'êtes pas aussi heureuse que vous devriez l'être. [*C* 1, 203]

> My imagination wanders in all possible ups and downs since I've known that you are not as happy as you should be.

In this way, communication appears curiously short-circuited. Stendhal suggests a kind of *psychopathology* of epistolary exchange[31] in which the addresser finds it impossible to control the impact of a message which reveals him in spite of himself, in which the addressee fails, in a movement of narcissistic recoiling, to succeed in getting out of the circle of apprehensions into which too much imagination thrusts him. In the last analysis, there is not much that "corresponds" in these correspondences. In his correspondence Stendhal himself anticipates this moment when

> vous n'aurez plus rien à me dire, vous ne m'écrirez plus qu'avec ennui, et bientôt vous n'écrirez plus du tout. Alors tout sera fini." [*C* 1, 201]

> you'll have nothing left to say to me, you'll no longer write me but wearily, and soon you won't write at all. Then it will all be over.

This anguish of *ending,* of stopping communication, no doubt finds its most obvious formulation in the following letter, written to Clémentine Curial on 24 June 1824:

> Tu ne saurais te figurer les idées noires que me donne ton silence. . . . En rêvant devant mon bureau, les volets fermés, mon noir chagrin s'est amusé à composer la lettre suivante, que peut-être tu m'écriras avant peu; car, enfin, que t'en coûtait-il de m'écrire un mot?
> Voici donc la lettre que j'aurai la douleur de lire:

31. See "Erreurs de lecture et d'écriture," in Freud, *Psychopathologie de la vie quotidienne* (Paris: Payot), 115–42; "Misreadings and Slips of the Pen," in Sigmund Freud, *The Psychopathology of Everyday Life,* 6, trans. James Strachey (London: Hogarth Press, 1960), 106–33. Freud gives numerous examples of the way in which "the reader's preparedness . . . alters the text" (112). French text reads: "le désir secret du lecteur . . . déforme le texte" [the reader's secret desire . . .] (122).

"Tu as exigé de moi, mon cher Henri, la promesse d'être sincère. Ce commencement de lettre te fait déjà prévoir ce qui me reste à ajouter. Ne t'en afflige pas trop, mon cher ami, songe qu'à défaut de sentiments plus vifs, la plus sincère amitié ne cessera jamais à m'unir à toi. . . .

Adieu, mon cher ami, soyons raisonnables tous les deux. Acceptez l'amitié, la tendre amitié que je vous offre, et ne manquez pas à venir me voir à mon retour à Paris.

Adieu, mon ami" [*C* 2, 35]

You couldn't imagine the gloomy ideas your silence gives me. . . . Dreaming at my desk, with the shutters closed, in deep sorrow I amused myself by composing the following letter, which you'll write me perhaps in a little while; since, in short, what would it have cost you to write me a note?

Here then is the letter that I'll have to suffer the grief of reading:

"You wrested from me, my dear Henri, the promise of sincerity. This introduction should prepare you for what I have to add. Don't be too distressed, my dear friend, consider that lacking more intense feelings for you, I'll always be united to you in the most sincere friendship. . . .

Goodbye, my dear friend, let's both be reasonable. Accept my friendship, the tender friendship I am offering you, and don't fail to come see me when I return to Paris.

Goodbye, my friend."

The possibility of *copying*, suggested to the addressee, is found again here. But Stendhal goes farther, materializing the degree zero of an epistolary communication in which sending and replying are confused, and in which the addresser writes and answers in the same gesture.

The epistolary machine certainly gives rise to confusion. There is no escaping the fact that originality can disappear behind a jumble of borrowed phrases, of literary reminiscences that may come to a writer's pen, or that his meaning may overflow, or that the addressee may decipher this meaning all wrong. Consequently it is not at all surprising if Stendhal's characters hesitate to pass through the double mediation of the letter—in that it obliges them to give a written form to highly problematic speech[32]—and if, for show, Stendhal gives the form of a pirouette to his anxiety, shying away from the responsibility of saying *I*.

32. Cf. M. Crouzet, *Stendhal et le langage* (Paris: Gallimard, 1980), which treats this problem as a whole while emphasizing its historical foundation; see also P. Brooks, "L'Invention de l'écriture (et du langage) dans *La Chartreuse de Parme*," *Stendhal Club*, 78 (January, 1978), which shows how writing curiously constitutes only a transient stage of the communication between Fabrice and Clélia.

Stendhal stands thus in a perfectly equivocal position concerning the letter. On the one hand, he tends to minimize the inevitably dialogical nature of the letter and to write for himself, likening the genre to autobiographical prose. This is particularly the case in the letters making up the beginning of the Correspondence. Stendhal is inclined to go from his notebook to his stationery and vice versa without feeling any necessity other than the imperative of *putting into writing (mettre par écrit)*. Hiding behind desire that is the feeling which will be the prime mover in his whole literary undertaking to be recognized one day at last as a writer—which he certainly is not at the time of his writing to Pauline—and sooner or later to bring into existence the ideal reader, his soul mate. In this connection correspondence is really *literature* for Stendhal from the very beginning, when he merely had his sister read him before there were others. On the other hand, this resolutely literary option leads to the writing games Stendhal indulges in throughout his epistolary practice. Its form invites him to, since, for him, it is above all *novelistic*. For Stendhal, an unconditionally enthusiastic reader and admirer of "classical" works of the epistolary genre, everything beckons toward literature. He uses and abuses it until he loses his own voice. This does not occur without a paradox: while he fully puts into play the form's properties, Stendhal rebels, however, against the coded aspect it inevitably presupposes. A "blank,"[33] the letter hampers him with its imposed style, with its attached insincerity. In this he comes up against precisely what constitutes this genre's internal contradiction. The letter implies spontaneity, naturalness, and originality, "whereas its gestation is characterized by the practice of artifice and stereotype."[34] Jean Rousset and Tzvetan Todorov have analysed this point brilliantly for the epistolary novel: as a novel, this genre looks to "become more natural" in its sumptuously staged correspondences.[35] Nevertheless it seems surprising that this type of analysis has not been extended beyond the scope of the novelistic form, and that the consequences of this

33. R. Barthes, *Fragments d'un discours amoureux* (Paris: Seuil, 1977); *A Lover's Discourse: Fragments*, trans. Richard Howard (New York: Hill and Wang, 1978) defines the letter in this way: "forme vide (codée) et expressive (chargée de l'envie de signifier son désir)" (187) ["blank (encoded) and expressive (charged with longing to signify desire)" (157)].

34. "alors que la pratique de l'artifice et du stéréotype caractérise sa gestation." A. Viala, "La Genèse des formes épistolaires en France," *Revue de Littérature Comparée*, 2 (1981), 173.

35. Cf. J. Rousset, *Forme et signification*; T. Todorov, op. cit.; see also R. Bray, *L'Art de la lettre amoureuse: Des manuels aux romans* (Paris-La Haye: Mouton, 1965).

contradiction have not been measured for all types of letters, a fortiori for those whose authors intend to make literature their profession. If the naturalist undertaking long influenced the destiny of novels,[36] it still continues to influence heavily the writing of the letter, as well as its reading. The letter *speaks* (*porte parole*). This is the way in which Stendhal understands it:

> pour avoir un bon style épistolaire, il faut dire exactement ce qu'on dirait à la personne si on la voyait, ayant soin de ne pas écrire des répétitions auxquelles l'accent de la voix ou le geste pourraient donner quelque prix en conversation. [*C* 1, 3]

> to have a good epistolary style, it is necessary to say exactly what you would say to the person if you were to see him, being careful not to write repetitions to which intonation or gestures could give some value in conversation.

The letter is a *herbarium*, the trace of a dried voice, and as such necessarily close to truth. Here we must recognize the argument that Jacques Derrida has patiently dismantled. In the direct line of rationalists of the seventeenth century, Rousseau made writing a *supplement*, condemned it to be forever "fallen, secondary, instituted"[37] vis-à-vis voice which won the guarantee of veracity and naturalness. The letter then may remain as the last avatar of naturalism and "representation." A formal stylization from the very outset, the letter dreams constantly however of a speech whose exact copy it would be, whose ideal nature would assure it a truthful character. The letter claims to *take the place of* speech and through this link with speech, presumed more true than writing, assures itself—in spite of its history, which formalizes and fictionalizes it straightaway—of the same benefits as speech. The use made of the letter does not refute its claims: the letter is *read* as if it were true, a continuation of the process J. Derrida calls "phonemic limitation."[38]

36. Cf. R. Barthes' remarks in *Mythologies* (Paris: Seuil, Points, 1970), 227 ff.; *Mythologies*, trans. Annette Lavers (New York: Hill and Wang, 1972), 140 ff.

37. "déchue, seconde, instituée," J. Derrida, *De la grammatologie* (Paris: Minuit, 1967), 29; *Of Grammatology*, trans. Gayatri Chakravorty Spivak (Baltimore and London: Johns Hopkins University Press, 1976), 17.

38. "limitation phonématique," J. Derrida, *La Carte postale*, 493. Derrida makes this remark in the context of his text "Le Facteur de vérité" ["The Factor of Truth"], in which he accuses of being idealistic the way in which Lacan, in his "Séminaire sur la lettre volée," understands the epistolary phenomenon. The implication according to Derrida is "a phonemic limitation of the letter, an interpretation of the *phoné* which spares it divisibility as well. Voice provokes such an interpretation of itself: it has the phenomenal characteristics of spontaneity, of self-presence, of circular return to itself. It keeps better for the belief that it may be kept without external accessories, without paper and envelope: it is, it tells us, always available wherever it is."

Stendhal's attitude vis-à-vis the letter cannot be isolated and considered as being specific to his epistolary activity. The letter is autobiographical prose, just as autobiographical prose is letter: this is the model evoked as much for *Les Souvenirs d'Egotisme* ("Je me suis imposé d'écrire ces souvenirs à vingt pages par séance, comme une lettre" [I've decided to make myself write twenty pages of these memoirs at each sitting, like a letter]) as for *La Vie de Henry Brulard* ("J'écris ceci, sans mentir j'espère, avec plaisir comme une lettre à un ami" [I am writing this, I hope without lying, with as much pleasure as if I were writing a letter to a friend]).[39] We discover here in fact his whole behavior toward language. From the beginning of his literary career, Stendhal comes up against a major difficulty: making his own voice heard. He finds fault with language for making in particular the voices which preceded him heard, voices in which for a long time he harbored his literary illusions. Did he not go as far as wondering if he shouldn't *speak* like Rousseau?[40] If he accuses language of being above all socialized speech, a code which others expect you to use adequately, making an ape of yourself in the living room (*une singerie de salon*) in an act which has lost its claim to sincerity for ever, if he accuses the literature of his time of not being suitable for the portrayal of feelings because the age is mercenary, he nonetheless studies diction and declamation with the actor Dugazon and he begins nonetheless by writing pastiches and plagiarizing.[41] The same one who calls so violently for the understanding of souls, who tries desperately to drive out hypocrisy from discourses and minds, who does not have enough sarcastic remarks for *society*, is regarded as a brilliant yet boastful speaker in the eyes of his contemporaries, as a powdered histrion, practically a caricature;[42] he hides himself behind a pseudonym, puts on an act, even though he wants to be understood as *the rebel*.[43] He feels *ambivalence:* language is traitorous, and it would be better not to speak (his lovers would rather exchange glances than write or speak), all is literature and in that case welcomes

39. Respectively, for both quotations, *Oeuvres intimes*, 2 (Paris: Gallimard, Bibliothèque de la Pléiade, 1982), 452 and 536; *Memoirs of an Egotist*, trans. David Ellis (New York: Horizon Press, 1975), 61; and *The Life of Henry Brulard*, trans. Jean Stewart and B. C. J. G. Knight (New York: Funk and Wagnalls, 1968), 6.

40. *Oeuvres intimes*, 1, 61; *Private Diaries*, 52. On this subject see M. Crouzet's remarks in *Nature et société chez Stendhal* (Lille: Presses Universitaires de Lille, 1985).

41. See J. J. Hamm, "Stendhal et l'autre du plagiat," *Stendhal Club*, 91 (April 15, 1981), 203–214.

42. Cf. Mérimée's description of Stendhal in *Portraits historiques et littéraires* [Notes et Souvenirs, HB] (Paris: Champion, 1928), and J. Starobinski's remarks, op cit., 205.

43. Cf. Michel Crouzet, *La Vie de Henry Brulard ou l'enfance de la révolte* (Paris: Corti, 1982), and the beginning of *La Poétique de Stendhal*.

the use of an infinite potential for play. The voice which says *I* would like very much to find a base somewhere, but at the same time the temptation to come out of oneself and become a *character* is too great. With fiction and reality confused, one has to face the facts: for Beyle, Mocenigo, Brulard, or the baron of Cutendre, as soon as language is involved, life is a novel.

Translated by Mark Gross
with Alan Stoekl

LOUIS LE GUILLOU

Lamennais: A Happy Ending

Others will speak of their suffering as editors of correspondences and, indeed, someone who plunges into an important enterprise of correspondence publication has to be crazy or have the faith to move mountains. Fortunately the editor judges only very imperfectly, at the start, the obstacles that await him! For he must first discover the documents—and they are not found as easily as canned peas at the grocer's—gather them together, decipher them, classify them, analyze them, date them, annotate them, and all of this already requires a wealth of patience and erudition. I too have experienced all this and it was not without some difficulty that I managed to publish my nine substantial volumes of *Correspondance générale de Lamennais* (Paris: A. Colin, 1971–81, 7500 pp.) boasting more than 6,000 letters, 4,400 by Lamennais himself. No. What I would like to talk about is my joy, the great joy I experienced in searching out, finding, exhuming certain documents that were thought to be lost forever. For beyond the difficulties inherent in all research is a profound joy in having arrived, if not at one's goal—for will there ever be a truly complete correspondence?—at least close to it. Who can express, for example, my satisfaction when I received from Belgium the photocopy of one of Lamennais's letters, with its postmark, which was published initially as dating from 17 March 1833 and which was in reality, as I had shown, of 21 May 1834. It implied, surely, a certain boldness on my part, that I felt impelled to change so much, not only the year but also the month and the day!

The following passage by Emile Forgues can be found in the *Revue des questions historiques* of 1922:

> Every morning of his life, Lamennais devoted two or three hours to his
> correspondence. If, someday, someone managed to collect it in its

169

entirety, we would find in this inexhaustible mine a living and detailed chronicle of the period spanning the years 1809 to 1854. No richer source will ever be found for the material and moral history of France and of religion during this most eventful half century, whose last echoes we are still picking up today. But can we ever hope to find that man, both lettered Benedictine and audacious, clear-sighted editor, willing to attempt gathering all of the scattered materials of this gigantic edifice? In his remarkable work on *Lamennais avant l'Essai sur l'indifférence*, M. Anatole Feugère undertook to compile a list of all of Lamennais's published letters: it exceeds 2,500 entries [in fact many fewer if we are concerned with published letters, for many are only mentioned and have not yet been found!] and his work, although remarkably accurate for the time when it was published [1906], is already outdated and incomplete. If we bear in mind that this is approximately two-thirds of the total, we recognize the dimensions of this arduous task, to which we would have to invite young and noble minds that are sufficiently unselfish. May our century witness the completion of this glorious monument to the memory of our precursor Lamennais and contribute at last to rendering him the full and complete justice that he has been denied for so long! [218]

As for myself, I do not think that I have been a Benedictine, lettered or not, but I am happily fortunate to have succeeded better than Forgues imagined. One-third more than 2,500 would have yielded 3,750. However, I reached 4,400 letters by Lamennais, that is, seventy-five percent more than what was known, just a few years ago. And now, since 1981, I have garnered over fifty unpublished letters, certainly of great importance, to Liszt, to the baron d'Eckstein, and others, and many more addressed to Lamennais, including an unpublished and very beautiful one from Victor Hugo and another from Lamartine. For Lamennais's regular correspondents, besides the baron de Vitrolles, the count and countess de Senfft, Saint-Victor, Montalembert, to mention only a few, were named Joseph de Maistre, Chateaubriand, Hugo, Lamartine, Sainte-Beuve, Béranger, Victor Cousin, Michelet, Quinet, George Sand, Liszt, d'Ortigues, David d'Angers, and so forth—that is, the century's best. This is what explains the historical, literary, philosophical, and religious interest of this correspondence.

The journal *Studi francesi*, in 1972, observed that the *Correspondance générale de Lamennais* was "one of the most important documents for the intellectual history of the first half of the [nineteenth] century," *Projet* judged it to be "a milestone in the history of publishing," and Jean Gaulmier, in the *Revue d'histoire littéraire de la France*, wrote in 1979: "I scarcely know of any other work, in these last years,

*Lettre de Lamennais au baron d'Eckstein. Aut., collection Louis Le Guillou.
Unpublished. With the permission of Louis Le Guillou.*

To the Baron d'Eckstein

I have not yet read, honored and dear friend, your article on ancient religions, but I have read the one on M. Guizot, and I hasten to thank you for the pleasure. It is full of reason, insight, and truth. The Doctrinaires resemble men who think that th y have planted trees after fixing in the ground rows of wooden stakes cut to the same length. I find only one point on which we would not seem to agree. Christianity will live on. It is immortal; but Christianity's organization, the Church, as it has been formed by time and events, seems to have run its course; in my opinion it is destined henceforth to offer only the ever woeful spectacle of more or less gradual decomposition; in my view, it is but an exhausted body from which the soul withdraws to form a new one. Please continue your most remarkable work and accept the sincere affection of your devoted friend,   F.L.

December 29

Monsieur
Monsieur le Baron d'Eckstein
rue Mondovi 5

which, in documentary wealth and in human value, rivals this one." The list of these laudatory comments, which were made in all languages, could go on and on.

But the satisfaction of the completed work—which can be truly assessed only once it is published (for to bring out a large edition of a correspondence and to carry it to fruition, is a feat in itself: my edition was stopped and threatened with foundering twice!)—for me was tempered with several questions: of what use was such an edition of correspondence? in other words, was Lamennais's correspondence worth publishing, and if so what does it bring to the scholarly community?

In my humble opinion these nine volumes are an exceptional contribution to literary, political, social, and religious history, to the flow of ideas over a half-century. Once the Mennaisian world becomes a bit familiar, one reads Lamennais's correspondence as one reads Balzac's *Comédie humaine*, with the pleasure of rediscovering one or another character who reappears episodically. The historian will find his due there, interested as he is in the account of contemporary events—in the nineteenth century, a century without radio, a fortiori without television, and in which newspapers are quite different from those of today, people describe what they saw, they try to breathe life into the event— voyages, the cost of land, food, manners, and, as J. Onimus pointed out in the *Revue des sciences humaines* of 1973, "At the level of the history of ideas such a publication is well worth all of the works of synthesis." The linguist will be interested in the epistolary style of the period, the vocabulary and the spelling. Finally the scholar of literature will not fail to discover in it one of the three most beautiful correspondences of the nineteenth century, along with those of Flaubert and of George Sand (for how many very great writers are, in other respects, mediocre letter writers!) and in addition a storehouse of useful or picturesque information on the life of the time.

Finally and above all the interest of this correspondence, the one which in retrospect gives me the greatest satisfaction, lies in restoring to us the sensibility of a man and his many-faceted personality. All of Lamennais's letters—where he takes us more freely into his confidence than in a more carefully crafted literary work—tremble with the ardor of his polemic, with his anger at the stupidity and cowardice of those who, in his eyes, betray the exigencies of the truth. From the time he became a priest, in 1816, until his death in 1854, as a worthy descendant of the corsairs of St. Malo, Lamennais was always at the breach to defend, in one way or another, the rights of man that were constantly attacked and violated. In 1831, quite naturally, for example, he was to be found at the side of the Poles, bishops and priests to the fore, who were struggling for their liberty and the recognition of their national rights, flouted since the treaties of 1815. He upheld them in their fight, made known to the world their problems, and roared his indignation at the "30,000 warriors of Bar and the 20,000 citizens of Praga, dying for faith and liberty, for the Lithuanians bludgeoned to death or expiring in the mines, for the inhabitants of Oszmiana massacred in their churches and homes, for the soldiers slaughtered by the Prussians at Fischau, for those who were knouted to death by the Russians at Kronstadt," to quote the funereal litany of "The Books of the Polish Pilgrims" by the great Polish poet Mickiewicz, who was himself to declare one day that if many Frenchmen had understood the Poles, Lamennais was the only one to have "felt" them, that is to have understood them in his heart, beyond all reasoning and any other consideration: "Poland and we are but one," he used to say, "our heart is there and our hope also."

It is certain that the atrocious repression that followed the capitulation of Warsaw, the indirect support given czar Nicholas I by Pope Gregory XVI—himself a temporal sovereign whose lands were in full upheaval—in his letter of June, 1832, to the bishops of Poland, in which he denounced the malevolent agitators who had plunged their country into an abyss of misery and reminded them of the obedience due to legitimate governments, bore a fatal blow to the hopes that Lamennais placed in the Papacy. In approving the use of brute force, in appearing to ally himself with Nicholas, Gregory XVI had, for Lamennais, betrayed his mission: "He had divorced Christ, the savior of mankind, to fornicate with all of his executioners." The "assassination" of Poland, the opportunistic politics of the Pope, led Lamennais to serious reservations about the attitude of the conservative Catholic hierarchy of his time, and all this well before the denunciatory encyclicals *Mirari vos*, in 1832, and *Singulari nos*, in 1834.

A few years later, in 1835, he is on the side of the accused in the great April trial, having accepted the position of one of the defenders for the 121 prosecuted for their participation in the insurrections in Lyons and Paris of 1834, but who fought, he claims, for the "sacred principles of equality and liberty to which the people will owe their emancipation and the world a better future." He starts funds for their families, who had been reduced to destitution. He stands beside the poor, the persecuted, the humiliated.

In 1848, when the Republic had triumphed, Deputy Lamennais, on the extreme left of the time, will be a defender of the people and will strive to create for it a better social order and a more equitable distribution of credit, through mutual benefit societies, in particular.

Poland, the defendants of April, 1848: the same struggle, the same fundamental appeal for the rights of the individual. All of Lamennais is summarized in this desire to help the world organize a new society founded on justice, liberty, and solidarity. Under this nascent society—"We are witnessing, he confides to his friend Charles de Coux in 1834, the birth of a new world"—Lamennais wants to rebuild the evangelical foundation from which, century after century, it had drifted: "Ministers of Him who was born in a manger," he writes to his clerical colleagues in an October, 1830, edition of *L'Avenir* [The Future], his renowned newspaper bearing the epigraph "God and liberty," "return to your source, replunge yourselves voluntarily into poverty, into suffering, and the word of the poor and suffering God will regain on your lips its original efficacy. With no other support than this divine message, descend, like the twelve fishermen, into the midst of the people and begin anew the conquest of the world. A new era of triumph and glory awaits Christianity."

This will be possible however only when the priest has become free from temporal power, free from the mighty of this world. His absolute detachment, his independence in relation to the authorities, must be complete, money and honors being in general the mark of servitude. The crust of bread that is thrown to the clergy is the sign of its oppression, and it is in order to win independence and dignity simultaneously that Lamennais advocates the suppression of the ecclesiastical budget, just as he will insist in *L'Avenir* on the separation of Church and State, the freedom of religion and conscience, education, the press, and association, and on extended suffrage and decentralization.

One has only to reread the *Correspondance générale* of Lamennais and the major articles of *L'Avenir*—indeed those of *Le Monde, Le Peuple constituant*, or *La Réforme*—to be struck by their modern, extremely contemporary character. "The question of the poor, which is not just a question of economics but a question of life or death for five-sixths of mankind, is more than ever one of those which call for a prompt solution in Europe." "At the same time when, in Europe, Asia, and America, there are those who grumble about a glut of useful goods, as valueless as they are unused, the common man languishes in his destitution and in poverty without precedent. Call that order if you will. I feel like Job, *plenus sermonum*, when I come to consider these gigantic disorders, which those who profit from them seek to consecrate in the name of Heaven."

With an almost prophetic conscience of historical evolution and social dynamics, Lamennais had brilliantly understood that the conditions for the presence of the Church in the developing new world were liberty, independence, and poverty. For him the problem was to know whether the priest who performed, undoubtedly with zeal and devotion, the daily tasks of his ministry, who received any and all visitors with good will, who accepted the respect, indeed the honors due to an official personage, still had the apostolic and evangelical impulse; whether this religion which was often presented as a rampart, a brake against social disorder (this is the role that Thiers assigns to it as did also many manuals of the time written for ecclesiastics), is still the religion of Christ; whether this Church which opposed peoples' aspirations to wrest their political liberties, which condemned the Polish revolt of 1831, had not, through its association with the party of order, kings, and the mighty, become a hindrance to the progress of humanity; in short, whether it had not become the prisoner of its own power, what Dostoevsky, perhaps drawing on Mennaisian ideas, will popularize in "the myth of the grand inquisitor" of the *Brothers Karamazov*.

Is it possible for someone to proclaim himself a Christian—even were he to observe the exterior practices of religion—if he is villainous, covetous, hard, cruel to others? Is not the spirit of the Gospel charity, openness, mutual understanding, does it not exclude all dogmatism, all intransigence that generates persecution, violence, and hatred? It is this ideal of justice and love that Lamennais attempted to transmit in his works; certain of them, *Paroles d'un croyant* and *Le Livre du peuple* in particular, literally astounded his contemporaries—and not only those who were French, because they were translated into almost all of the languages of the earth, Lamennais's disciples being numbered even in the most distant countries: Mexico, Chili, Peru, Argentina.

Because he was an upright man, he always rejected compromise and diplomatic gamesmanship. Because he was a champion of liberty, of that true liberty which has nothing to do with laxity and anarchy, it was inevitable that one day or another he would clash with the established powers, temporal and spiritual, and be crushed.

But of what importance is immediate success, compared with the judgment of posterity! Indeed, the historian Adrien Dansette, in his *Histoire religieuse de la France contemporaine*, wrote in 1948: "He [Lamennais] in the religious domain and Karl Marx in the social are the two great visionaries of the nineteenth century. We can reject their ideals, but we cannot deny their perspicacity: the future has obeyed their prophecies." The real drama is that it took—whatever our judgment of the fact may be—three-quarters of a century to realize, willy-nilly, through ordeal and anguish, the separation of Church and State. It took a century and a half, through the terrible Renanian and modernist crises, for religious freedom to be recognized by Vatican II, and for first *Pacem in terris* and then John-Paul II to affirm the importance of natural rights and the rights of the individual.

In conclusion let me say that this adventure with the correspondence of a magnificent writer, a brilliant prophet of the modern world, has been most enriching for me. It is as sociologist, as ethnologist, that I often had to judge my work as historian, philosopher, even theologian, when it was not as an emulator of Sherlock Holmes, satisfied to have completed an investigation which did not present itself a priori as one of the easiest. An editor of correspondences enriches the intellectual world of his contemporaries but he especially enriches himself, at least intellectually. *Exegit monumentum,* as Horace would have said.

Translated by Erec Koch

SHEILA GAUDON

On Editing Victor Hugo's Correspondence

In 1824, prefacing a selection of letters by Voltaire, Victor Hugo, who was at the time twenty-two years old, wrote:

> It is always in a man's letters, more than in his other works, that one must seek the imprint of his heart and the trace of his life.[1]

More than fifty years later, in 1875, he gave in his literary testament precise instructions concerning the publication of his own letters:

> I want after my death all my unpublished manuscripts, with their copies, if any exist, and everything written by my hand whatever its nature may be . . . to be gathered together and put at the disposal of the three friends herein named: Paul Meurice, Auguste Vacquerie, Ernest Lefèvre. . . . I ask them to publish, with intervals that they will determine between each publication: firstly the completed works, next the partially completed works, finally the fragments and scattered jottings
> . . . .
> Independently of these three categories of publications, should it be judged appropriate to publish my letters after my death, my three friends are expressly entrusted by me with this publication, by virtue of the principle that letters belong not to their recipient but to their writer. They will sort them out and will decide the conditions of propriety and suitability for this publication.[2]

These two declarations leave no doubt about the legitimacy, for

1. *Choix moral de lettres de Voltaire*, précédé d'une notice sur la vie et les ouvrages de cet écrivain, 4 vols. (Paris: A. Boulland, 1824), Préface de l'éditeur, x.
2. Victor Hugo, *Oeuvres complètes*, édition chronologique publiée sous la direction de Jean Massin, 18 vols. (Paris: Club français du livre, 1967–1970), 15/16, 961–62. Hereafter cited as *M*.

Hugo, of publishing his letters. In both cases the need for selection is implicit, although the author proposes no precise criteria on which a selection might be based. In 1824 Voltaire's letters are paralleled with his "other works," indicating a clear recognition of their literary status. In Hugo's own case the terms of his will suggest that the problems raised are somehow different. His literary executors are first charged with "publishing *everything* written by his hand, whatever its nature may be." The addition of a separate paragraph devoted to letters may simply be attributed to a desire to assert his right of literary property: the content of all manuscripts, including letters, belongs to the person who wrote them, and, for the duration stipulated by law, to his heirs. It is however significant that letters are set apart from other writings and that the responsibility both for the appropriateness of such a publication and for the eventual selection of its contents is left to the judgment of his executors. This text, standing alone, reveals some hesitation if not outright ambivalence on the part of the writer.

Few prominent figures in the nineteenth century were solicited as often as Hugo to take a public stance on moral or political issues, but he had also on occasion had the unpleasant surprise of discovering in the press letters that were never destined for publication (reading in 1853, in a French newspaper, letters by his parents, he had immediately asked the offender, a well-intentioned journalist, to return them to him).[3] He knew by experience that any correspondent outside of his close family circle was liable to use his letters for personal advantage and he was, in 1865, to deplore this tendency: "This continual publication of my letters is, as you know, something I would prevent if I could. I except of course letters relating to the public interest."[4] Even during his lifetime, authentic letters nourished *Souvenirs* and *Mémoires* and were from an early date coveted by collectors, but so many forgeries were in circulation by the end of the 1860s that it was not unusual for a journalist to insist on the authenticity of the letter he was publishing.[5] On these

3. Unpublished letter to Léon Laurent-Pichat, 5 July 1853 (Yale University, Beinecke Library). With his reply of 21 July 1853 (Maison de Victor Hugo, 2117) the journalist enclosed the two letters. They were later published by Madame Victor Hugo in *Victor Hugo raconté par un Témoin de sa Vie* (Brussels and Paris: A. Lacroix, 1863), 1, 25–27.

4. Letter to Auguste Vacquerie, 5 March 1865, quoted in *Actes et Paroles 2, Pendant l'Exil* (Paris: Ollendorff-Albin Michel, 1938), 481. All references to *Actes et Paroles* will be to this edition, forming part of the *Oeuvres complètes de Victor Hugo* in 45 vols. known as the Edition de l'Imprimerie nationale. Hereafter cited as *IN*.

5. See the note preceding a letter addressed by Hugo to E. Coupy, 15 January 1896, in *Le Courrier de l'Europe* (*AP* 2, *IN* 357).

accounts alone an edition prepared by friends in whom he placed his trust was entirely justifiable.

The date of Hugo's literary testament may throw some additional light on his attitude. In 1875–1876 were to appear the three volumes entitled *Actes et Paroles*, the first collected edition of his major political speeches and letters from 1841 (his election to the Académie française) to 1876, when he became a Senator. Although Hugo had, at significant times, arranged for updated collected editions of his speeches,[6] this was the first of which he was to say that he was "opening wide his life to his contemporaries."[7] His long introduction to the first volume, "Le Droit et la Loi," is a profession of faith and the occasion for a return to the past, retracing for posterity a moral and political itinerary from childhood to old age. It is a moment when he takes stock, as it were, of his life, giving an "official" version, set with the author's seal. What is of special import here is that this edition of *Actes et Paroles* grouped together for the first time a wide range of political interventions corresponding to the years between 1854 and 1869. Although he was deprived of any official tribune, Hugo's world stature was such that appeals for his public support during these years were numerous. With the exception of speeches delivered at funerals or banquets, his exclusive vehicle of communication was the open letter. A glance through the second volume of *Actes et Paroles*, *Pendant l'Exil*, might lead the reader to believe that here was a first edition of Hugo's letters, carefully selected by the author. Moreover, certain terms of his introduction to the third volume, *Depuis l'Exil*, suggest that these "acts and words" had in the author's eyes a function similar to that of Voltaire's letters: "A whole life is in these volumes. It is complete. . . . This book has the true form of a man."[8] It is not surprising then that a literary testament providing for the publication of his letters—his own literary property—should be drawn up at the time when he had in fact just made a partial selection of those he considered of public interest.

From the above remarks, it would seem that Hugo's ambivalence springs from a conception of his life as a public life. From 2 December 1851 the image of the opponent to Napoleon III was to dominate his public *persona*. Were he to have written his memoirs, one could surmise

6. In 1851, 1853, 1854 and 1872. For details see Talvart et Place, *Bibliographie des Auteurs modernes de la langue française (1801–1948)* (Paris: Aux Horizons de France, 1949), 10, 46 and 95–96.
7. "Le Droit et la Loi," *AP* 1, *IN*, 20.
8. "Paris et Rome," *AP* 3, *IN*, 7.

that he would have found more inspiration in the model of *Les Mémoires d'Outre-Tombe* than in Rousseau's *Confessions*.

The terms of Hugo's will, and no doubt some oral instructions, appear to have determined the orientation of the two editions of his letters undertaken by his literary executors: a two-volume anthology, published from 1896 to 1898 by Paul Meurice and Jules Simon,[9] was almost completely reproduced and considerably augmented to form the last four volumes of Hugo's complete works, edited in the same spirit by the successors of Paul Meurice.[10] Here the aims are clearly stated: Hugo's letters are presented chronologically in order to illuminate more clearly the life of the poet and public figure who had made an imprint on the whole of the nineteenth century.[11] This option rests, however, on a relatively small and careful selection of letters, a considerable number of which are only partially reproduced and occasionally "corrected," perhaps for the reasons of "propriety and suitability" invoked by their writer. This obviously no longer corresponds to our notion of what an edition of correspondence should be.

Since the conception of the above editions, two important trends have changed our approach. The former arbitrary treatment of the letters of literary figures has gradually given way to a more objective intention, based on the principle of completeness. Put into practice as early as 1880 by Louis Moland in his eighteen-volume edition of Voltaire's letters,[12] this principle determined the course of Theodore Besterman, whose monumental *Voltaire's Correspondence* is enriched by numerous more recent discoveries. It guided Jean Bonnerot in his *Correspondance générale de Sainte-Beuve*[13] and has since been the aim of all major editors of collected letters in France. The notion of completeness implies that all of the letters, however brief or "uninteresting," are to be made accessible and whenever possible collated on the autograph manuscript. The amount of fresh material provided by editions of this type interests different categories of readers whose preoccupations are not necessarily literary, especially when it is accompanied by annota-

9. Victor Hugo, *Correspondance*, 2 vols. (Paris: Calmann-Lévy, 1896–1898).

10. The *IN edition*. The *Correspondance*, published from 1947–1952, was edited by Cécile Daubray.

11. "Avertissement de l'éditeur," ibid., 1, 287.

12. Forming part of Voltaire's complete works (Paris: Garnier Frères, 1880–1882), Moland's edition contains over 10,000 letters by Voltaire, presented chronologically.

13. Première série, vols. 1–6 (Paris: Stock, 1935–1939); deuxième série, vols. 7–15 (Paris: Privat/Didier, 1957–1966). Incomplete on the death of Jean Bonnerot in 1964, the work has been continued by his son, Alain Bonnerot.

tion clarifying contemporary allusions that are no longer comprehensible. Although the focus remains the author himself, a wealth of information is available for historians, political analysts, sociologists, and linguists. These "other works" of writers have thus acquired for us another dimension. They have become, without losing any literary interest they may have, as informative as archives.

The perception of a potential historical value is not altogether new. In the words of Horace Walpole, "Nothing gives so just an idea of an age as genuine letters: nay, history waits for its last seal from them."[14] Indeed, the letters of those who direct events, the statesmen and military leaders who "make history," have long been a source of information for the historian. It was to this end, as much as to the greater glory of his ancestor, that in 1854 Napoleon III appointed a nine-man commission to "collect, coordinate, and publish" the letters of Napoleon I pertaining to "the different branches of public interest."[15] But it is only since the advent of a new conception of history, where the perception of events is considered as important as the events themselves, that genuine letters of other members of the community, illustrious or not, have come to be regarded as historical documents. The light they shed on the day-to-day realities of life, the evidence they contain of the impact of events on those who suffer them, is valuable research material for the modern historian. Editors of letters of major literary figures, from Voltaire to George Sand, while insisting primarily on what they reveal of the life of the writer, on the insights to his personality, do not fail to point out their contribution to our knowledge of the age.

A second significant development has been the renewal of interest in exchanges between two correspondents. The publication in 1904 of the correspondence between George Sand and Gustave Flaubert, containing 318 letters written by two close friends over thirteen years (from 1863 to the death of George Sand in 1876), was an immediate success, and a second edition appeared the following year. The unsigned foreword states in simple terms the main reason for this choice: "All correspondence is a *duo*, and it cannot be said that one knows it when only one of the parts is known. Can a response be understood without the

14. Quoted by W. S. James, *Selected Letters of Horace Walpole* (New Haven and London: Yale University Press, 1973), xv.

15. *Correspondance de Napoléon* publiée par ordre de l'Empereur Napoléon III, 35 vols. (Paris: Imprimerie impériale, 1858–1859), 1, iii.

182 Yale French Studies

182182 Yale French Studies

question, can one be 'satisfied with the question without the response?"[16]

These two approaches to editing the letters of famous writers have helped to no small extent to shape the strategy adopted by the group which for a number of years has been preparing a new edition of Victor Hugo's correspondence.[17] Our first concern—that it should be as complete as possible—led us to concentrate on the formidable task of collecting letters written by Hugo over a period of seventy years to men and women from all walks of life and from all corners of the world. The question that arose from the onset was that of the mode of publication to be adopted. Several possible solutions presented themselves: to publish only the already numerous letters of Hugo himself, following in the tradition of collected letters ("Correspondances générales"); to clarify Hugo's letters where necessary by the addition of extracts from his correspondents' replies, in footnotes (the method adopted by Roger Pierrot and George Lubin in their editions of the letters of Balzac and George Sand);[18] to append selected responses at the end of each volume, on the model of Lamennais's correspondence;[19] or to insert relevant replies from time to time in the main body of the text, as was done by Jean Massin in the chronological edition of Hugo's complete works. We decided from the start on a more radical approach: to abandon the monologue in favor of a dialogue, of a *correspondence* in the full etymological sense of the word.

To this major consideration may be added another, yet more decisive in respect of Hugo. When we read the letters of Madame de Sévigné to her daughter we have but small concern for Madame de Grignan, whose only function appears to be that of passive recipient. Copies of Mme de Sévigné's letters circulated during her lifetime in a

16. *Correspondance entre George Sand et Gustave Flaubert* (Paris: Calmann-Lévy, 1904), note preceding the first letter. A new edition of this correspondence, containing 422 letters and richly annotated by Alphonse Jacobs, appeared in 1981 (Paris: Flammarion).

17. The group, composed of scholars from several countries, is sponsored by the C.N.R.S. and has its geographical base at the Maison de Victor Hugo, 6, place des Vosges, 75004 Paris, France. The codirectors of the edition are Jean Gaudon, Sheila Gaudon, and Bernard Leuilliot. Publication, by the Editions Laffont (Collection "Bouquins"), will begin in 1987 and will continue at the rate of one volume a year.

18. Honoré de Balzac, *Correspondance*, textes réunis, classés et annotés par Roger Pierrot, 5 vols. (Paris: Garnier Frères, 1960–1969). George Sand, *Correspondance*, textes réunis, classés et annotés par Georges Lubin, 17 vols. published (Paris: Garnier Frères, 1964–).

19. F. de Lamennais, *Correspondance générale*, textes réunis, classés et annotés par Louis Le Guillou, 8 vols. and supplement (Paris: Armand Colin, 1971–1981).

society passionately interested in the arts of literature. Her letters belonged to a recognized literary genre, a genre which Victor Hugo appreciated[20] and of which Voltaire was to be the undisputed master. Beyond the avowed recipient, implicitly or explicitly, the author was addressing a much wider audience. The *épistolier* has his place beside the novelist, poet, or essayist.

But the letter cannot be, for writers of Hugo's generation, the vehicle it was for Mme de Sévigné or for Diderot writing to Sophie Volland. As Pierre Larousse comments, with undue pessimism perhaps but with some perception: "Having cast all its brilliance over the sixteenth, seventeenth, and eighteenth centuries, correspondence is dying in the nineteenth. It may even be said that correspondence is dead, and it is an irreparable loss for literature and science."[21] Although correspondence as it was understood in the wake of its glory was perhaps to rise from its ashes, and although we may quarrel with this apparently peremptory judgment, it intuitively reflects a perceptible phenomenon. It has always been considered that one of the characteristics of Romanticism was a hypertrophy of the self. Whatever reservations one may care to make about this excessively simplifying vision, it is certain that writers of the first half of the nineteenth century, whether or not they wear their hearts on their sleeves, place the self at the center of their works. This is true of Victor Hugo who, although one of the least openly "confidential" writers of his age, is also the one who uses most often the first person singular. The complex strategy proceeding from this apparent paradox takes from the letter a large part of its function as a representation of the self. It may be said without exaggeration that *le Moi* is more effectively represented in *Les Contemplations* or in *Les Misérables* than in letters, which contain in the end fewer "imprints of the heart" of the author. In consequence the magnitude and force of Hugo's works may make his letters seem inadequate, and all the more so if they are compared with seventeenth- or eighteenth-century models.

But this in no way diminishes their interest. Apart from what we can expect from such documents—information about the man and the age, glimpses of certain aspects of his personality and his daily life—they reveal the extraordinary place held by Victor Hugo in his century, a

20. "The other genres have rules; this one has only secrets. . . . It is in the models of the *genre* that one must seek these secrets; it is from the letters of *Mme de Sévigné, Voltaire, Jean-Jacques* that must be drawn the lessons of this art which is not an art" (*Choix moral de lettres de Voltaire*, 1, 8).

21. Pierre Larousse, *Grand Dictionnaire universel du XIXe siècle*, 16 vols. and supplement (Paris, 1866–1877), article "Correspondance."

place which is comparable to that of Voltaire or Goethe. They bear testimony above all to his social and political status. Through the power of his pen alone Hugo acquired an international stature equalled by no other writer of his time. His influence and opinions were sought and respected worldwide by those concerned with justice and equity. The record he kept in his notebooks of the endless procession of visitors to his home in exile and in Paris after his return there give but a meagre idea of the prestige he enjoyed.[22] In 1869, his son tells us, "he writes twenty pages and ten letters a day, and smiles to the future as to a friend coming towards him."[23] But there were also times when the servitudes of prestige bore heavily upon him, when its attendant correspondence became overwhelming. Apologizing in 1863 for the brevity of a reply to his publisher, he reveals some measure of exasperation: "[This letter] is short, but the days are shorter. I do not know how to manage at the same time my work, my business affairs, and the colossal correspondence with which I am honored by the four winds. I have on my table at the moment at least three hundred letters awaiting replies."[24]

His correspondents were from all groups of society, from kings and heads of state (the Emperor of Brazil twice visited him in 1877), ministers, poets, critics, to political exiles, convicts, beggars, and psychopaths. By 1867 he was receiving fifty letters a day,[25] an increasing proportion of which he kept. On his death many of those concerning his works were classified along with the manuscripts and found their way to the Bibliothèque Nationale. A large number of others were donated by his descendents to the Maison de Victor Hugo in Paris. The existence of this collection of letters from more than sixteen hundred correspondents, many of which are inscribed with an *R* indicating that Hugo had replied, was a further incentive to include (as far as possible in any undertaking of this nature) all the letters by the poet and the letters addressed to him.

The collections of the Bibliothèque Nationale and the Maison de Victor Hugo are the richest single sources of documents, but the disper-

22. See Hugo's *Agendas* and *Carnets* from 1855 onwards, published by Bernard Leuilliot in *M*, 10 to 16[2].

23. Charles Hugo, *Les Hommes de l'Exil* (Paris: Lemerre, 1875), 341.

24. From an unpublished letter to P.-J. Hetzel, 10 December 1863 (Private collection).

25. "It is midnight and I am beginning to feel tired, having been up since five o'clock this morning. I receive fifty letters a day" (letter to Paul Meurice, 31 March 1867, in *Correspondance entre Victor Hugo et Paul Meurice* [Paris: Charpentier, 1909], 248).

sion of the poet's letters, even among public collections and archives in France, makes it difficult to establish as we go along a definitive inventory. To the resources of various other Parisian and provincial libraries must be added the holdings of public collections as far apart as Leningrad and Washington, Bucharest and Manchester. The number of letters in private collections cannot be assessed with any degree of accuracy, but the generosity of many collectors has already contributed significantly to increasing our corpus. To date some nine thousand letters have been collected, a figure which does not include the 14,000 letters addressed to the poet housed at the Maison de Victor Hugo. We are, however, well aware that many others have yet to come to light.[26]

This immense body of material presents problems, the first of which is the precise definition of the corpus of the correspondence. Should open letters to the press—and therefore much of *Actes et Paroles* 2 and 3—be included? Hugo's letter to Lord Palmerston, protesting against the execution of Charles Tapner in 1854, is exemplary. Along with others (the appeal for a reprieve for John Brown in 1859, his attempt to prevent the execution of the emperor Maximilian, for example), it is an important contribution not only to Hugo's constant duel with the death penalty but also to the history of abolitionist movements. The spate of related correspondence provoked by public letters of this nature requires for its comprehension that the original be before the reader's eyes. Hugo's long letter to Nadar, destined for immediate publication, is somewhat different. Written in response to a request from Nadar who needed to raise money to finance the construction of a flying machine, a "helicopter," it was not, for diverse reasons, published at the time. One might argue that an eleven-page exposition of the problems that modern aviation has conquered is more of an essay than a letter and has its place among Hugo's literary writings. But until it was reinserted as a letter by Jean Massin in his edition of Hugo's complete works, this prophetic text had only found its way into print posthumously, in an appendix to the *IN* edition of *Actes et Paroles*. As the letter to Palmerston, it is the core of an extended correspondence with Nadar and others.

We shall also include letters that appeared as prefaces to the works of younger authors. Hugo's encouragements to budding writers were legendary. Reflecting his unfailing and often excessive generosity, they are an ever-present facet of his literary activity. The letters written

26. We should be very grateful if readers who may know of the existence of letters to and from Victor Hugo in collections other than those of the major libraries would communicate with me at the Department of Romance Languages, Wesleyan University, Middletown, CT 06457, or at the Maison de Victor Hugo, 6, place des Vosges, 75004 Paris.

during Hugo's summer journeys are in a category of their own. Are they authentic letters or are they really material for a book, a *récit de voyage?* Those written during his excursions to the Rhine Valley in the summers of 1838 to 1840 were destined from the outset for publication, and *Le Rhin* appeared in 1842. Being essentially a literary convention, these letters do not have a place in a volume of correspondence. Although the above examples do not lead to a definition of decisive criteria, they set a common-sense rule: each text has to be examined separately and within its context.

Letters from correspondents pose problems of a different nature. Their number and diversity make it very unlikely that Hugo's reply—if indeed there was one—will always have been conserved or that it will be discovered. Among the 14,000 letters held by the Maison de Victor Hugo are many that do not bear the *R* attesting a response. This does not necessarily preclude one, for Hugo's indications were not throughout his life systematic. But even if we have no trace of a letter from Hugo, it is evident, for instance, that the begging letters the author received and later attributed with only slight modifications to Thénardier in a particularly dramatic chapter of *Les Misérables* (3, 8, 3), should be published. An example such as this, though perhaps exceptional, shows that no a priori distinction between correspondents can be made. In the perspective of a contribution to history a letter from a political prisoner, a beggar, or any of his innumerable solicitors may be considered as a more important document than one from an illustrious contemporary or even from Victor Hugo himself.

Only the letters from Juliette Drouet are a case apart, and they present the most serious difficulty we have yet encountered. Some 20,000 are known to be in existence, 18,000 of them at the Bibliothèque Nationale. The 271 letters from Hugo to Juliette that have survived, together with his annual entry in her "Birthday book," published by Jean Gaudon in 1964, present no intrinsic problem. Entrusted to the Bibliothèque Nationale in 1913 by the daughters of Paul Meurice, they remained sealed until 1964. The delay, which has been attributed to excessive prudishness, was without doubt a way of respecting to the letter all of Hugo's intentions—his concern for propriety and suitability, as well as his desire that the letters should eventually be published. It is not impossible, as I conjectured above, that oral instructions were given to this effect. Thus the first two editions of Hugo's letters ignore the presence by his side from 1833 to 1883 of his devoted companion, but on the other hand his wishes, expressed in a letter to Juliette, have been carried out: "I do not want this trace of your life in mine to be erased for ever. I want it to remain, I want it to be found again, one day, when we are both nothing but dust and ashes, when the revelation can no longer break anyone's heart. I want it to be known that I have loved you. . . ."[27] As the extraordinary numerical imbalance shows at a glance, Juliette's daily—often twice daily—missives brought forth few replies, and such does not appear to have been their intention. They are the ever-renewed expression of Juliette's love and, despite their repeti-tions, the writings of a natural *épistolière*. To publish them in their entirety would be materially impossible—they alone would fill some forty volumes—and yet they cannot be left aside. The method adopted by Jean Massin points a way: Hugo's infrequent communications will be interspersed with a greater number of letters from Juliette—her replies to messages received, questions that may have been answered *viva voce*, pertinent news and comments, and so forth.

A mass of correspondence of this magnitude calls for a new approach to the presentation of the letters. Two different methods have been used in two recent editions of correspondences comparable to that of Victor Hugo by their scope and duration and by the systematic inclusion of both letters and responses. They are *Voltaire's Correspondence* and *The Correspondence of Horace Walpole*. Theodore Besterman, presenting "a close-up of the society of an entire epoch in all its grandeur and baseness,"[28] proceeded according to strict chronological order, the number of Voltaire's correspondents being relatively small. An edition of Hugo's correspondence consisting of a simple chronological presentation, letter by letter, of the numerous exchanges of vastly unequal duration and importance would, however, be unreadable. The very question of chronology is complicated in the case of Hugo by the circumstances of his life and by his work habits: the time that might elapse between the moment a correspondent posted a letter and the day Hugo wrote his reply varied considerably. Although relatively predictable when the author was in Paris, the normal time lapse (three days from Brussels or Paris to the Channel Islands) was often greatly extended during the eighteen years of his exile. In order to avoid interception of his letters by

27. Victor Hugo, *Lettres à Juliette Drouet 1833–1883. Le Livre de l'Anniversaire,* texte établi et présenté par Jean Gaudon (Paris: J.-J. Pauvert, 1964), 3.

28. Voltaire, *Correspondence and related documents,* definitive edition by Theodore Besterman (1966–1977) in *Complete works of Voltaire* (Institut et Musée Voltaire. Geneva; University of Toronto Press, then Voltaire Foundation at the Taylor Institution, Oxford), 85[1], xv.

the police of Napoleon III, Hugo would entrust them to personal messengers returning to the continent or send them to friends in Brussels who then posted them on to Paris. Letters arrived for him under an assumed name, at an agreed address where they then had to be collected. Although at times Hugo did reply to letters by return, during the frequent periods of intense creative activity he answered his correspondence only once a week, on Sundays. A chronological presentation based upon the date or postmark would therefore mean intercalating between a letter and its reply all the other letters and brief notes received in the interval. A solution such as this would annihilate the dialogue. The resulting fragmentation would render any coherent reading extremely difficult, if not impossible.

The concern for readability was one of the main reasons put forward for the presentation adopted by the editor of Horace Walpole's correspondence, Wilmarth S. Lewis. He rejected a strict chronological arrangement in favor of a series of separate dialogues between Walpole and a single correspondent, stating: "Walpole's letters gain greatly in interest by being restored to his correspondent's. They can now be read for the first time, as they were written and answered, with 'ease and opportunity,' in Stevenson's phrase."[29] For W. S. Lewis even fifteen letters during the course of one month, arranged chronologically become "a maze of unrelated subjects."[30] Both of these editions possess excellent indexes permitting numerous cross-references that allow for other readings.

No two collections of letters are alike, and the heterogeneity of Victor Hugo's interlocutors, the extreme brevity of some of the exchanges, are only the first features that distinguish his correspondence from those of eighteenth-century writers. Nevertheless its publication in the form of a series of separate exchanges permits, firstly, a readable presentation of extended dialogues. When Hugo enters into an epistolary discussion with one or even several people or is in more or less continuous correspondence with someone over a period of years, only the separate presentation of the exchanges allows the reader to follow, without encumbrance, their development and evolution. But, one may ask, is it at all possible in this format, to translate the very diversity and profusion that also characterize Hugo's relations? This aspect of his public life should also be discernible, even though the material difficul-

29. *The Yale edition of Horace Walpole's correspondence*, 48 vols. (New Haven: Yale University Press, 1939–1983), 1, xxxv.
30. Ibid.

ties are enormous. The essential question is how to reconcile the inherent dichotomy: at the same time to preserve the diversity of the correspondence without sacrificing readability along with the dialogue.

Bernard Leuilliot's *Victor Hugo publie "Les Misérables"* (1970)[31] made it possible for the first time to circumscribe the problem and envisage a solution. For although subtitled "Correspondance avec Albert Lacroix," this volume also contains letters exchanged by Hugo and Louis Verboeckhoven, the associate of Lacroix in Brussels. The transition from *duo* to *trio* did not, however, go far enough; other correspondents could have been integrated if Leuilliot's project had taken into consideration the Paris edition of Hugo's work.[32] The correspondence between Victor Hugo and another publisher, Pierre-Jules Hetzel, proved to be infinitely more complex. The first volume marked a development in polyphony and provided a key for future procedure. This may appear paradoxical for a correspondence that testifies to a collaboration and friendship commencing in 1852 and continuing, though not without ups and downs, until the death of Hugo in 1885. When he left Belgium for Jersey in the summer of 1852, the poet mandated Hetzel to take charge of his literary affairs in Brussels and Paris. Although Hetzel's name does not appear on the contracts, or in the books, he played a decisive but discreet role in the publication of the first two works Hugo wrote in exile, *Napoléon-le-petit* and *Châtiments*.[33] Consequently the author communicated not only with Hetzel, the principal coordinator of the undertaking, but also with the publishers and printers directly concerned with the making of the books. During the eighteen-month period of the printing of these works, and even though Hetzel was the director of operations, Hugo corresponded with ten other collaborators. A similar pattern has emerged with respect to *Les Contemplations* and *La Légende des Siècles*, both published simultaneously in Paris and in Brussels. The mass of letters to and from Hetzel appeared at first sufficiently homogeneous to constitute a comprehensible and readable dialogue. But their content, the frequent allusions to problems raised by other collaborators, Hugo's referral of them back to Hetzel, or his direct replies led to three- or even four-way exchanges on the same question. It

31. Paris: Klincksieck. The letters in this volume cover only the period of the revision and printing of *Les Misérables*, from August 1861 to July 1862.

32. The two editions were to appear simultaneously, but Hugo corrected only the proofs of the Brussels edition. In Paris the type was reset and the proofs corrected on the spot.

33. *Correspondance entre Victor Hugo et Pierre-Jules Hetzel I (1852–1853). Publication de "Napoléon-le-petit" et de "Châtiments,"* texte établi, présenté et annoté par Sheila Gaudon (Paris: Klincksieck, 1979), passim.

became imperative to include these other letters. From a single correspondent, envisaged at the outset, there emerged a group of people writing to Hugo on closely related matters. Correspondents were limited to those who were technically collaborators in the production, but within the framework of Hugo's collected letters other people who crossed the writer's path on this occasion—booksellers, would-be agents abroad, informants, clandestine distributors—would have a place. This expansion is not to be regretted; we have every interest in broadening as much as possible the range, within the bounds of relevance, in order to include documents that have no relevance elsewhere.

The above example illustrates what appears to be a characteristic feature of Hugo's mode of communication and is at the origin of our decision to base the series primarily on groups of correspondents rather than on a single interlocutor. From an early date the abundance of Hugo's creative activity, the rhythm of his output, and the consequent overlapping of a current work with the next project means that discussions rarely centered on one work alone and usually concerned more than one correspondent. Especially evident in the broad field of literature, this phenomenon is equally perceptible in other aspects of his epistolary relations. In the political arena, Hugo was in contact with individuals and groups episodically and over longer periods of time. His interventions in the Legislative Assembly from 1848 to 1851, his public protests on the issue of capital punishment, his support of independence movements in Greece, Italy, or Crete, his defense of Poland, or his opposition to Napoleon III brought him a constant flow of letters from home and abroad. These concerns varied at different times in his life with the urgency of the question under debate. They fall into broad areas, involving sometimes a single correspondent, sometimes a number of individuals who may or may not form a group. The discontinuity in style, tempo, and tone which ensues may be considered an advantage in terms of readability and will no doubt increase the interest of the series to be called "Political correspondence." Several series are envisaged: the poet's literary relationships, his work in the theater, political life, relations with publishers, and so forth. But the first that comes to mind is the family correspondence.

Comprising some three thousand documents, this is the largest and most important mass of autographs we possess, the members of this closely knit clan having rather systematically kept each other's letters. Not only does it span the whole of the poet's life, but it crosses over the boundaries of specific concerns revealing them in different perspectives. At certain periods it furnishes a day-by-day account of Hugo's private life, and altogether it establishes a solid biographical framework for the rest of the undertaking. We therefore decided to begin by Hugo's correspondence with his family. It was a denomination which at first sight appeared to pose few problems of content: exchanges between Hugo and his parents, wife, children, cousins, uncles, aunts, and so on will indeed constitute the main body of material. Although one might, in principle, adhere strictly to the basic conception of correspondence with Victor Hugo, third-party exchanges were found to have, on occasion, considerable interest. Letters sent to each other by Hugo's parents reveal episodes in the poet's childhood and adolescence that were to be of great consequence in his adult life. Similarly, some of the correspondence between Madame Victor Hugo and her sons or between François-Victor Hugo and his sister Adèle, during the latter's flight to Halifax and the Barbardoes, illuminates the life and works of the exile of Guernsey. Documents such as these have their place in the correspondence of a family group, even though they are not addressed to the head of the household.

Alongside the family, the two men who came closest to intimate friendship with Victor Hugo, Auguste Vacquerie and Paul Meurice, had a special status setting them apart from other correspondents. After the death, in 1843, of Léopoldine Hugo and her husband, Auguste Vacquerie was gradually to be seen as "one of the family." Writing to a colleague a few years after the tragic accident at Villequier, Hugo expressed a sentiment that was never belied: "Monsieur Vacquerie, whose brother died so nobly and whose death was so painful for us, has become for me as one of my children." Both Vacquerie and Meurice enjoyed the dubious privilege of sharing with Charles and François-Victor Hugo, in the autumn of 1851, their first experience of Louis-Bonaparte's repression, becoming, through their participation in the newspaper *L'Evénement*, members of Hugo's political family. From 1852 until 1859 Vacquerie lived with the Hugo household in Jersey and in Guernsey and later acted as an essential link when Mme Hugo and her sons returned to take up more or less permanent residence on the mainland. His affectionate relationship with all members of the family and his participation in their daily life makes his correspondence assimilable to that of the other children. His letters complement many other exchanges and provide yet another point of view on contemporary events. They will be grouped with the family correspondence.

While Vacquerie shuttled back and forth to Belgium and France, Paul Meurice, in Paris, was Hugo's devoted factotum, his intendant, not only responsible for administering the family's finances and managing the author's literary affairs, but also a generous collaborator in the actual publication of the works he so ardently admired. He was Hugo's representative in all manner of business and remained so to the last. He was the intermediary with publishers, theater directors, musicians, critics, journalists, creditors, and bankers. But he was never, perhaps because he did not take his daily bread with the illustrious exile or play billiards with Charles and François-Victor, on the same intimate footing as Auguste Vacquerie. The duration and importance of the exchanges between Hugo and Paul Meurice demand that this correspondence not be dispersed. It stands apart as a testimony to a unique relationship in the life of a man who maintained cordial but not intimate relations with his fellows. This dialogue will be published separately.

On the specific level of textual editing, the grouping of letters as defined above alleviates one of the first tasks awaiting the editor: the identification of correspondents. Although the majority are civilly and socially identifiable through the use of the excellent research tools available, there remain those ephemeral writers who do not weigh heavy on the social scale and whose precise identity, even if it is to be found in parish registers, would enlighten us little more than the content of their letters. Such are the convicts, beggars, solicitors of all sorts, the legion of obscure admirers, male and female. Hugo's replies may stand small chance of having survived, but the letters are nonetheless informative documents and their pertinence within the envisaged series is, in the balance, of greater import than the discovery of a certificate of birth, marriage, or death.

As many of his contemporaries, Hugo rarely dated informal letters. On some he may have noted only the day, on others he may have omitted the year. Techniques of dating are common to all editors of nineteenth-century letters and hardly need be discussed here: from almanachs and perpetual calendars to the scrutiny of faint postmarks, when they exist, the resources are well-known. Changes in the form of French postal obliteration, albeit relatively infrequent, the tardy introduction to general use of the separate envelope (letters, folded, were addressed on the last page, thus ensuring the survival of a first element of information), are useful guides for narrowing down date limits. In the case of Hugo himself a study of the paper and the characteristic evolution of the handwriting also contribute to circumscribing a broad time period. Exact dates however are more usually reached from internal evidence—allusions within the letters also verifiable from other sources—and from confrontation with other correspondence. A particularly probatory example are the letters handed secretly to Victor Hugo by his fiancée between 1819 and 1822. When Hugo himself did not inscribe on them the date they were received, the absence of postmark, name, and address means that the chronology can only be restablished by studying their content and confronting it with Hugo's replies. Need it be pointed out that this basic editorial task is facilitated and the annotation reduced when letters and responses coexist?

The major textual decision confronting the editors is that of diplomatic transcription. Should letters for which we have an autograph manuscript be reproduced as they were written, preserving all of the writer's irregularities or excentricities in what W. W. Greg, in an important article on "The Rationale of copy-text,"[34] has qualified as accidentals—punctuation, capitalization, and spelling—or should they be normalized to conform to modern typographical conventions? The theoretical discussions that have fed into scholarly journals for many years on this side of the Atlantic regarding Greg's hierarchical distinction between substantives—the actual wording of the text—and accidentals, a hierarchy that has been vigorously called into question in its application beyond a limited category of texts within a limited time period,[35] have found no echo in Europe,[36] but in the actual practice of textual editing there is often a tacit adherence to these principles. It is not, however, for scholarly reasons that in many cases punctuation and spelling are modernized, not because timorous publishers, seeking wider readership and easier proof-correction, impose their conventions on editors. Although French orthography is now relatively stable, the use of punctuation fluctuates in no small degree. In view of widespread levelling trends it is perhaps not irrelevant to reiterate here, at the risk of stating the obvious, the importance of punctuation both to determine meaning and as the written sign of "juncture, pitch, and stress" of the spoken language,[37] in short, its integral appurtenance to the style of the writer.

With respect to Victor Hugo's correspondence four aspects of the thorny and perhaps insoluble problem of punctuation and spelling in-

34. In *Studies in Bibliography*, 3 (1950–1951), 19–36.

35. In particular by Morse Peckham, "Reflections on the Foundation of modern Textual editing," *Proof*, 1 (1971), 122–26.

36. Fredson Bowers notes that "Greg's position has been substantially accepted in the U.S. and in England, although not on the continent" ("Current theories of copy-text," in *Essays in Bibliography, text, and editing* [Charlottesville: University of Virginia Press, 1975], 279).

37. Peckham, 124.

vite discussion. When collating letters of Hugo published in the *IN* edition of his complete works, we have frequently restored punctuation which appears to have been "normalized" and which does not always correspond to that of the autographs. The humble comma is the first object to strike the conscience of zealous copy editors, and this is not a development of the twentieth century. Hugo's letters contain numerous complaints about printers who bespeckled his texts with commas. The following especially colorful protest expresses his indignation about the Belgian edition of *La Légende des Siècles:* "As for the Belgian edition . . . it has one defect. Here it is: in certain climatic periods locusts invade Egypt and commas invade punctuation. Belgian printing is particularly hit by this scourge. Under this excess of commas the carefully worked out subordinate clause becomes the parasite of the sentence, and all the breadth of the line, all amplitude of style disappears. My proofs arrived tatooed with this vermin. I was obliged to delouse them several times."[38] On the other hand, as Bernard Leuilliot has pointed out, Hugo complained that the proof correctors of *Les Misérables* removed commas whenever they preceded the conjunction *and.* "The comma, Hugo insists, should often be placed before a conjunction: it depends upon the meaning. Follow scrupulously my punctuation."[39] For Leuilliot the study of Hugo's punctuation shows the skill of a writer who knows his craft and who punctuates with "concerted precision."[40]

What is true of literary works is equally valid in letters. Commas, semi-colons, full stops are used with the utmost care. The absence of capitalization—a customary practice of Hugo and most of his contemporaries—may sometimes cause us to hesitate, but our hesitations are infrequent. We strive to reproduce accurately the author's punctuation, reinstating only the capital letters at the beginning of sentences. We also respect the paragraphs of a writer who constantly refused to make changes, saying "I cannot add a paragraph. . . . Paragraphs are chapters,"[41] or "You must not suppress my new paragraphs . . . nor add any more,"[42] and threatened to demand another set of proofs if his instructions were not carried out.

The letters of Hugo's correspondents cover perhaps the whole range of skill and concern about punctuation. Here, as in other textual mat-

38. Letter to P.-J. Hetzel, 20 September (1859), in *M* 10, 1322.
39. Note in Hugo's general instructions to the printers of *Les Misérables,* cited by Leuilliot, 80.
40. Leuilliot, 82.
41. From an unpublished letter to Noël Parfait, 19 July 1855 (Private collection).
42. Note to Albert Lacroix, 5 February 1862, in Leuilliot, 152.

ters, a sustained exchange may allow us to note a pattern corresponding to a style. Hetzel, for example, very often replaced the full stop by a dash, but the lack of capitals makes it difficult to decide a priori whether the dash has the value of a full stop, comma, or semi-colon. His special mode of punctuation has been preserved, capital letters being reinstated where the substantive reading of the text appeared to warrant it. The frequent use of brief paragraphs is yet another characteristic of his style. Along with his extremely cursive handwriting, it reflects a haste usually confirmed by the content of the letter. On the other hand no pattern is discernible in the letters of the future Mme Victor Hugo, whose rare punctuation, somewhat whimsical at the best of times, tends, with the exception of the full stop, to disappear when she writes under the stress of a strong emotion. In any case, as typographical conventions impose capitalization, this inroad on the rigorous diplomatic reproduction is inevitable.

Orthographic particularities fall into three categories: *lapsus calami*, "personal" orthography, current usage. We all have our lapses, and who has never forgotten an *s* at the end of a plural noun? When this is not habitual to the writer, it may be generally assumed that it is a *lapsus calami*. But when Victor Hugo insists that *poète* be printed *poëte*, prefers *lys* to *lis* [lily], and when he writes *bleuet* [cornflower], refusing to admit the spelling *bluet* of the sixth edition of the *Dictionnaire de l'Académie* of 1835, his choice is a personal one which he justifies: "*Bleuet* comes from *bleu*. Take no account of the stupid spelling of dictionaries which are all made by asses."[43] He had already insisted on retaining this spelling in *Les Contemplations:* "The word *bleuet* is pretty only because it contains *bleu*."[44] It is appropriate to respect a decision of this kind, imposed by the poet himself: "I have to a certain degree my spelling and my punctuation. Every writer has, beginning with Voltaire. The intelligence of the printer consists in respecting the spelling *which forms part of the writer's style*."[45] Unfortunately the distinction between *lapsus calami* and personal orthography is not always so clear. In the case of Hugo himself, what one might call spelling mistakes are not frequent enough to be pertinent, and correcting them would be neither a gain nor a loss. No doubt that being a conscientious craftsman he would have made the corrections as he read over his proofs. We have therefore always added missing accents, for Hugo, writ-

43. Note accompanying corrected proofs of *Les Misérables*, 12 February 1862, ibid., 165.
44. To Noël Parfait, 19 July 1855.
45. Letter to Paul Meurice, in *M* 10, 1308. The italics are mine.

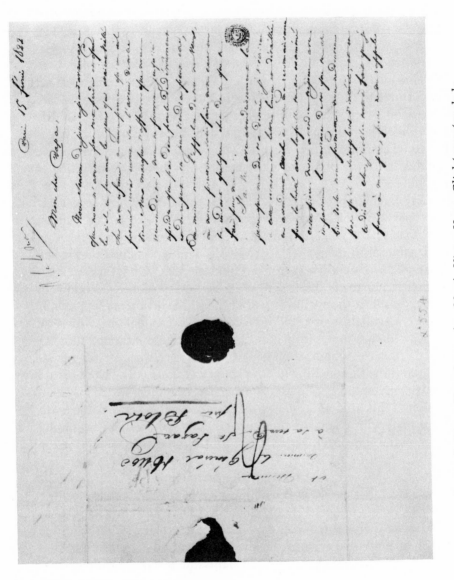

Lettre de Victor Hugo à son père. Musée Victor Hugo. Cliché musées de la Ville de Paris.

ing correctly but cursively, was exceedingly economical with accents both in his manuscripts and letters.

The orthographical variations and syntactical aberrations in letters of correspondents are numerous and usually pertinent. They reflect a level of education and are important indications of social stratification and a potential contribution to a history of literacy. Within the framework of a correspondence that mirrors a century it would be inconceivable to obliterate these signs. The letters of Adèle Foucher are among the first elements of this correspondence recording the relatively sound education of the daughter of a middle rank civil servant during the Napoleonic era and early Restoration. Her grammatical errors are not numerous enough to impair seriously the comprehension of her letters, as the following extract, in its diplomatic transcription, shows:

> *C'est la dernière fois qu'une lettre aussi longue suivra une si courte* cela s'appele parler en maitre tu crois que quand je ne t'écris que peu c'est de ma faute et je puis t'assurer que tous le momens que je peux te consacrer je les recherche avec le plus grand empressement. je n'ai pas certainement à ma possibilité seulement un quart d'heure par jour, mais toi, Victor, ne devrais tu pas m'en écrire encore plus long et cependant je ne me plains pas. tu dois m'en écrire au moins trois pages contre moi une. mais ne parlons plus de cela car tu dois être persuadé du bonheur que j'éprouve à t'écrire.[46]

The improvement in spelling and syntactical accuracy between this and later letters written after years by her husband's side, reading and copying his manuscripts, is striking. Likewise Hugo's sons and daughters came to express themselves well in their native language, writing with increasing correctness and elegance. It is perhaps not uninteresting to follow their progress.

These historical and sociological considerations naturally lead to the question of the evolution of usage. The replacement of *tems* by *temps* or *événemens* by *événements*, the disappearance of the circumflex accent on *vîte* or *remercîmens*, with a transitional period when the two spellings exist indeterminately, has exactly the same interest as the change in measures of distance from the league to the kilometer or in the monetary system from the pound to the franc. There is no reason to deprive the reader and the historian of language of this type of information. In short the adoption of a diplomatic reproduction, tempered by

46. Unpublished letter, Bibliothèque Nationale, Mss., nouvelles acquisitions françaises 13414, fo. 223.

only minimal typographical exigencies, is a necessity in a correspondence, especially when it is based on dialogue.

Long frequentation of the considerable body of material that constitutes Victor Hugo's correspondence has strengthened our belief in the value of the undertaking. When brought to completion it will be an indispensable instrument of research for all scholars of the nineteenth century.

We are, however, convinced of the wisdom of the remarks made by Jean Pommier in his opening address at the symposium on the editing of letters held in Paris in April 1968: "the heterogenity of the material makes it impossible to dictate general rules or establish norms that would be appropriate for all editions."[47] We have not sought originality at all costs, but we realized at an early stage that a search for new solutions was a requisite for the advancement of the project and, indeed, that its very existence depended on them. We are aware that no solution is perfect and that the method we have adopted can only be effective if it is constantly moderated by a pragmatic approach. Once the principle of grouping within series is adopted, maximum flexibility must be maintained. All combinations should be possible, from correspondence with one individual to exchanges with much larger groups, allowing thus for the inclusion of isolated letters which otherwise could not be integrated. Some decisions will no doubt be considered arbitrary, and we are quite happy to accept this reproach. Arbitrariness ceases to be an objection when it is counterbalanced by a system of indexes and cross-references that invite each reader to circulate as he chooses within and between the volumes, thus imposing his own arbitrary reading on the whole.

If I have invoked the reader in concluding, it is because we hope that Victor Hugo's correspondence will not only be a work of reference consulted in libraries but that, being readable, it will be read. In an age when the public is avid for memoirs, for the correspondence of convicts, military men, explorers, great artists, or the working man, it would be surprising if the fabulous trajectory of a writer who fascinated and occupied a whole century left the reader indifferent.

47. *Les Editions de Correspondances.* Publications de la Société d'Histoire littéraire de la France (Paris: Armand Colin, 1969), 6.

PHILIP KOLB

Proust's Letters

Flaubert once remarked caustically that people were ecstatic about Voltaire's correspondence, "but," he added, "he never was capable of anything else than *that*, poor man!"[1] The general attitude toward Proust is exactly the opposite. People seldom elicit raptures about his correspondence, but not even his most carping critics fail to recognize his immense capabilities. It is precisely because of that profusion of gifts as a novelist, ranking Proust today among the great masters of world fiction, that his correspondence does perhaps suffer by comparison.

The fact remains, however, that Proust's letters constitute an important segment of his writing. So it may be worth considering what lends them such interest and why that interest appears to have accrued over the years to a degree that has indeed surprised some critics. His correspondence belongs in a special category and is, in a sense, unique, because Proust is one of those writers who kept no diary, who wrote no memoirs. Not only that, but he took considerable care to dilute the autobiographical elements of his great novel. They are indeed so tenuous that any who scan *Remembrance of Things Past* in search of an image of its author are risking self-delusion. In consequence Proust's letters represent the only authentic record we have of his inner self and of his earthly existence. We find in them the day-to-day record of his activities, his feelings, his opinions on every conceivable subject, his methods and practices in composing his works—in short, what constitutes his life and his personality.

That being so, one may wonder why interest in Proust's correspon-

1. *Oeuvres complètes de Gustave Flaubert. Correspondance Deuxième série (1850–1854)* (Paris: Louis Conard, 1910), 348, letter to Louise Colet, Trouville, août 1853, *Vendredi soir, 11 heures*. The translation is mine.

One of Proust's last letters, to Gaston Gallimard. With the kind permission of the Beinecke Rare Book and Manuscript Library, Yale University, the Proust family, and the Librairie Plon.

dence has varied so greatly over the years. As we shall see, that interest goes back to the time of the author's death, and its evolution is due in large part to three factors, having to do with Proust's purpose in writing his letters, the fact that he seldom bothered to date them, and the manner in which the early editions presented them.

Proust wrote vast numbers of letters, and his purpose in writing most of them was simply to convey the many thoughts that crowded into his powerful brain to the innumerable people with whom he wanted to keep in contact. He was perfectly capable of writing the sort of "anthology" letter that Voltaire loved to write in order to impress people. We have plenty of examples of such letters in Proust's correspondence. But for the most part he simply wrote to communicate his thoughts of the moment. Perhaps that is one reason that he did not attach enough importance to them to trouble to date them. We shall return to this last question in speaking of the early editions.

The story of how Proust's letters came to be published is a curious one. It appears that he himself was opposed to the idea of their ever being published. At one time, at least, he expressed such an opposition in forthright terms. In a letter written to Madame de Clermont-Tonnerre he asks her to destroy a previous letter and adds: "I want absolutely (I'll tell the reasons publicly at the beginning of *Swann*) none of my correspondence to be preserved, still less published."[2] One may wonder why he expressed himself so forcibly on this matter and, having done so, why his wishes in that respect appear to have been disregarded. In Céleste Albaret's memoirs she speaks of the many letters Proust used to write and claims that, late in life, he began to worry that he had written too many of them and to express his regret at having done so. She recalls his announcing an intention to take precautions against their publication. Apparently he consulted two friends on the matter, Henry Bernstein, the playwright, and Horace Finaly, a banker. According to Céleste, their attitude gave Proust no comfort. Then he went to see his attorney. According to her the attorney replied that it would be of no use for Proust to forbid such a publication, stating: "Any letter from you that is in the hands of the addressee is that person's property. He (or she) can do with it what he or she wishes."[3] As for Proust's opposition to such a

---

2. Mme de Clermont-Tonnerre, when she published a fragment of the letter we quote, took care to suppress that portion of the letter. See *Robert de Montesquiou et Marcel Proust* (Paris: 1925), 234. My dating is: *3 January 1921*. The letter has not yet been published.

3. Céleste Albaret, *Monsieur Proust. Souvenirs recueillis par Georges Belmont* (Paris: Editions Robert Laffont, 1973), 245–46. My translation.

publication, Céleste's memory is corroborated by the letter we quoted to Mme de Clermont-Tonnerre, of which Céleste presumably had no knowledge. It is also true that Proust had no right to reclaim any of the letters he had written to other persons, because, in the eyes of the law, such letters were the property of the recipient. But on another point Céleste's memory has been less faithful. Certainly no attorney-at-law would have told Proust that the recipient of a letter was free to do with it as he pleased, because that would have contradicted French law and constituted misinformation. The recipient of a letter is the owner of that letter only as a physical entity, that is, the paper and the ink. Its text remains the property of the author. It is hardly surprising that Céleste's memory, remarkable as it is, has become clouded on that point after so many years.

Nevertheless since we know that Proust was, at least at the time we indicate, opposed to the publication of his correspondence, one wonders why he took no effective measures to have his wishes respected. He had three possible courses of action. First, he could have indicated his wishes on the matter in his last will and testament. Another way would have been to notify his publishers, as he apparently intended doing when he wrote the letter to Mme de Clermont-Tonnerre. Or finally, he might simply have told his brother what his wishes were on this question. There appears to be no evidence that he took action in any of these ways. We know that his brother came to see him shortly after he wrote the letter we quoted. And we know that Proust had some twenty months yet to live, so he had plenty of time to make his wishes known on this matter. But we also know his temperamental disinclination to make decisions. He evidently decided against the idea expressed in that letter to make a public statement at the beginning of *Du côté de chez Swann*. Gallimard would have pointed out that such a statement was not customary and that his novel had little to do with his correspondence. Yet it is difficult to believe that he never discussed the question with his brother. He died on 18 November 1922. On 1 January 1923 a special number of hommage to Proust's memory was published in the *Nouvelle Revue Française*. Jacques Rivière, who was responsible for that publication, would assuredly not have included the several Proust letters that appear in that number without the express authorization of Robert Proust. It does indeed appear as if the latter had already decided to honor his brother's memory by the publication of his correspondence. What lends support to such a supposition is the fact that, shortly afterward, Robert Proust acquired at auction some 260 of Marcel Proust's letters addressed to Robert de Montesquiou. We shall examine presently the motives he may have had in making such an acquisition.

The first decade after Proust's death, it should be noted, saw the publication of a very considerable number of his letters. They were to come out in newspapers, periodicals, and books.[4] The first of the books, strange to say, was to be published by the very person to whom Proust had written to state his opposition, in no uncertain terms, to any such public dissemination of his letters. That was the volume entitled *Robert de Montesquiou et Marcel Proust*, by Elisabeth duchesse de Clermont-Tonnerre. It came out in 1925. I can find no evidence that Robert Proust ever indicated his opposition to that or any of the similar publications that came out subsequently. On the contrary, we have Robert Dreyfus's word testifying to the fact that it was Robert Proust who had persuaded him to publish the letters he had received from Marcel Proust.[5] He published some of them in a booklet entitled *Marcel Proust à dix-sept ans*, and almost immediately afterward he gave the bulk of his collection of Proust letters in a volume under the title *Souvenirs sur Marcel Proust* (1926). Another important publication was Louis de Robert's *Comment débuta Marcel Proust: lettres inédites* (1925). More letters were published at about the same time in *Le Salon de Madame de Caillavet*, a booklet containing Proust's letters to Camille Vettard, and a selection of the letters to Robert de Montesquiou included in a sort of hommage volume published anonymously under the title *Marcel Proust*, all issued in 1926. This last volume must have had Robert Proust's consent since it contained some of the letters he had recently acquired, as we have said, at auction. In 1928 Princesse Marthe Bibesco brought out her *Au bal avec Marcel Proust*, which was to be reissued in a number of subsequent editions. That same year, Léon Pierre-Quint gave his *Comment travaillait Marcel Proust*. Lucien Daudet published his *Autour de soixante lettres de Marcel Proust* in 1929. The following year saw the publication of Robert de Billy's *Marcel Proust: lettres et conversations*, and Pierre-Quint's *Comment parut Du côté de chez Swann*.

An explanation for these numerous publications of Proust letters

4. See my bibliography of the correspondence in *La Correspondance de Marcel Proust: chronologie et commentaire critique* (Urbana: The University of Illinois Press, 1949), 325–29. See also Douglas W. Alden, *Marcel Proust and his French Critics* (New York: Russell & Russell, 1973), 171–259.

5. Robert Dreyfus, *Souvenirs sur Marcel Proust avec des lettres inédites de Marcel Proust* (Paris: Bernard Grasset, 1926), 143–44.

seems to come from Robert Proust, who, in 1930, gave expression to his views on the subject in his preface to the first volume of the *Correspondance générale*. There he tells how, after several vain attempts, he had been faced with the impossibility of obtaining possession of the originals of all of his brother's autograph letters. Since they were being dispersed widely at auction and were already circulating freely, he had decided that it would be preferable to assemble as many as possible and make them available to Proust's true friends, the readers of his works, through their publication in an edition of *Correspondance générale*.[6] It appears, therefore, that Robert Proust had not disregarded his brother's wishes on the matter, but had given his consent to the publication of the letters only because their wide dispersal had made it impossible to suppress them.

Proust himself seems to have failed to foresee such a situation. In any event, his attitude toward the matter was anything but consistent. If he opposed the publication of his own letters, as we have seen, we have his word for the fact that he expressly condemned any suppression of the letters of other men of distinction. He felt that such letters belong to the common heritage of mankind and that private collections ought to be placed at the disposition of the public. On that question, he asks, disapprovingly: "What would one say of a gentleman who kept for himself, as autograph letters, Voltaire's or Emerson's correspondence?"[7] Apparently he did not subscribe to the dictum that "what is good for the goose is good for the gander." He wanted to keep his own letters to himself, but he was indignant at the idea that anyone else might sequester the letters of Voltaire or Emerson. He denied the critic's right to examine the writer's private life. But Proust himself, as we know, was extremely curious about the private lives of other creative artists. We have abundant evidence of that attitude in his correspondence.[8]

This brings us to the question of the early editions. When Robert Proust embarked upon the enterprise of publishing his brother's correspondence, he was, so to speak, setting sail on what for him were uncharted seas. He had chosen, as we know, to follow his father's example

6. *Correspondance générale de Marcel Proust publiée par Robert Proust et Paul Brach. 1. Lettres à Robert de Montesquiou 1893–1921* (Paris: Librairie Plon, 1930), ii. Robert Proust's purchase of Proust's letters to Montesquiou is confirmed by Céleste Albaret in *Monsieur Proust*, 310.

7. Marcel Proust, *Correspondance générale de Marcel Proust publiée par Robert Proust et Paul Brach*, 5 (1935), 64, letter dated *10 juillet 1919*, addressed to Walter Berry.

8. See Marcel Proust, *Correspondance: Texte établi, présenté et annoté par Philip Kolb. Tome 1: 1880–1895* (Paris: Plon, 1970), 9–13.

by entering the medical profession. He had published his thesis and some medical treatises but had never ventured, until then, beyond the realm of his own field of surgery.[9] It would be unfair to imply that his manner of operating on his brother's letters was a slaughter. Nevertheless if his purpose in publishing them was to enhance Marcel Proust's reputation, he went far beyond his depth. His method of procedure was simply to gather together, along with the letters he had purchased at auction, whatever others his brother's correspondents were willing to contribute, without concerning himself about the manner in which they were supplied. He had a typist make copies of all of those letters; then he deleted any passages that he deemed to be unflattering to his brother or to other persons, and also deleted names of many of the persons mentioned in the letters. If the text happened to be garbled, that did not seem to matter. There were other problems, to which we shall return presently. That seems to be the way he managed to produce the five volumes issued before his death in 1935. They met with little public favor.

That first volume of Robert Proust's *Correspondance générale* seems to have doused cold water on his entire enterprise. The reasons can readily be surmised. That volume set an unfortunate tone. The 252 letters to Robert de Montesquiou were presented in almost total disarray, with only an occasional explanatory note. The tone of the early letters is obsequious. There are so many unexplained allusions in those letters that they are largely incomprehensible. The second volume contained fifty letters to the poetess Anna de Noailles. Those letters all contain Proust's style of excessive flattery, but in this case they have a graceful bantering tone that has its charm. The fact is, Mme de Noailles's letters to Proust contain that same sort of flattery. But here Mme de Noailles's letters are presented out of context. They met with not much more favor than the ones to Montesquiou.

The principal reason for the failure of Robert Proust's edition, however, lies elsewhere. He had been unable to deal with one major difficulty. That was the fact that his brother had never dated his letters. Save for an occasional day of the week, most of them are undated. In the early editions the only letters that bear dates are those for which a postmarked envelope has been preserved. But there is no assurance that the envelope and the letter were posted at the same time. In consequence, few of the letters are presented in their proper sequence. Most are undated, or partially dated, a considerable number misdated. The

9. *Titres et travaux scientifiques du docteur Robert Proust* (Paris: 1932), 239–[250].

texts, as we have said, are not always complete nor exactly transcribed. A number of additional volumes of Proust letters were published separately, but in the same haphazard manner as the *Correspondance générale*. Many other letters appeared in periodicals or newspapers and were, in consequence, available only to those who could consult them in the Bibliothèque Nationale in Paris or similar places. To take one characteristic example, for instance, the letters to Maurice Duplay were published in *La Revue nouvelle*, a periodical. In those letters Proust quotes numerous passages from Duplay's novels. Despite that fact, the texts are badly garbled, and the few datings indicated are unreliable. In a volume of *Lettres à Madame C.*, we find erroneous dates indicated for more than one in three of the letters presented.

Such was the chaotic state in which Proust's correspondence had been published when I began work on it. My purpose was to try to bring order to the available correspondence. I was at work on my dissertation in Paris when Proust's niece, Madame Gérard Mante, asked me to assist her in preparing Proust's letters to Monsieur and Madame Emile Straus. I dated all of the letters in that collection, which was published as volume 6 of the *Correspondance générale* in 1936.[10] For my Ph.D. dissertation (Harvard, 1938) I confined myself to the study of the published correspondence. After the hiatus of the second World War, I gathered together the results of my dissertation, along with my work on subsequently published letters, in a volume intended to be useful for future Proust studies. It was published by the University of Illinois Press in 1949, under the title *La Correspondance de Marcel Proust: Chronologie et Commentaire Critique*. In it I gave the justification for my datings of Proust's letters and a critical commentary of the letters, discussing any problems they presented. The study dealt with approximately 1,450 letters. Included in the volume are a bibliography of all correspondence published before 1949, a general index listing, in alphabetical order, all references in the letters to persons, places, titles of works of art, music, books, etc., a chronological index listing all dated letters, a list of Proust's correspondents, and an index of the letters in the principal collections.

The publication of that volume led to an invitation by Proust's niece and the Librairie Plon of Paris, publishers, to undertake an edition of all available correspondence of Marcel Proust, to be presented in chronological order, with full annotations, introductory material, chro-

10. The datings I ascribed to some of those letters in 1936 are at variance with those I indicate in my current edition.

nology, and indices. Such an edition is at present in progress. The Librairie Plon published volume 12, containing the letters for the year 1913, in 1984.

As a rule, Proust's letters require precise dating and ample background information in order to be fully comprehensible and useful for scholarly investigation. Elsewhere I have given an example showing why the dating of the letters is indispensable for their proper evaluation, and how scholars have been misled into false hypotheses on important points when they were unable to date a text accurately.[11] One further example should suffice on this question. It concerns a letter that Proust wrote to berate a young friend who had failed to meet him at an appointed hour at the seashore after having agreed to do so. The letter has a considerable interest, because Proust, in venting his spleen, uses certains expressions and imagery which he will use again in his novel. The words are precisely the ones Swann will use to scold Odette one evening when she refuses to stay with him and goes off to see a vaudeville with the Verdurins. That letter was first published by Bernard de Fallois, who ascribed no precise dating for it did and did not identify the person to whom Proust was writing, except to indicate that it was a young man eighteen years of age. He does state, however, that it is "probably the only love letter Proust has left us," a claim that is indeed wide of the mark.[12] In point of fact, the letter simply expresses Proust's extreme annoyance at what he thinks is the young man's lack of respect for his elders and a lack of appreciation for Proust's kindness toward him. When we know exactly when he wrote the letter, and under what circumstances, it becomes perfectly clear and understandable. The circumstances are indeed even dramatic. On that particular evening Proust was invited to the annual dinner of the Golf Club of Cabourg. When young Nahmias failed to appear at the appointed meeting, Proust was displeased. He went back to the hotel and began his letter. He interrupted it to go to dinner, then later he finished it. The tragicomic aspect of the incident is the fact that the young man was innocent of any intention to be discourteous toward Proust. He had gone to Deauville for the afternoon and no doubt was hurrying to return to Cabourg for his meeting with him when his automobile ran over a little girl. Proust knew nothing of the accident; he did not learn about it until the following day, possibly because the young man's family may have tried to

11. See my introduction to the first volume of my edition of the correspondence, *Avant-propos*, 21–23. (See note 8 above.)

12. See Marcel Proust, *Correspondance*, 11, letter 102. See also my introduction to the volume.

suppress the news. In any case, the letter is anything but a "love letter."
And Bernard de Fallois did not notice that the wording of the letter was
to recur in a passage of *Un amour de Swann.*

The reader can judge for himself. Here is the text of the letter, in my
translation, with my dating and other clarifications of it:

[Cabourg, Tuesday evening 20 August 1912][13]

Dear Friend,

Despite my fatigue and my haste to be ready for a dinner that I
have to attend this evening,[14] I want to write you this so that, if you
hear I'm inviting some young people from Cabourg and elsewhere, you
will not suppose, before I explain, that the fact of my not inviting you
is a petty proof of resentment, as unworthy of you, I dare say, as of me.

You know that a small incident, insignificant as it may be, can
often, when it provokes supersaturation of an invisible but overbur-
dened state, assume great importance. I wasn't well yesterday, but as
you had agreed to meet me between six and seven on the pier, and as I
thought you might have hastened your return from Deauville on that
account, dead or alive I'd have been there.[15] And besides, having
learned that some attractive young persons from Houlgate were in
Cabourg, I used all my wiles to keep them here for your entertain-
ment.

Naturally you didn't come, you didn't take the trouble to let me
know, nor even inform me whether Helleu had left (it's of no importance, for I sent Nicolas to Trouville and he spoke with him about it).

While dining in the Casino restaurant afterward, then in the Music Hall, I was thinking sad thoughts whose melancholy enumeration
I spare you.[16] My dear Albert,[17] you must pardon me. I have been
spoiled by friends who were older than I. I have seen Alphonse Daudet
at the height of his fame and of his sufferings, who could no longer
write a line without tears for the pain it caused his whole body, writing

13. The text of the letter, first published in *Le Disque vert,* special number of *Hommage à Marcel Proust,* December 1952, is presented by Bernard de Fallois. He gives an
inexact dating for it, and does not identify the addressee, suppressing his first name. I
indicate in my annotations the evidence that the letter was addressed to Albert Nahmias,
Jr. My dating is based on references to "a dinner that I have to attend this evening" (note
14) and the reasons for Nahmias's missing his appointment with Proust (note 15).

14. Proust was invited to a dinner preceding a dance given on 20 August 1912 by the
Golf Club of Cabourg, presided over by his friend the Vicomte d'Alton.

15. Nahmias was prevented from coming to meet Proust at the appointed time by
an automobile accident in which he ran over a girl on the road from Deauville to
Cabourg. The accident occurred on the same day as the dance given by the Golf Club of
Cabourg.

16. Here Proust continues the letter, which he had interrupted to go to dinner.

17. The name is omitted in the published text. See notes 18 and 23.

twice to me at seven o'clock when I was having dinner at his house at eight, to find out whether some insignificant detail of the meal wouldn't give me more pleasure by sitting next to a friend. I have seen France put off an excursion to Versailles eight days in a row so I might be included, and each day sending word to me to find out if it wouldn't tire me . . . and I purposely only cite little things, and I could cite a thousand of them. I was well in those days; an outing, a meeting weren't what they are for me now. And when I see you, living as you do so close by,[18] having nothing to do, allow me in my haste not to take the time to explain what you understand quite well.

If my letter didn't have as its purpose to spare your feelings, in consideration of a deep and true friendship that I had for you, it has none. For I know that you are not perfectible. You aren't even made of stone, which can be sculpted if it is lucky enough to encounter a sculptor (and you could meet a greater one than I, but I would have done it with tender care), you are made of water, plain water, elusive, colorless, fluid, sempiternally inconsistent, flowing in as fast as out.[19] One watches you go by, if that amuses one, but you have no character.[20] I who have had a real affection for you, I can only feel like yawning, or weeping, or wanting to drown myself.

So excuse me for wanting to say good-bye forever to your shores. I guessed what your true nature was the day you said to me with such energy: "But I can't, on account of the Foucart party."[21] But one always wants to hope, one doesn't like to have made a mistake. And so nicely, too nicely, for the budding lilacs of those days were better than the foul odor of the stale lilacs of today, you have proved to me how different your character is.

And in fact that friendship (I'm speaking of my own) which I thought so fragile, I felt it had a rare solidity. You are one of the only ones I've seen this year. You can say that you've seen a wonderful possibility of a friendship pass you by, and you botched it.

18. Nahmias's parents had the Villa Berthe, not far from the Grand Hôtel de Cabourg.

19. "You see, your *Nuit de Cléopâtre* (what a title!) has no bearing on the point. What I must know is whether you are indeed one of those creatures in the lowest grade of mentality and even of charm, one of those contemptible creatures who are incapable of forgoing a pleasure. And if you are such, how could anyone love you, for you are not even a person, a clearly defined entity, imperfect but at least *perfectible. You are a formless water that will trickle down any slope that offers itself, a fish devoid of memory, incapable of thought, which all its life long in its aquarium will continue to dash itself a hundred times a day against the glass wall, always mistaking it for water.*" Marcel Proust, *Swann's Way. Translated by C. K. Scott Moncrieff and Terence Kilmartin* (New York: Random House, 1981), 316. Italics mine.

20. The transcription from the original appears dubious here.

21. Mr. and Mrs. Léon Foucart, and their son André, had given a party in their place at Cabourg.

Let me finish; I know that Mr. D. and Mr. V. are not any more than you down to 11.75,[22] but at least their company doesn't make me sad, because I never did believe in them. I had no illusions about them. And perhaps they are more harmonious than you, for, basically similar, they don't have that broken flight, that effort toward something better that they didn't attain, those inclinations that one could take for talent, etc. . . . If I were well, I would make up my mind to see my ex-friend. I hate to be a bore, and when you hypocritically take on your sad look, I am so unhappy that I yield at once. But I am the victim.

You aren't even capable of coming to the pier at seven o'clock! And I, for whom that represents so much fatigue etc., I'm the one who suffers. I am too tired to see a friend who even materially, by missing a meeting, etc., is a cause of nervous irritation and fatigue. I need friends who spare me such things, not one who gives me more of them.

My dear friend, have pity for my health, don't look for the decoy of a reconciliation that you aren't capable of maintaining even for a month. What you call your troubles are what you think are pleasures, a dance, a game of golf, etc. Some day I'll paint those characters that will never know, even from a vulgar standpoint, what it means to have the elegance, when one is ready to attend a dance, to give it up in order to stay with a friend.[23] They think they are society people, but they're just the opposite.

I don't have time to write another line, and I leave you for good. But I want to tell you in closing that I don't want you to think I say all this with a light heart; I had, I tell you so because I think it gives you pleasure and some pride, deep sorrow; and my heart is not one of those that without a bitter pang put in the past tense what (even often a simple object) was as you were the predilection of their present and the hope of their future. Send this letter back to me, and allow me to give you the handshake of a friend.

—Marcel.

22. Proust borrows a term in use among stock brokers. Young Nahmias worked for a broker.

23. Earlier in the scene quoted above from *Swann's Way*, Swann is distressed at the thought that Odette, "after living for more than six months in daily contact" with him, "hasn't yet reached the stage of understanding that there are evenings when anyone with the least delicacy of feeling should be willing to forgo a pleasure when asked to do so." There is a similar instance in *Guermantes' Way*, when the Duchesse de Guermantes, learning that Swann has only two or three months to live, hesitates a few moments before going off to dinner with the Duke.

Contributors

CHARLES A. PORTER, Professor of French and Director of Summer and Special Programs at Yale University, has written about Restif de la Bretonne and Chateaubriand and teaches courses on pre- and early Romanticism and the contemporary French novel.

JANET GURKIN ALTMAN, Associate Professor of French at the University of Iowa, is the author of *Epistolarity: Approaches to a Form* (1982) and two forthcoming books on Jean Cocteau, as well as articles on Proust, Balzac, Mme de Graffigny and epistolary and diary fiction.

MIREILLE BOSSIS is a research scholar in French literature at the University of Nantes and is finishing her thesis on the Novels of George Sand. She has written several articles concerning Sand and participated in a number of colloquia, including several that have considered Correspondences.

KAREN MCPHERSON is a graduate student in the French Department at Yale University. She is currently completing her doctoral dissertation "Criminal Passions: Guilty Women in Four Twentieth-Century Novels," a "criminal investigation" of works by Beauvoir, Duras, Woolf, and Hébert.

MARIE-CLAIRE GRASSI completed last year her *doctorat d'état* with a thesis on *Correspondances intimes* (1700–1860). She is *Maître de conférences* at the University of Nice.

NEIL GORDON is a graduate student in the French Department at Yale University and is doing research on his doctoral dissertation.

DEIDRE DAWSON received her undergraduate and Master's degrees from L'Université Paul Valéry in Montpellier, France, where she wrote her thesis on Voltaire's correspondence with the Duchess of Saxe-Gotha. She is currently a graduate student in the French Department at Yale University and plans to continue working on the *Correspondance* for her dissertation.

ENGLISH SHOWALTER, JR. was executive director of the Modern Language Association from 1983–1985 and is currently Distinguished Professor of French at Rutgers University, Camden. He is the author of books and articles on the eighteenth-century French novel and on Albert Camus. He is currently working on a nine volume edition of the letters of Mme de Graffigny.

PIERRE RIBERETTE, *Directeur de recherches* at the Centre national de la recherche scientifique, is the editor of the ongoing Correspondence of Chateaubriand.

LOUIS LE GUILLOU is Professor at the University of Bretagne Occidentale (Brest) and Director of the coordinated research group (Gréco) sponsored by the CNRS to work with nineteenth and twentieth-century correspondences.

EREC KOCH is a graduate student in the French Department at Yale University. He is currently completing a dissertation entitled "Order and Disorder in Pascal."

MARTINE REID, Assistant Professor in the French Department at Yale University, has participated in several colloquia in the United States and abroad and published articles on Stendhal, Racine, Nerval, and Proust. She has received a Mellon Fellowship to write a book on Stendhal and representation.

MARK GROSS is a graduate student in the French Department at Yale University. He is currently writing a dissertation on Gérard de Nerval entitled "The Palimpsest of Memory: Reading and Rewriting in *Les Filles du feu.*"

ALAN STOEKL is Assistant Professor of French and Comparative Literature at Yale University. He is the editor of Bataille's *Visions of Excess* and author of *Politics, Writing, Mutilation* (both published by the University of Minnesota Press).

SHEILA GAUDON is Associate Professor of French at Wesleyan University and one of the coeditors of the Correspondence of Victor Hugo.

PHILIP KOLB, Editor of the ongoing Correspondence of Marcel Proust, is Professor Emeritus of French at the University of Illinois.

Leur lévrier industrieux
Aux Dames Manet va remettre
— Côtes-du-Nord, à Portrieux
La Roche Plate — cette lettre .

Sans t'endormir dans l'herbe verte
Naïf distributeur , mets-y
Du tien : cours chez Madame Berthe
Manet, par Meulan, à Mézy

Deux adresses en vers de Stéphane Mallarmé. 1890, 1894. Photos du Musée de la Poste.

The following issues are available through **Yale University Press,** Customer Service Department, 92A Yale Station, New Haven, CT 06520.

63 The Pedagogical Imperative:
   Teaching as a Literary Genre
   (1982) **$12.95**
64 Montaigne: Essays in Reading
   (1983) **$12.95**
65 The Language of Difference:
   Writing in QUEBEC(ois)
   (1983) **$12.95**
66 The Anxiety of Anticipation
   (1984) **$12.95**

67 Concepts of Closure
   (1984) **$12.95**
68 Sartre after Sartre
   (1985) **$12.95**
69 The Lesson of Paul de Man
   (1985) **$12.95**
70 Images of Power:
   Medieval History/Discourse/
   Literature
   (1986) **$12.95**

71 Men/Women of Letters:
   Correspondence
   (1986) **$12.95**
72 Simone de Beauvoir:
   Witness to a Century
   (1987) **$12.95**
73 Forthcoming Issue
   (1987) **$12.95**

Special subscription rates are available on a calendar year basis (2 issues per year):

Individual subscriptions $22.00
Institutional subscriptions $25.90

- -

ORDER FORM   **Yale University Press,** 92A Yale Station, New Haven, CT 06520

Please enter my subscription for the calendar year
☐ **1985** (Nos. 68 and 69)   ☐ **1986** (Nos. 70 and 71)   ☐ **1987** (Nos. 72 and 73)

I would like to purchase the following individual issues:

_____   _____

_____

For individual issues, please add postage and handling:
Single issue, United States $1.00
Each additional issue $.50
Connecticut residents please add sales tax of 7½%.

Single issue, foreign countries $1.50
Each additional issue $.75

Payment of $ _____ is enclosed (including sales tax if applicable).

Mastercard no. _____

4-digit bank no. _____ Expiration date _____

VISA no. _____ Expiration date _____

Signature _____

SHIP TO: _____

_____

_____

- -

See the next page for ordering issues 1–59 and 61–62. **Yale French Studies** is also available through Xerox University Microfilms, 300 North Zeeb Road, Ann Arbor, MI 48106.

The following issues are still available through the **Yale French Studies** Office, 2504A Yale Station, New Haven, CT 06520.

19/20 Contemporary Art $3.50	43 The Child's Part $5.00	57 Locus: Space, Landscape,
23 Humor $3.50	44 Paul Valéry $5.00	Decor $6.00
32 Paris in Literature $3.50	45 Language as Action $5.00	58 In Memory of Jacques
33 Shakespeare $3.50	46 From Stage to Street $3.50	Ehrmann $6.00
35 Sade $3.50	47 Image & Symbol in the	59 Rethinking History $6.00
38 The Classical Line $3.50	Renaissance $3.50	61 Toward a Theory of
39 Literature and	49 Science, Language, & the	Description $6.00
Revolution $3.50	Perspective Mind $3.50	62 Feminist Readings: French Texts/
40 Literature and Society:	50 Intoxication and	American Contexts $6.00
18th Century $3.50	Literature $3.50	
41 Game, Play, Literature	53 African Literature $3.50	
$5.00	54 Mallarmé $5.00	
42 Zola $5.00		

Add for postage & handling

Single issue, United States $1.00   Single issue, foreign countries $1.50
Each additional issue $.50   Each additional issue $.75

- -

YALE FRENCH STUDIES, 2504A Yale Station, New Haven, Connecticut 06520

A check made payable to YFS is enclosed. Please send me the following issue(s):

Issue no.   Title   Price

_____   _____   _____

_____   _____   _____

_____   _____   _____

                                                                            Postage & handling   _____

                                                                                          Total   _____

Name _____

Number/Street _____

City _____ State _____ Zip _____

The following issues are now available through Kraus Reprint Company, Route 100, Millwood, N.Y. 10546.

1 Critical Bibliography of	11 Eros, Variations...	25 Albert Camus
Existentialism	12 God & the Writer	26 The Myth of Napoleon
2 Modern Poets	13 Romanticism Revisited	27 Women Writers
3 Criticism & Creation	14 Motley: Today's French Theater	28 Rousseau
4 Literature & Ideas	15 Social & Political France	29 The New Dramatists
5 The Modern Theatre	16 Foray through Existentialism	30 Sartre
6 France and World Literature	17 The Art of the Cinema	31 Surrealism
7 André Gide	18 Passion & the Intellect, or	34 Proust
8 What's Novel in the Novel	Malraux	48 French Freud
9 Symbolism	21 Poetry Since the Liberation	51 Approaches to Medieval
10 French-American Literature	22 French Education	Romance
Relationships	24 Midnight Novelists	

36 37 Stucturalism has been reprinted by Doubleday as an Anchor Book.
55/56 Literature and Psychoanalysis has been reprinted by Johns Hopkins University Press, and can be ordered through Customer Service, Johns Hopkins University Press, Baltimore, MD 21218.

Jean-Baptiste Carpeaux
Sculptor of the Second Empire
Anne Middleton Wagner

With **wit, elegance, and scholarship,**
Anne Wagner discusses the career of
Jean-Baptiste Carpeaux, perhaps the
most successful French sculptor of
the mid-nineteenth century. Her
book is not only a fascinating biography but also a penetrating account
of the circumstances that shaped
modern art in nineteenth-century
France.   261 b/w + 6 color illus.
$50.00

Painters and Public Life in Eighteenth-Century Paris
Thomas E. Crow

A highly original examination of
how public opinion about the arts in
eighteenth-century France—the
tastes of the authorities, the state,
and the crowds of salon visitors—
increasingly affected the ambitions
of the artists of the period. Watteau,
Greuze, and David are among the
artists whose work is discussed and
portrayed.

"Excellent." —Anita Brookner, TLS
150 b/w + 8 color illus. $40.00

Yale University Press
Dept. 294
92A Yale Station
New Haven, CT 06520

The City as a Work of Art
London, Paris, Vienna
Donald J. Olsen

A provocative and entertaining
architectural history of nineteenth-
century Paris, London, and Vienna.

"A marvelous book, which brilliantly
relates the form and functions of
these three great cities to the political cultures and social values
which moulded and created them.
Written with wit, warmth and
wisdom, it is . . . a **superb** piece of
urban history."—David Cannadine
142 b/w + 8 color illus. $35.00

Family Plots
Balzac's Narrative Generations
Janet L. Beizer

A fascinating exploration of the role
of family motifs in the narrative and
language of Balzac's fictions.
Balzac's "plots" about the family,
inextricably engaged with schem-
ings *against* the family and burial
sites *for* the family, attest to the
interrelated disintegration of family,
narrative, and language paradigms.

"A superb piece of criticism, valuable
both for its brilliant readings of individual Balzac texts and for the more
general resonances of its argument."
—Ross Chambers $21.00

Now available in paper

The Academy and French Painting in the Nineteenth Century
Albert Boime

Using words and works of both
pupils and masters of the French
Academy of Beaux-Arts, this fascinating book provides a wealth of
information about the environment
and studio practices of French official art from 1830 to 1890.

**"This excellently researched work
makes a very important contribution** to the study of modern
painting." —*Times Literary Supplement*   Illus. $19.95